THE IMPROBABLE BISHOP

Also by John S. Peart-Binns

Blunt
Ambrose Reeves
Cornish Bishop (J. W. Hunkin of Truro) with Alan Dunstan
Eric Treacy
Defender of the Church of England (Ronald Williams of Leicester)
Living with Paradox (Archbishop John Habgood of York)
Wand of London
Archbishop Joost de Blank
Maurice B. Reckitt
Graham Leonard
Edwin Morris, Archbishop of Wales
Hugh Montefiore
Rebel and Sage – Tom Heron (with Giles Heron)
A Heart in My Head. Richard Harries
Gordon Fallows of Sheffield
Gravitas With A Light Touch. Edward Luscombe: Bishop and Primus

THE IMPROBABLE BISHOP

IAN RAMSEY OF DURHAM

by

JOHN S. PEART-BINNS

The Memoir Club

© John S. Peart-Binns 2010

First published in 2010 by
The Memoir Club
Arya House
Langley Park
Durham
DH7 9XE
Tel: 0191 373 5660
Email: memoirclub@msn.com

British Library Cataloguing in
Publication Data.
A catalogue record for this book
is available from the
British Library

ISBN: 978-1-84104-511-5

Typeset by TW Typesetting, Plymouth, Devon
Printed by JF Print, Sparkford, Somerset

Dedication

Margaret Ramsey
whose unsparing love, strength and self-surrender
provided her husband with earthed stability
and a home for their family.

Contents

List of Illustrations

Acknowledgements

Paul Ramsey holds primacy of place for gratitude. He has furnished vital material including a number of Ian Ramsey's diaries, generously locating and copying House of Lords *Hansard* Reports containing his father's speeches and interventions. He has also compiled the Index. Throughout our meetings and correspondence he, and his wife Gail, have been enthusiasts for this undertaking. It is Paul and his brother Vivian who have made the publication of *The Improbable Bishop* possible.

A draft manuscript of this modest biography was completed many years ago, since which some contributors have died. It was my good fortune to garner the perceptions and notable recollections of Alec Hamilton, former Bishop of Jarrow, Kenneth Skelton, Assistant Bishop of Durham, and Maurice Harland, Ian Ramsey's predecessor. I am grateful for the insights of Tony Hart, Domestic Chaplain to both Harland and Ramsey. Deaconess Diana McClatchey presented me with a number of Harry McClatchey's Durham papers. Alec Vidler kindly sent a copy of his two lectures on William Temple. Gordon Dunstan responded to my searching questions and gave me his memories and appraisal of Bishops Robert Mortimer and Ian Ramsey.

From the recollections of people who knew and served with Ian Ramsey I have selected a representative sample which encompasses and illuminates what others were saying. My huge thanks go to the following clergy – Sam Burrows, Richard Davison, Bert Galloway, Hilary Jackson, Jeremy Martineau, Peter Moss, Harold Saxby, Noel Swinburne, Keith Woodhouse, Philip Wright and Ian Zass-Ogilvie.

The Memoir Club has been disciplined and exemplary at each stage of bringing this work to publication. I salute with gratitude Lynn Davidson (Managing Director), Jennifer Soutter (Editor) and the staff.

Without the memoir by David L. Edwards of Ian Ramsey (1973) it is doubtful if I would have had the courage to research anew and present this offering! I also wish to take this opportunity of placing on record my tribute to David Edwards who has lavished his brilliant gifts as a thinker and historian on the Church of England. His published work should not be allowed to gather dust.

Finally, without the patience, care, criticism and love of my wife Annis, none of my biographies would have seen the published light of day. She is married to a computer illiterate (I almost used the word Luddite) who, even now, has never visited the parallel universe of the internet.

John S Peart-Binns
Hebden Bridge
August 2010

Preface

By Divine Providence

On 6 October 1972 one of the most versatile and loved Church of England bishops of the twentieth century was taken away in the noontide of his power, in the climax of his opportunity, at the height of his influence. Ian Thomas Ramsey was an unlikely bishop and one of the most improbable figures ever to be elevated to the historic and illustrious See of Durham.

The Bishop of Durham is marked off from his episcopal colleagues by some honorific distinctions which arouse curiosity and challenge explanation. After the archbishops of Canterbury and York he takes rank next to the bishop of London: he is one of the three bishops (London, Durham and Winchester) who sit in the House of Lords by title of their sees, not in the order of their own consecration: in his official documents he uses a style distinctive of archbishops, writing himself 'by Divine providence', not, as is usual, 'by Divine permission'; the mitre which surmounts the arms of the see is bound with a ducal coronet; and he has the privilege of supporting the Sovereign on the right side at a coronation. These honorific distinctions may, perhaps, be regarded as the last surviving relics of the splendour of the Palatine Jurisdiction which the bishop of Durham, alone among the bishops of England, once possessed, and which survived the changes and chances of history only to perish in the year 1836 with Bishop William van Mildert, the last of the bishops of Durham who possessed the rights and dignity of Earl Palatinate. The palatine bishops were not only great spiritual magnates, but rulers, statesmen, diplomatists, even commanders.

By the mid-twentieth century bishops were treated as though they had inordinate authority when they had in fact very little. Yet their responsibilities still amounted to the greatest scope and privilege.

A new bishop coming to a diocese will give a fresh interpretation to episcopacy and create a distinctive style. But the work he is set there to do is essentially what it has always been – to enable the Church to live out the Gospel. Unfortunately a treadmill was created upon which chief pastors became slaves of time and motion, restlessly straining forward from yesterday to tomorrow. Bishops are prone to that strange condition described by an American tourist, suffering from an indigestible diet of attractions, as 'cognitive overload!' The only effective resistance which obscures a clear recognition of God is vigorous discipline, rigorous pruning, discriminating judgement, and a stripping of the activity alibi which can harm the spiritual life. These are features which will not be markedly visible in the ninety-first bishop of Durham.

The purpose of this work is to rekindle interest in Bishop Ian Ramsey. Public figures rapidly fade into obscurity, often oblivion, following their deaths. Only a select few of them are resuscitated for entries in the *Oxford Dictionary of National Biography*. Academia has its own way of remembering its own by researchers producing dissertations, doctoral theses, and articles in learned journals. In that closed-circuit environment the thought and insights of Ian Ramsey as philosopher, theologian and scientist still resonate. Of greater permanent significance is the Ian Ramsey Centre in the Faculty of Theology, University of Oxford. The Centre was first mooted in 1973 for the study of the ethical problems created for the Church and for society as a whole by technological change, especially in medicine and in the biological sciences. Ian Ramsey in effect designated his own memorial when, in a University sermon delivered in St Mary the Virgin, Oxford on 14 June 1964 he called attention to the fact that 'the most stubborn problems which beset contemporary society are those which occur on the frontier between different disciplines' and urged that they should be studied 'in a Research Centre or Institute within the precincts of a University or otherwise in close association with one.' Peter Baelz, Canon of Christ Church, Oxford and Regius Professor of Moral and Pastoral Theology at Oxford, and later Dean of Durham, was prepared to be the first Director of the Ian Ramsey Centre. It did not come to pass until 1985 with Canon Arthur Peacocke, a biochemist and theologian, as its first Director. He was awarded the £700,000 Templeton Prize for Progress in Religion in 2001.

This biography is modest in proportion and limited in scope to Ian Ramsey as Bishop of Durham from 1966 to 1972. It includes an essential account of his background, early life and education together with a specific chapter devoted to his contribution to medical and social ethics. In exploring, portraying and appraising Ian Ramsey it aims not only to massage and extend the memories of those who knew him, but also to introduce the essence of his life and the flavour of his episcopate to a new generation of Anglicans and others. It eschews analysis and evaluation of new concepts and theories that he developed on philosophy, theology and science which are covered in his published books and contributions to learned journals.

Honest tribute embraces the complete person, bounty and blemishes, strengths and frailties alike. There is a certain éclat about a bishop as he moves about his diocese. In most places and situations the metaphorical carpet is rolled out in welcome. Ian Ramsey was not a person to succumb to flattery or toxic obeisance. But there *were* temptations. Was there the possibility that he may slide from virtuous 'popular' to dangerous 'populist'? He appeared not to dislike the limelight. Were there very occasional glimpses of self-importance? Only he knew if he battled with pride or struggled with humility. What if his mapped-out road paved with good intentions – faithfully, strongly and obstinately pursued – became self-sufficing ends in themselves and deified?

> Sin grows with doing good –
> Servant of God has chance of greater sin
> And sorrow, than the man who serves a king,
> For those who serve the greater cause may make the cause serve them,
> Still doing right
>
> (T.S. Eliot *Murder in the Cathedral*)

By best fortune we know that Ian Ramsey was moral, loving and good, and spent his life searching and striving to do God's will and nourished by the Sacraments. He was a man under authority in his daily coming and going. Christianity is a history of paradox, and when closely examined the paradox of that history is the paradox of Christ. Victory is through defeat; restoration is through humiliation; strength is through weakness; life is through death. Whatever 'signs', 'symbols', 'prophecies', 'visions' and 'disclosures' that became an integral and vital part of Ian Ramsey's thought and experience, the paradox of the Incarnation, the paradox of a Redeemer who wields the might of Godhead in and through a manhood which is perfected through sufferings, the paradox of Jesus Christ and Him crucified, had to be faced and accepted.

As a very busy university lecturer and college chaplain at Cambridge, and a professor at Oxford he was the sole arbiter of the many pressures on his time and work where there was no one to whom he could delegate. That was an embedded trait which continued at Durham, where there were ample resources and many able hands to assist him. Kenneth Skelton was Bishop of Matabeleland when Ramsey invited him to be rector of Bishopwearmouth and Assistant Bishop in the diocese. In character and temperament they were opposites; in most aspects of theology and doctrine they were allies. Skelton, who became Bishop of Lichfield, one of the largest and oldest dioceses in England, inaugurated a collegial system with three area bishops retaining for himself oversight of the diocese. It worked! How different in Durham, as Skelton observed:

> Ian Ramsey used to complain that everything landed on his desk, but if it didn't he complained even more loudly. It is quite true that he couldn't say 'No'. After his death it was discovered that in the midst of what would have been a very busy period he had accepted an engagement to preach outside his diocese for a priest who had no particular claim on him but who was notorious for 'collecting' bishops. And he once suggested that the Bishop's Council might meet on Easter Eve because there was nothing in his diary on that day. I'm not sure also that because of over-work he was always 'master of his brief'. I was a little shocked to find him preparing his sermon in a corner of the vestry at Bishopwearmouth twenty minutes before the Induction service began.

Inauspiciously the waning of episcopal authority led to a waxing centralised bureaucracy in most dioceses and at Church House, Westminster when the corridors of persuasion were not so subtly transformed into corridors of power similar to those across the road in the Houses of Parliament. The Church appeared to forget or overlook that administrative tasks are an essentially diaconal ministry. The bishop is no more than a head servant whose service is enabling

things to happen, keeping things in order, directing other servants of
the Lord, or allowing them space, by taking care of the routine,
organising the whole community for its task. It is an illusion that
societies are able to function bottom up! How will Ian Ramsey fit
into his new surroundings? The majority of bishops have three
vocational indelibilities in their lives – marriage, priesthood and
episcopacy. The first is often neglected with occasional catastrophic
and calamitous results. Some bishops hurtle into episcopacy, fulfilling
their secret desires or more evident ambitions, without sufficiently
considering the immense emotional and physical upheaval experienced by their wives and families, with lamentable results. Bishops
may lose any adventurousness or newness in their spiritual lives.
Tiredness of mind, physical exhaustion and spiritual dryness lead to
vain repetition. Bishops live in the midst of words, and need time for
the silence that disturbs and the quietness which renews. Church of
England bishops would find a modest but searing rebuke in words of
the late Bishop Azariah of Dornakal, South India, who recognized
the zeal, energy and commitment of European missionaries, but who
said to them, 'One thing only have you failed to give us. You have
failed to give us love.' And in a number of overseas dioceses where
bishops are elected in the Anglican Communion today a primary
consideration is that their bishops should be holy!

In 1966 Durham required a bishop who would polish the jewel that
is Anglicanism so that it would glint and shine. Not, on the one hand,
to hold on with timorous tenacity to theological opinions, albeit
sacrosanct by time, which are disallowed by modern knowledge; nor,
on the other hand, to let go the fundamental verities, which are
eternally valid, necessary and morally energizing; nor to float on the
stream of popular fashion which is equally confident and fleeting. Ian
Ramsey never allowed the treasured Anglican *via media* with its balance
of Word and Sacraments to become lopsided in emphasis or practice.

The ingredients in Ramsey's character were widely and divergently
mixed. He was straightforward and elusive, popular and enigmatic. He
revealed himself as a complex but not a mysterious man, a paradox but
not a puzzle. Unlike many dignitaries there was not the slightest hint of
pomp or circumstance about him, none of the chameleon-like
characteristics of shiftiness, duplicity, smoothness and barely concealed
ambition, which inflict some would-be or could-be leaders. On the

surface the postman's son – small, stocky, unpretentious – with a Lancashire accent, and owl-like appearance was abundantly blessed with a first-class honours brain and an attractive personality. His academic excellence and proficiency in mathematics, moral science and theology were gathered and expanded over twenty-three years in the Universities of Cambridge and Oxford. Words of the Venerable Bede, who died in Jarrow in 735, apply to Ramsey, 'I took sweet pleasure in always learning, teaching, or writing'. These are not the only Bede features which apply. Bede may have lived in the calmness of a monastery but his life was marked throughout by conscientious industry. Idleness was unknown to him. His fame as a scholar was deep, extensive and widespread. He had a passion for learning which, even in his own lifetime, brought recognition and intellectual eminence.

Ian Ramsey distributed rather than hoarded knowledge and did so with urgency, gusto and stimulation, avoiding the professorial temptation of intellectual conceit. He was saved from academic arrogance by never closing his mind. Dogmatism and fundamentalism were anathema to him. That is why he was an opponent of glib Christian statements which he described as 'a patchwork of principles and prejudice'. Christianity is not a prescriptive religion with rules and regulations and directions for daily life, so clear, so precise, and so sufficient, that there will be no need for thought, reflection, consultation and arrangement. For Ramsey the biblical record is not the last word on any subject, it is the first word. It is impossible to journey very far with him before the key words of 'vision' and 'disclosure' fall from his lips.

There are few twentieth-century bishops who can be described as 'great' or who have left a permanent legacy. But the majority may be described as 'good men all and true', faithfully following the precepts conveyed to them when the Holy Bible was delivered to them at their consecration. The language was succinct and potent:

> Be to the flock of Christ a shepherd, not a wolf; feed them, devour them not. Hold up the weak, heal the sick, bind up the broken, bring again the out-casts, seek the lost. Be so merciful, that you be not too remiss; so minister discipline, that you forget not mercy.

These words from *The Book of Common Prayer* are etched into Ian Ramsey's duties and responsibilities. Individual bishops bring a combination of their distinctive natural gifts and acquired skills with them. It is often claimed that one of the weaknesses of the Church of England is the isolation of the bishop from his people; he does not start as one of them, but is wished upon them by a remote authority and has to labour long before he can identify and be identified with them. Further it is perceived as an additional burden, handicap and limitation if the bishop has never been a 'vicar'! This is an erroneous assumption. Pastoral experience and parish experience are mistakenly confused. From the outset Durham knew that they had a people's bishop in Ian Ramsey. It was in his nature to be interested in other people, and courtesy had become an invariable habit. He had a sharp eye for the details of common life, and relished any item of news which demonstrated the decency and good sense, as well as the struggles, of ordinary people, and their refusal to be bamboozled by those in authority. He enjoyed talking to everybody, and liked to bring people out. He was completely devoid of 'class' or 'side', being everywhere 'at home', in a railway cafeteria, at the Athenaeum with the high and mighty of the land, in a miner's cottage, conversing with a taxi driver and being late for a meeting, at parish bun-fights. His writings and sermons were full of homely illustrations, usually humorously illustrated. In one of his books on the mystery of religious awareness he observes: 'It is as though having seen some junior archdeacon "come alive" when he exchanges apron and gaiters for linen apron and dishcloth; one can then see the most prelatical-looking bishop as "having a human heart".'

Occasionally he, and his wife, Margaret, were mistaken for others, as he recalled:

> There was the electrician at Auckland Castle who asked my wife if she worked part-time. 'No', said my wife truthfully, 'full-time'. In my gaiters – welcome now in many youth groups as 'mod gear', I have been mistaken from the rear for the head waiter, by a visitor in a Durham restaurant. But my wife can cap that, entering a certain civic building to open a sale, she had a bouquet of flowers thrust into her hand with the words of a very harassed lady, 'Just take that up the stairs dear – it's for the opener'. So she had the unusual experience of being presented with the same bouquet twice in the same day.

Professor Basil Mitchell has a pertinent insight:

It is said of certain mystics and magicians in Tibet that they had the power of manifesting themselves in different places at the same time – a tall story, but one to which acquaintance with Ian Ramsey lent some credence. And 'manifesting himself' rather appropriately describes the way in which one would become aware of his presence at a gathering without having noticed his entry. An unassuming *persona* is unusual in a leader.

Ian Ramsey was already a man of academic distinction, wide sympathies, pastoral perception, personal probity, and of generous spirit when he was nominated for the bishopric of Durham. It was a time when the episcopal administrator with bureaucratic tendencies was beginning to be trapped in the snare of busyness, a snare often set by the bishop himself. It continued to grow so incessantly that the Church of England was in danger of having an episcopate deprived of men of just insight and far-seeing wisdom, independently-minded scholars, forthright and disturbing prophets, historians providing knowledge, proportion and perspective to contemporary issues, and those with the capacity of being bishops of England not merely of their own dioceses. Then, into their midst came the most unusual and extraordinary figure, often wearing apron and gaiters when most bishops had put them into an ecclesiastical museum. Yet here was a bishop who could 'connect' with an amazing range of people of every class and age. The Church could no longer rest on conventions, albeit deeply entrenched in popular acceptance, sacrosanct by antiquity, and freighted with memories. Yet in spite of confusions, in spite of anomalies, in spite of the apparent and deplorable weakness of its system the Church of England still embodied for many thoughtful Christians a type of Christianity which uniquely attracted, the loss of which would inflict a grievous wound on the Religion of Christ.

In the secularized and secularist society of the 1960s and 1970s the challenge for the Church was to justify its character as the 'salt' and the 'light' of the world. It appeared that Ian Ramsey was motivated and propelled to do just that. Every fibre of his being vibrated with opening minds, ears, eyes and hearts to a vision – his vision! He spoke, served and witnessed to the condition of the age. Bishop George Bell wrote of William Temple:

he had all the vividness and swiftness of a flame. It was like a flame that he sped through our whole firmament, filling every corner of it with a new splendour. It was like a flame that he communicated warmth and light to all who saw and heard him. We cannot expect to look upon his like again in our lifetime.

Could that also be said of Ian Thomas Ramsey?

CHAPTER 1

Lancashire Roots

THERE WERE NO INDICATIONS of outcomes in the antecedents of the boy who was born on 31 January 1915. Nor did the unpretentious red-brick terrace house at 9 Ivy Grove, Kearsley, Bolton, provide the slightest hint of future life in a Cambridge court, Oxford quad or a castle in County Durham. What was firm and constant was the rootedness in firm Lancashire soil for Ian Thomas Ramsey.

The Ramseys had for many generations lived in Manchester or in Bolton. Thomas Joseph Ramsey was born on 1 March 1861 at Coopers Row off Deansgate in Manchester. He married Ann Bagnall, the daughter of Edward Bagnall, a farrier, on 24 May 1886 at Stowell Memorial Church, Salford. They had two sons and then moved to live betwixt mill, where Thomas worked as a millwright, and Bolton Railway Station. The couple's youngest son, Arthur, was born on 12 June 1894 in Bolton. He attended Great Lever Church of England School leaving at thirteen to be a telegraph boy or Post Office messenger at the General Post Office in Bolton. If they could, the boys avoided Belmont as it was a long haul of four miles from the town centre and their remuneration of one penny was identical to that received for less arduous routes.

Arthur met May Cornthwaite of Kearsley, Bolton. Her father, John Cornthwaite, was a cotton carder until there was a slump in trade when he became a miner. Arthur and May were married in 1914 and the following year their only son Ian Thomas, was born. As with most children born at or near the outbreak of the First World War, their fathers joined the armed forces and it was very hard on mothers left with the sole responsibility for bringing up children. Arthur served with the Seaforth Highlanders/Royal Engineers mostly in France.

After the war Arthur returned to the Post Office and by sustained perseverance he moved steadily upwards. It was a long haul for someone who was ambitious. He knew the ceiling of promotion at Bolton was low so he would have to look elsewhere for the advancement he sought. It was a gradual process, but in 1938 he was Public Relations and Publicity Officer at the General Post Office at the Manchester Headquarters. From August 1939 he worked at the North West Regional Office of the Ministry of Home Security until, in May 1940, his ability was rewarded by appointment as Head Postmaster at Rochdale. He was also Commanding Officer of the Post Office Home Guard; member of the local National Savings Committee; and member of the Parochial Church Council of Christ Church, Healey. In 1944 he became Assistant Head Postmaster at Liverpool, and then from 1949 until his retirement in 1954 he was Head Postmaster at Norwich which had the largest geographical postal area in the United Kingdom. At Norwich he laid the foundations for the postcode sorting. His reputation was one of diligence and meticulous method, gaining him considerable respect. These moves involved five house changes. Fortunately for Ian, these occurred long after he had left home for Cambridge.

We return to Ian's childhood when the family moved from Ivy Grove to a semi-detached house at 366 Manchester Road, Clifton, which they called St Kilda, where Ian spent most of his boyhood. Much benevolent attention was showered on Ian by his maternal grandmother, who lived with them, and by the paternal grandparents who lived nearby. He was aware of two pressures, one to succeed, the other to be good. They attended St John's, Farnworth. This was fortuitous. During the first half of the nineteenth century Bolton was 'governed' by Canon James Slade, who was vicar from 1817–1856. He was a majestic Evangelical personality whose pastoral concern stretched from the preaching of the Gospel to all in his care and beyond, to the provision of education for both the young and the old, to supporting hospital work and establishing a savings bank in the town. Twelve churches in and around Bolton were built during his incumbency, St John's being one of them. Ian, turned five years, was a late entrant to St John's Primary School.

We have his mother's recorded recollections. Although self-evidently biased and romanticised, they contain memories which have a bearing on the future, and are best included unadorned. Moreover, the mother outlived the son. She died on 10 January 1988 at Blackpool.

Ian could not speak until he was about three, and then it was his own language when he did. Could not say Ian so called himself 'Nini'. Of course he was very charitable even at five. I always took him and met him from school and went for a walk. This day it was very cold, and I suggested he turn back for his coat. He said he had not got a coat. I told him he could not go for a walk without his coat. Mr Jabbert said, 'Mrs Ramsey, you'll find it on one of the other boys – Dan Neery.' Ian told me that Dan Neery was so cold that he gave him his coat. Ian came home one day and told me that the Neerys were very well-off since they had eight brothers and two sisters. Ian would not go out to play with the other children but walked about with the teachers. He could tell the right time in the baby class and his teacher told him to watch the clock for him.

Ian did not like to go to the barbers – he did not like the chair so we bought him a little stool and he called this his 'sit upon' and he took 'sit upon' every time he went to the barbers.

He had a very happy time at St John's, but when the coal strike was on they were giving the schoolchildren free meals. Ian was very upset because he could not go to the 'party'. I went along to school and told his teacher that Ian was upset – so next day Ian took a basin and a mug – but he could not eat the dinner!

Some of the mothers complained that there were children coming to school dirty and they told me Ian did not play with them. I told them that he had to learn to grow up with both kinds and then make a choice. Years later when Ian was on a bus in Manchester he was recognised by his old school friend Dan Neery and given a free ride because Dan worked on the buses. Ian was thrilled to see him again.

We had family prayers every evening and then I read Ian a story. One story was about playing the game. One night Ian had not gone to bed when he ought to and he was very worried that he had not been 'playing the game'. He was always worrying in case he trespassed – and when he grew up he was just the same.

During the war Ian would go to work with me and sit under my desk on a ledger. There he would play with his trains or read. Then when I went out to deliver the post Ian would go along with me. Ian always had his hands behind his back.

A doting mother of an only child constantly visiting the school may have been an embarrassment. He later observed, 'I think of my own primary school; woe betide the parent who dared cross the threshold! It was worse for her or him than for the boys or girls.'

With the move to Clifton there was a change in the place of worship. The family attended St Anne's, Clifton. It was 'low church' before evangelical entered the normal vocabulary. Ian was friendly with the vicar, Trevor Wright (of St John's College, Durham and the London College of Divinity), and was taught in the Sunday school by a miner, Tommy Marsh. He was confirmed in 1931 by the Bishop of Middleton, Richard Parsons. He probably never saw 'Jumbo' (a nickname because of his size) Parsons again, and would not realise that he was a close friend of William Temple with similar broad interests.

At the age of ten Ian went as a scholarship boy to Farnworth Grammar School (coeducational and partly fee-paying), a single tram ride from his home. At first he concentrated on Latin and then discovered science, achieving distinctions in pure mathematics and physics. He rapidly rose to top of the class and eventually became head prefect. Two of his teachers have memories. Alice Ashcroft remembers him sitting in the midst of the class, two at a desk. 'His owl-like appearance and the fact that his eyes never left my face made me find out his name.' May Rankin has a reflection: 'Although Ian's achievements were exceptional, they were the result of sheer hard work combined with the desire for understanding and accuracy in all that he undertook. It is greatly to the credit of his parents that their only child although clever was not conceited.' He responded to all requests to take part in school activities, for example he was secretary of the Scientific Society, a member of the Geographical and Photographic Societies, contributed to *Lumen*, the school magazine, including tongue-in-cheek reports of the Temperance Society! Although he had no sporting prowess he enjoyed arranging the school lists for fixtures. Lists would be a feature of his life! Mr McCarter, the headmaster, said 'we cannot teach him how to say "no".' Ian left unsung but not unhonoured.

As Ian leaves Farnworth there are emerging characteristics − a few transitory, mostly permanent. First, Ian's love for his mother was and remained paramount. This would lead to problems when he married. The bond between mother and son was natural, the closeness enhanced because of his father's absence at war during his early years of childhood. But that was the lot of many children and does not, as we shall discover, explain the depth and closeness of this mother and son, as if the umbilical cord had never been broken. Secondly, Ian's relationship with his father later gathered pace and they became close. Together they went on a long cycling holiday to Scotland and, as with any holiday in the future, Ian made detailed notes, recalling miles travelled, details of people met and places visited. Arthur had a streak of independence and on one occasion went on a deep sea fishing trip out of Fleetwood on the steam trawler *Erna*. When Ian decided to build/design his own house named High Quarry at Harcourt Hill, North Hinksey, Oxford, his father built the walls round the drive, laying stone after stone all taken from digging the garden – he was an amateur and expert gardener – and both parents moved into High Quarry Flat! At Cawston, their home near Norwich, he was on the Parochial Church Council and Chairman of the Parish Council. He was Churchwarden at the time the rood screen was restored in 1952, and his initials are recorded for posterity on a small plaque by the side of the screen. Thirdly, the effect of being an only child cannot be underestimated. Gail, who married Ian's first son Paul, is herself an only child and has these perceptions:

> It is easy to generalise about 'onlys' but I know from personal experience that these children develop in a different way from those with siblings. Parents may work hard to ensure that the child is not spoilt – as Ian certainly was not. However, 'only' children tend to relate better to older people rather than their peer group – and tend not to be 'team' players. Never having had to co-operate in play with other children in the intimacy of the family, they find it difficult to allow others to take the lead. If you have spent most of your childhood devising your own games and organising your own time, it is easy to see how hard it is to relinquish control in adult life. 'Only' children may not be selfish but they are used to seeing the world only through their own eyes.

Fourthly, although young Ian took a normal part in church life, it made no great impact on heart or mind.

Ian won a scholarship to Manchester University, but perhaps against his parents' initial expectations, then achieved a place at Christ's College, Cambridge. Ramsey went to Christ's College as a 'swot', little distinctive personality, and somewhat socially out of his depth with the public school undergraduates. He began to read philosophy in addition to what appeared an easy ascendancy in mathematics. As for his future, perhaps a career in the Civil Service? Nothing certain. What gave him a compelling sense of direction was the result of tragedy and overcoming it. To an extent he had been molly-coddled at home and when left to his own devices at Cambridge he studied as many hours as the day and evening and some of the night provided. His lodgings were remote from the college and he neglected his health. A cold became severe, developed into bronchitis and led to tuberculosis. At the age of nineteen he was admitted to Papworth Sanitorium. Including a period of convalescence it was eight months before he recovered. On many occasions in the future he referred to returning health and new life, as a sign of the loving kindness of God. The influence of friends was likewise an instrument for changing direction, not least that of the college chaplain, H.F. Woolnough. These were the days before centralised bureaucracy of the Church of England at Church House, Westminster, so, in addition to chaplain, Woolnough was also General Secretary of the Central Advisory Council of Training for the Ministry (CACTM). Ramsey often pondered on the subject of vocation. In the Old Testament the Jews are a people 'called' to their divine destiny. The initiative lies with God. In the New Testament Jesus 'calls' people and they follow. In both Testaments there is the idea of 'calling out'. God calls the whole Church to a life of faith, obedience, service and worship; this is the meaning of Christian vocation in the teaching of the New Testament. Every Christian has a vocation in this biblical sense. Ramsey was puzzled when the term was used to mean 'occupation' or 'profession'. Nowhere in the New Testament is this use to be found. Paul was 'called' to be an Apostle; he was not called to be a 'tent-maker'. God does not call people to be doctors or engineers: he calls doctors and engineers to be evangelists, pastors, etc. A priest's profession must be thought of in the same way. The New Testament nowhere suggests that one may be called to the Church as a profession. Rather every member of the Church receives a call to the ministry which certain men express in the particular ministry of the Word and Sacraments. Vocation to the ordained ministry has two sides. Firstly, a conviction that one is called to serve. Secondly, the Church one is to serve has to be convinced that he is the best person to serve it. Too often a young man is invited to offer himself before the Church calls. He is expected to know and be sure of his vocation before half of it exists. It appears that for Ian Ramsey the interior and exterior calls coincided. His path may have led in a different direction had he not been in Papworth Sanatorium and if Woolnough had not been the college chaplain.

Ian's vocation was an expanding not a narrowing horizon. Theology was part of his exhilarating new life – 'enlivening' is too modest a word. And brilliance followed him, with the following results: 1st class Mathematical Tripos part I (1936); B.A. (1st class Moral Sciences part II) and Burney Prize, 1938; 1st class Theological Tripos part II (with distinction, 1939). He decided not to proceed with a doctorate but headed straight for theological college. Until he became Bishop of Durham he was not technically qualified to be called 'doctor' – at Oxford he was officially 'Professor Ramsey' but 'Ian' usually sufficed. Later he received honorary Doctorates of Divinity from Oxford (1966), Durham (1967), and Glasgow (1968).

There was only one theological college which was a perfect setting for Ian Ramsey. He was already a 'Modern Churchman' in embryo and to Ripon Hall, Oxford, he went under Principal H.D.A. Major. Ripon Hall represented the determinative principles of the type of Anglicanism which has persisted and developed under the successive designations of 'broad', 'liberal', and 'modernist' churchmanship, and Ramsey fitted each of that trinity of descriptions. Later he would be a Governor and Treasurer of the College, and a member of the Council, and Vice-President of the Modern Churchman's Union, a speaker at their annual conferences, and contributor to its periodical *The Modern Churchman*. He was nicknamed 'Panda' at Ripon Hall.

Ian Ramsey was made deacon in 1940, ordained priest in 1941 and served his curacy at the Church of the Holy and Undivided Trinity, Headington Quarry, Oxford, under the Revd T.E. Bleiben. The population of the village was 3,700. Bleiben was a Classical and Greek scholar, and in addition to his parochial duties he was an assistant master at Magdalen College School, and chaplain of New College, Oxford. Was this an early bad example for Ramsey – a vicar who had numerous appointments and duties running concurrently? He had been on the receiving end of hospital visiting, and knew the importance of the 'presence' of a person not their endless chatter. As Bleiben was chaplain of London Road Hospital Ramsey began to learn of the importance of empathy and listening, when he went hospital visiting. He was popular and energetic in the parish.

However, Headington Quarry was the place where his personal life was changed for ever and for better. It is here he met Margretta (Margaret) McKay. Born on 5 June 1918 she was the youngest of nine children whose parents were John and Janeanna, both from Northern Ireland. John McKay worked in Belfast for a time, but his home was in Coleraine in County Londonderry where he worked as a draper, but the business folded. He was variously a member of the Portstewart Masonic Lodge, the Urban Council, the select vestry of St Patrick's Church (of Ireland), Coleraine. He was a Unionist and belonged to the Orange Order. Janeanna was born and died in Coleraine. Their house, where Margaret was brought up, was in the centre of Coleraine.

Margaret went to Sunday evening Pierrot shows, and mimicked these when she got home, having said, 'Save my share of the washing up for me'. After schooldays she went to a secretarial college in Londonderry, thence into the Civil Service. In the late 1930s she came to London to work in the Civil Service, lived in Streatham and travelled by tram to work. The office overlooked the Circle Line near Farringdon. It was a good life of work and friendships. Seriousness and lightheartedness mingled. Following the outbreak of war she was evacuated to Oxford and worked at Merton College with the Ministry of Aircraft Production. She lodged with a Mr and Mrs Frank Spooncer in Headington Quarry. From the moment Ian and Margaret met it was 'love at first sight', a rapid engagement, and they were married on 17 June 1943.

It is important to pause at this point and understand that she was beyond doubt the stabilising influence in Ian Ramsey's life, and that of their two children Paul (born in 1945) and Vivian (born in 1950). There is no hesitation in recognising her place as the bedrock in their lives and in the home. Ian's diaries are full of expressions of his love and adoration for Margaret. If Ian had moved from his curacy to an incumbency their lives and their futures would have been different. But in the year of their marriage Ian returned to Cambridge as Chaplain of Christ's College. The flower of his brilliant academic achievements came to full bloom. If Ian's home was his foundation for the future – and it was – his self-absorption should not be minimised. He was the world's theological and philosophical waiter, and would or could never recognise that the restaurant was fully booked. There was always a student who wanted a meal, or a group of philosophers who required a table. Somehow room would be found for them. In today's language he became, if slowly, an academic 'celebrity'. When he was appointed Nolloth Professor of the Philosophy of the Christian Religion and Fellow of Oriel College, Oxford in 1951, the queues at the restaurant were round the block. What was he doing besides teaching and pastoring? He commenced reviewing books in 1945 in the *Cambridge Review, Cambridge Journal* and *Theology* on a regular basis. His sermons and lectures were appearing in print. There was an early BBC Discussion with C.A. Coulson on 'Science and Religion' (printed as a Church Pastoral Aid Society Fellowship Paper). His name was beginning to be noticed and he was reading papers at the International Congress of Philosophy, the International Conference on Patristic Studies, and the International Congress in New Testament Studies. He was invited to give the Forwood Lectures, F.D. Maurice Lectures, the Alden-Tuthill Lectures, Whidden Lectures and Riddell Memorial Lectures in various universities in the United Kingdom and overseas. Some of them were transformed into books, notably *Freedom and Immortality* (1960), *On Being Sure in Religion* (1963), *Religious Language* (1963), *Religion and Science: Conflict and Synthesis* (1964), and *Christian Discourse: Some Logical Exploration* (1965). Ramsey spread himself to an absurd extent. There were notable exchanges between, for example, H.D. Lewis, Professor of the History of Philosophy in the University of London and Ramsey on 'Freedom and Mortality' (*The Hibbert Review* 1961), and between Professor Ninian Smart, H.G. Wood Professor of Theology, in the University of Birmingham on 'The Intellectual Crisis of British Christianity' (*Theology* 1965). He also had preaching engagements throughout the country. His daily diaries have entries naming ten people he might meet and converse with in a single day, as well as researching and writing, teaching and attending groups and committees.

Meanwhile, what about his family? His father retired from the Post Office in 1954. Ian had built a house at Harcourt Hill, North Hinksey, Oxford. Margaret Ramsey suggested that a flat be built over the garage for his parents and so they moved, with an aunt, into High Quarry Flat in 1956. Margaret Ramsey was approachable and friendly. She enjoyed cooking and catered for parties in their rooms at Cambridge. As Treasurer of Ripon Hall on Boar's Hill, Oxford Ian was in constant contact with the nearby college. In fact having looked without success for a house in Oxford itself, in which to move, the solution was to live in the otherwise empty Hostel at Ripon Hall in 1951. There the gardener called in for coffee each morning with Margaret and she had close friendships with the wives of college staff, particularly Anne Baelz and Muriel Whiteley, and she enjoyed meeting friends from wartime years, with Charlotte Cluness visiting often. Margaret was hit hard when Muriel and Charlotte died of cancer. Her own sisters Helen and Jennie were also visitors in Cambridge and Oxford. Margaret was at her best when entertaining at home, preferring the intimacy of the few, although there were dinner parties when she relished opportunities of experimenting with new dishes. She enjoyed parties with people she knew. There was late night cooking when Ian or the boys returned home. The wives of Oriel dons used to go to each other's homes whilst their husbands were feasting in College. In Oxford she had a shopping routine, walked to the nearest bus stop at North Hinksey, catching the C5X to town. She would call in to Twinings on George Street to order her weekly delivery, and call in at the Cadena Café for coffee. There were friends to meet.

All this is a normal picture of a don's wife. Alas, it is a partial, even superficial, account of her life. Slip beneath the surface and there are acute, recurring and severely damaging tensions. Her sister, Helen, a tough and single-minded nurse, later Matron at the Evelyn Nursing Home in Cambridge, was quick to spot the nature of the problem. It was Ian's mother. The brilliant academic could not recognise that anything was wrong, such was his supreme love for his mother. Margaret desperately needed support, a point made by Helen to Paul on several occasions. Ian Ramsey appeared to neither see nor comprehend what was evident to others. When mother May and daughter-in-law Margaret were in close proximity there was an over-current of tension. Margaret spoke of the humiliation when she had prepared everything for greeting and entertaining her in-laws during the last year of the war, but everything she and Ian had prepared was more than matched by what May had brought. When, shortly after Margaret's own mother had died in Ireland, she returned with Ian after a post-funeral visit to be met at the Liverpool landing stage by Arthur and May, May's first words were 'Well, he'll (Paul) have only one to call Grandma now.' Margaret felt she was being observed at all times, her every action scrutinised – and perhaps criticised. Such was the seriousness that she saw a psychiatrist in the late 1950s. But did anyone point out the problem directly to Ian Ramsey? No! His mother remained paramount. Auckland Castle would increase the 'observation' and 'isolation'. Is it any wonder that Margaret said she would love to live in a three-bedroomed house? This is one of those insoluble puzzles for a man who was concerned with mental and general health. Did he either see or feel her pain? The wife of a bishop, even more than of a professor, sees the delights of ecclesiastical success. She may also know the dire disappointments and failures of and for her husband. She may have to prick the bubble of inflation as well as provide support and comfort. Can she also deflect his gaze from the organisational Church of which her husband is a servant, to the Christian goals which are the ultimate source of his ministry? But Ian Ramsey seemed self-sufficient, and always much too occupied. It was ever thus.

Even at Cambridge Ramsey relished his work in and out of college. He was the College ARP and Fire Officer during his time as Chaplain. He undertook his demanding duties with efficiency and enjoyment. Quaintly dressed in tin hat and gown, and with his gas mask at the ready, one can imagine him bounding up and down the College staircases, a peripatetic philosopher yet sufficiently well earthed in reality to have been entrusted by the College with its safety in the event of an air raid on Cambridge.

Family holidays were wonderful times of release and recreation, although several included engagements. One notable holiday was in Canada and the USA in 1963, after Ian had been a visiting Professor at Colgate Rochester Divinity School for four months. The family started out from Rochester, N.Y. on 30 May and returned home to Oxford on 15 August. There were lectures and meetings and sermons but, above all recreation. Ramsey kept a journal with his usual meticulous care of detail. On the journey home from Montreal, it includes details of everyone he spoke to on the ship, and something about them. Menus of meals on the *Cairndhu* (Cairn-Thomson Line) are retained with comments on the food. The words 'wonderful' and 'splendid' recur with a tangible excitement. On land the number of miles travelled each day, number of tolls, prices of food purchased en route, motel bills, bus and rail fares and weather forecasts are carefully recorded. Eighteen colour films taken (thirty-six transparencies each). Distances including shipping and journeys in Scotland/England to and from port totalled 17,285 miles. The family (Ian, Margaret, Paul and Vivian) slept in forty-eight different beds. Such was Ramsey's interest in everything and everyone that he made a holiday an unforgettable experience for everyone else.

There are characteristics, some unchanged, some which developed during his Cambridge and Oxford years. He never discarded his roots. This kept him ordinary and unspoiled, never in danger of having 'ideas above his station' in life. Dropping an 'h' was not unknown. He was straightforward in his dealings with people though in his future dealings with northerners the language he used could be a barrier to people speaking plainly to him. There is a fortune to be made for anyone who collected the thousands of 'pennies dropped' and 'disclosures' made. He never 'played' to congregations, or softened his message to caress those listening to him. He never gave glib answers to inscrutable questions. If some sacred mysteries were hidden in darkness, he let them lie there in the darkness. A priest who knew him at Oxford and in Durham said, 'Our bishop seemed to prefer people leaving church scratching their heads and thinking about what he had said than leaving with a handful of answers to questions they had not asked.' Did he succumb to flattery? Was there any self-conceit? As Francis Bacon said, 'there is no such flatterer as is a man's self, and there is no such remedy against flattery of a man's self as the liberty of a friend.' Here there is a flaw, because we know that Ramsey heard but did not heed the advice of friends in matters affecting his personal life. There was no brake to change his behaviour. There is no evidence that Ramsey ever deliberately projected himself, but he could not but be unaware of the star status he achieved at Durham.

One deficiency in his life is the absence of silence and solitude. If he is not in his study, on a dais or in a pulpit we usually locate him in public, happily surrounded by people, articulate, not necessarily dominant. In a university milieu the wealth of words is expected. But has he cared for his spiritual life, that which is hidden? To date he has usually been speaking, lecturing and writing from the mouth and pen outwards. How deep is the spiritual well, and how fresh is the water in it that will sustain him at Durham?

It should not be overlooked or underestimated that although Ian Ramsey was very well known in the Church of England, there were areas in which this was not the case. His frequent visits to diocesan clergy schools to lecture drew many admirers. His books were well known, well read and well reviewed, but to a comparatively limited readership. However, there was one other area where he was also a name to be reckoned with. It was in the sphere of medical ethics. Before turning to this subject, there are some guiding words from him. The subject was specific – euthanasia – but the principles are the ones which guided his approach to all medical ethical issues.

> Let it be granted that some will always hope nostalgically for a leadership which gives them answers for immediate acceptance, and rules for unquestionable following. But whether this encourages genuine, does full justice to sound reasoning, or nourishes true faith is another question, and in any event it bespeaks the security of those who sit at ease in Zion, rather than the confident assurance of the pilgrim on his uphill road.
>
> Which reminds us that the Christian pioneer is another kind of leader – one who is fired by a vision, who by the light which the Gospels and the Christian tradition can supply (though even here not without hard work and controversy), explores problems of thought and action in all their complexity.
>
> There is a hard and testing road ahead. But some of us believe that the vision which a Church exists to purvey is best made evident when, like pioneers, we are bold enough to throw ourselves into the turmoil, not withdrawing into hard shells but wrestling with problems in such a way as makes clear to those around us the faith by which we live. There is, fortunately, this creative alternative to a united voice which neglects genuine differences, and an indecision which is overwhelmed by them.
>
> (Letter, *The Times* 2 April 1969)

CHAPTER 2

Ethical Imperatives

R OBERT MORTIMER, BISHOP OF EXETER, made a speech in a debate at Church Assembly on 4 July 1963 which was greeted with loud and sustained applause:

> The Church of England is beginning to pay the price for its neglect of, and even contempt for, moral theology during the last two or three hundred years. It is paying the price for an exaggerated exaltation of New Testament ethics at the expense of a Christian ethic which combines with the Gospel ethic the concept of natural law. The great work of the school men in reformulating the concept of the natural law as they found it in Aristotle and the making of it a basis and a support for the New Testament revealed ethic has been far too long ignored in Anglican circles. The result is that we have almost nobody within the ranks of Anglican theologians who is able to set out clearly and forcibly the concept of the natural law upon which, in fact, both Gospel ethics and ordinary sexual morality rest. What is urgently needed throughout the whole of Christendom is a reformulation in modern terms of the concept of natural law.

This 'reformulation' had been in progress for some time in the Anglican Communion and Ian Ramsey was in the vanguard propelling its movement forward. So was Basil G. Mitchell, a Fellow and Tutor of Keble College, Oxford who was a wonderfully collaborative colleague of Ian Ramsey, and will succeed him as Nolloth Professor and Fellow of Oriel College. Mitchell has an acute memory:

> Ian Ramsey had pre-eminently the gift of encouraging other people to make their own distinctive contribution to a co-operative enterprise. And any enterprise in which he engaged became a co-operative one. He was for this reason a superb chairman who could enable an initially heterogeneous group of people to develop a common mind without any overt exertion of authority on his part. He displayed this quality characteristically as chairman of a series of groups which reported on ethical problems in medicine and in the biological

sciences. In these discussions with doctors, scientists, lawyers and other experts Ian Ramsey was at his best, patient, quick in comprehension, humorous, fair and firm, impossible to shock and very difficult to disconcert. His improbableness was a great help here. No one ever looked or sounded less like a bishop or even a professor, so that from the start people were able to set aside their preconceptions and see and hear the man. Finding that he would listen to what they had to say, however abstruse and technical, and that he eschewed premature conclusions and artificial reconciliation, the experts quickly lost any suspicions that remained. He was seen to be totally lacking in the timorous anxiety which leads some churchmen to evade the rigours of careful empirical inquiry.

An early excursion into this terrain came prior to the Lambeth Conference of 1958. The Archbishop of Canterbury, Geoffrey Fisher, asked for a number of groups to prepare reports covering the major issues which would come before the Conference. The most far-reaching, important and controversial report was 'The Family in Contemporary Society'. Its basis was characterised in this way:

> Theology activates society when it is embodied in cultural forms: mediaeval Christendom became what it was because theology found an expression, not only in the liturgical, but also in the social and economic, life of men; it broke when theology became circumscribed, partly by authority, partly by its own logic, and so unable any longer to admit other aspects of knowledge and truth. That danger is present to Christians in every age. We would therefore recommend, as the means whereby in our own day a Christian culture may be developed, that the Church should encourage co-operative work on specific problems between those who are specialists working within the different disciplines of their diverse fields.

Ramsey was invited to join the group under the chairmanship of Canon Max Warren (General Secretary of the Church Missionary Society). It was evident that this was no ordinary ecclesiastical constellation. Its members included Richard Titmuss (Professor of Social Administration, University of London at the London School of Economics); T.S. Simey (Professor of Social Science, University of Liverpool); Sir Alexander Carr-Saunders (former Director of the London School of Economics); J.K. Thompson (Head of Social Services Department, Colonial Office); Sir Charles Jeffries (former

Deputy Under-Secretary for the Colonies); Miss E.M. Batten (Principal of William Temple College, Rugby); Canon Ronald Preston (Lecturer in Christian Ethics, University of Manchester); and Canon G.B. Bentley of St George's, Windsor. The Secretary was Revd Gordon Dunstan, Clerical Secretary of the Church of England Moral Welfare Council (later Professor of Moral and Social Theology, King's College, London), who became the knowledgeable and hard-working midwife to all the groups of which Ramsey was a member.

The group was set to study (a) problems of population; (b) economic and industrial development; (c) the reduction of mortality; (d) family planning; (e) social change; (f) related questions of Church discipline. The report itself was balanced, realistic and completely without emotional overtones. The writing distinguished when an argument was put forward from evidence that was conclusive and when ideas were being promulgated which were still in the realm of hypothesis. To the thirty-one pages of report were added 198 pages of appendices in which was provided a valuable collection of factual information from many countries. The evidence was excavated, studied and evaluated. It is extraordinary that the report itself was hatched from a group of nineteen members and signed with unanimity after only four days of discussion, with two additional days by the theologians alone, including Ramsey. This was not the usual route or procedure by which Anglican reports emerge – then or now!

The group held that the moral decision is taken by Christian men and women in the face of a situation which they are bidden to assess with their minds and judge in their consciences, each formed and informed within the life of the Church. Thus bishops, clergy and laity together both create a *consensus fidelium* – a common mind among the faithful – and submit to it. And while they submit today, they are already sensitive to the demands of tomorrow. Pure Ramsey! The Archbishop of Canterbury and the Lambeth Conference were receiving a report which was conspicuously different in tone and temper from the usual procession of reports, which was not necessarily to their liking. But you do not invite eminent people, chosen not for their dedicated churchmanship but for the academic and other peaks they have reached in their own disciplines, and expect them to reach prescribed conclusions. Mollification is not their natural milieu. Members had not been chosen in the usual way, ensuring that known views or convictions of one person must be balanced with contrary views from another person. The report came with a health warning!

> In our writing of this Report we have felt acutely a dilemma of authorship. We would gladly have furnished your Grace with such reading as, being set before your Grace's guests at Lambeth in July 1958, would have been to the satisfaction of them all. But if we had done so, we should have acted irresponsibly. The nature of our subject, and the responsibilities which our Christianity imposes upon us, oblige us to offer some things which the Bishops might understandably not have chosen for themselves, some from which their first inclination might have been to turn away, but things which, in our judgement, their Lordships may properly be asked to receive, and inwardly to digest, when they gather at your Grace's conference table. They will, perhaps, uphold our decision when they recall, as we do, the prayer of Archbishop William Laud:
>
>> Most gracious Father, we most humbly beseech thee
>> for thy holy Catholic Church. Fill it with all truth; in
>> all truth with all peace. Where it is corrupt, pirge it;
>> where it is in error, direct it; where anything is amiss,
>> reform it; where it is right, strengthen and confirm it;
>> where it is divided and rent asunder, make up the
>> breaches of it, O thou Holy One of Israel.

The bulk of the factual material dealt with the problem of over-population, and especially those of under-developed countries. The accumulated evidence undergirded by statistics from all over the world was thorough and refined, provided an assessment and theological consideration of the facts upon which the report was based. It is not difficult to imagine Ramsey revelling in this approach. The group was occasionally brutal in the interest of truth. If there is one thing more damaging than no hope it is false hope! The Lambeth bishops were pressed towards acknowledging realism. Of course, some of the predictions would be proved incorrect, even disproven but others, in the majority, were only too obviously reliable.

It was a long time since a Church of England or Anglican report had attracted major press attention with copious extracts and thoughtful leaders in the press. Birth control was the propeller. It was not simply a reaction to the Roman Catholic Church's strange and debilitating policy on the subject, but a disclosure of the policy and practice of some overseas Anglican provinces where tradition dictated against contraception. But in the report it was clear that family planning was not a preference but an imperative. The emphasis was emphatic, not entirely new but certainly of comparative recent origin. The history of this subject in the annals of twentieth century Anglican history is not very creditable. The case for family planning was rejected by the Lambeth Conference in 1908, and again in 1920, given only a grudgingly permissive acceptance in 1930.

The case for family planning appeared straightforward. If the Church supported the application of modern scientific knowledge to prevent disease or ameliorate suffering and ill-health and maternal and infant mortality, why should it then be reluctant to allow the use of new methods of controlling procreation which would prevent the dangers of overpopulation which may or would ultimately cause starvation in those countries with high birth rates and falling death rates? Such views were not as commonplace in 1957 as they would become a decade later. Details in the report both stimulated and irritated and nowhere more than when family planning was described as a positive good rather than as a *pis aller* suitable for an economic crisis. It was claimed that coitus has a value as expressing the relation between the man and woman and the love between husband and wife, and that these must be considered quite apart from its procreational value – the terms 'relational' and 'procreational' values were used. The symbolism of the union of the man and the woman, of the man's family and the woman's family, and of the intercourse permitting parenthood and that not giving the right of procreation, was common in African rituals of marriage, birth and death; but the mystic concept of coitus between a 'freely consenting man and woman' as constantly enhancing the unity and harmony of the marriage with children still further increasing that harmony was less often explicitly recognised in descriptions of Christian marriage.

The position of the family in the changing world was also discussed, dealing with the effects of automation in industry which gave more leisure at the cost of shift-working night and day, and the loss of individuality to the worker. To look at work as nothing but the necessary means, either to earn a living or to accumulate money and power, is a blasphemy on the dignity of labour. It logically leads to the justification of every form of commercial selfishness and calls by the name of common sense the self-seeking ambition to get as much as you can and to give as little as you must. The 'dignity of work' was a theme Ramsey carried with him to Durham.

Ian Ramsey later claimed that the ground-breaking *The Family in Contemporary Society*:

> marks the end of an era in which Christian ethics had been thought of primarily as the learning of a particular attitude to such topics as drink, gambling, and sex – an attitude which was, on the whole, negative and where what mattered most was skill in argument, the factual background being regarded as sufficiently understood by an intelligent man who was experienced in the world. The new era sees, first, a very different and far-reaching concern with the empirical facts, and secondly, both the status and function of theology as something very different from being *a priori* prescriber of answers, or dispenser of principles which are then applied by rule-of-thumb methods.
>
> (*Christian Ethics in the 1960s and 1970s*)

When the subject came before the Lambeth Conference in 1958 there was a rather lopsided committee. Of its thirty-eight bishops, seven were from England and sixteen from the United States. Only three bishops were nationals and non-white – one each from India, West Africa and the Sudan. Admittedly, at the time, there were no black bishops in South Africa, Central Africa or the West Indies. In West Africa, which included Nigeria, seven of its fourteen bishops were black. Elsewhere in Africa there were no Provinces, simply dioceses which came under the jurisdiction of the Archbishop of Canterbury. There was a single handful of black bishops (two in Uganda, one each in Kenya, Tanganyika (Tanzania) and the Nile). Four bishops covered the whole of South America (and they were part of the then named Protestant Episcopal Church in the United States of America) of which the bishops of Mexico and South-Western Brazil were nationals. Only in Japan were its four bishops nationals. The committee was fortunate in its Chairman, Stephen Bayne of Olympia, the future first holder of the Office of Anglican Executive Officer; in one of its Joint Secretaries, J.E. Hine of Texas (a future Presiding Bishop of the American Church); and in the English contingent which included Leslie Hunter of Sheffield,

Leonard Wilson of Birmingham, and Michael Gresford Jones of St Albans who had solid credentials to offer on a range of ethical issues. On the particular subject of marriage and family planning the Resolution of the Conference appeared to represent Anglican comprehensiveness:

> The Conference believes that the responsibility for deciding upon the number and frequency of children has been laid by God upon the consciences of parents everywhere: that this planning, in such ways as are mutually acceptable to husband and wife in Christian conscience, is a right and important factor in Christian family life and should be the result of positive choice before God. Such responsible parenthood, built on obedience to all the duties of marriage requires a wise stewardship of the resources and abilities of the family as well as a thoughtful consideration of the varying population needs and problems of society and the claims of future generations.

On marriage, the Conference was clear, affirming that:

> marriage is a vocation to holiness, through which men and women may share in the love and creative purposes of God. The sins of self-indulgence and sensuality, born of selfishness and refusal to accept marriage as a divine vocation, destroy its nature and depth, and the right fullness and balance between men and women. Christians need always to remember that sexual love is not an end in itself nor a means to self-gratification, and that self-discipline and restraint are essential conditions of the responsible freedom of marriage and family planning.

Marie Stopes, the English eugenicist who founded Britain's first birth control clinic lived long enough to hear what the Lambeth bishops said. She died in October 1958. The Conference dealt with other matters arising from the report, including artificial human insemination: 'Artificial by any other one than the husband raises problems of such gravity that the Committee cannot see any possibility of its acceptance by Christian people.' This would surface within a decade as would abortion, or infanticide, which involved the killing of life already conceived (as well as a violation of the personality of the mother) save at the dictate of strict and undeniable medical necessity. There were also resolutions on polygamy; gambling, drunkenness, and the use of drugs; migratory labour; and refugees and stateless persons.

An appointment in 1958 provided an opportunity for Ramsey's breadth and style of thinking to be brought to wider notice. The Church of England's Board for Social Responsibility was set up by resolution of the Church Assembly on 1 January 1958 and Ramsey was invited to be one of its first members. The work of the Board was to promote and co-ordinate the thought and action of the Church in matters affecting family, social and industrial life. Under its umbrella came supervision of the Church of England Moral Welfare Council and the Social and Industrial Council. Sir John Wolfenden, Vice-Chancellor of Reading University, was the Board's first chairman and, from the outset, the committees of the Board included some of the most imaginative and radical thinkers of the time. But there were severe growing pains and some of its members thought the Board would benefit from a strong clerical chairman. There were bishop members – Leslie Hunter of Sheffield and Michael Gresford Jones of St Albans – who had experience in some of the issues under consideration. But it can be an advantage to appoint a chairman of a board or commission who has no obvious expertise to offer. His chief contribution will be the manner of his chairmanship, the way he steers the ship.

Wolfenden stepped down in 1961. One of the last acts of Geoffrey Fisher as Archbishop of Canterbury was to call Ronald Williams, Bishop of Leicester into his study at Lambeth Palace and tell him that he would be the next Chairman of the Board for Social Responsibility. Williams was 'called' and 'told' not invited to consider the position. Professor C.H. Vereker, a former Professor of Political Theory and Institutions at Durham University was already a member of the Board. He considered Williams:

> essentially as an 'establishment' man, in the proper, not pejorative, sense of that term. He was moderate and middle of the road, as they say, in all things, he was extremist in none. He represented, and I think saw himself as representing, the unique partnership of Church and State established between 1689 and 1715 and mildly regretted any sign of instability. He was the quintessential Chairman: modest, quiet, firm, reconciling, seeking sensible compromises, indeed all the things needed by the Board when he took over. I should not describe him as an outstanding chairman in, say, the Attlee class, nor even as good as Lord Lindsay, the Master of Balliol, under whom I sat more than

once. Nevertheless he was impressive, commanding considerable respect and minimal criticism; and, because he sometimes went too slowly for the enthusiasts and occasionally too quickly for the conservatives, he was certainly well suited for the job.

Bishop of Leicester from 1953 to 1978, Ronald Williams was the greatest 'Defender of the Church of England' and, incidentally, John Betjeman's favourite bishop!

Ramsey was already well known to Williams. The former had a link with Leicester as one of the four Canons Theologian of Leicester Cathedral, an honorary and non-residential appointment dating from 1944. Ramsey never accepted an appointment without throwing himself into its 'possibilities'. It was not long before he had a warm place in the affections of both clergy and laity. He not only visited the diocese regularly for the Clergy School, where he often lectured, but, when he took his turn as a cathedral preacher, he stayed the weekend in one of the vicarages and preached in the parish churches on the Sunday evening. In this way he made a number of warm friends among the clergy and their families. Here an interesting footnote. From 1938 the Provost of Leicester was Herbert Arthur Jones who moved to Manchester in 1954 as Dean. When he retired in 1963, Ian Ramsey was offered the Manchester deanery but, sensibly, said 'No'. One wonders if he had been offered the deanery of Liverpool at the end of that year when his friend, Frederick William Dillistone, a theologian of note, stepped down to be Fellow and Chaplain of Oriel College, would Ramsey have likewise declined? Deans very rarely become bishops, and his influence in the Church would not have been as substantial or abiding. In terms of scholarship he could have written the 'great work' he never achieved, and his life may have been longer preserved – but there would have been no biography!

Before considering Ramsey's important contribution to working parties and reports of the Board we have Ronald Williams' views of him:

I found he was one of the Board's most lively and enthusiastic members. He tried never to miss a meeting although his engagement book was so full that he would often have to arrive late or depart early. While he was with us he took the very fullest part in our deliberations.

He could always bring a fresh and original contribution to every discussion. The whole slant of his mind led him usually to come down on the more radical, progressive or left wing side of debated issues e.g. marriage and divorce, gambling etc. It was, however, always clear that he had an anchorage of personal faith and devotion sustaining him through all these reappraisals. I remember one occasion when I asked him to take the morning Celebration, and we were all struck I think by his deep devotional approach to the Holy Sacrament. I will not say we were surprised, but another dimension was added to our appreciation of his character and outlook. He was, of course, very much at home in dealing with the inter-disciplinary consultations of which the Board had so many. He had been used to mixing with academics, and I suppose we have to face the fact that he really felt more at home with unbelieving academics than with simple believers, simply because their minds worked on the same lines as his even though they came to different conclusions.

There was a growing opinion, among doctors, magistrates, Members of Parliament, and others, that criminal proceedings were inappropriate against those who attempted unsuccessfully to commit suicide. Accordingly, the first subject the Board was asked to examine by the Archbishop of Canterbury in 1958 was suicide. The Board decided to invite a small group to undertake this work and 'small' in membership would be the watchword for subsequent working parties. Mr J.T. Christie, Principal of Jesus College, Oxford, chaired, and he was joined by Rupert Cross, Fellow and Tutor in Law of Magdalen College, Oxford; Dr Doris Odlum, psychiatrist and magistrate; and Ian Ramsey, with Gordon Dunstan as secretary. The Archbishop was receiving constant enquiries concerning the dependence on coroners' verdicts of the use of the Prayer Book Service for the burial of suicides, a matter also referred to the committee. The report – *Ought Suicide to be a Crime?* – was published within one year, 1959. They had looked at all aspects of suicide and attempted suicide, psychological factors and a moral and religious assessment. Their recommendations were succinct:

1. That attempted suicide should cease to be a crime, and that consideration be given to placing the law with regard to the liability of secondary parties to suicide on a more realistic basis by abolishing the felony of suicide and creating a new offence of aiding, abetting or instigating the suicide of another.

2. The coroners' verdicts should contain reference to 'other significant conditions' contributing to the death of a suicide.
3. That there should be an alternative Burial Service for use in
   certain cases of suicide.
4. That the needs of those tempted to commit suicide and of those
   who actually attempt it be specially commended to the pastoral
   concern of the clergy, and that the clergy be offered more help in
   understanding this part of their pastoral duty.

The case for these recommendations was carefully probed and argued.
Could the Church rightly separate suicide from every other sin?
Could there be a separate burial service without making the decision
as to its use invidious? In the eyes of the Church's teaching suicide
is a sin. It rests on the principle that a person is not the author of his
or her own life, but has received it from God. It is given in order
that a person may serve God in the body of this life. The period of
that service is not for a person to determine. Further, since the act of
suicide is in the nature of things a last and final act, it follows that a
person died in a state of unrepented grave sin. For this reason the
Church had denied to suicides the right of a Christian burial. The
conclusion of the report read, 'The Christian Church consistently
with its theology of death can, where necessary, justifiably provide a
special form of burial service, and in so doing this it also preserves a
moral judgment on some kinds of suicide which we believe it to be
important not to overlook.' The Bishop of Exeter chaired successive
working parties of which Ramsey was a member. When Mortimer
defended the traditional standpoint of the Church towards suicide he
was also clear in his judgment that:

> the Church is right in regarding suicide as a sin, but it does not seem
> to me that she is equally right in denying to suicides Christian burial.
> At least not on the grounds which are usually put forward. In the first
> place, who can tell what may or may not have happened in the last
> few seconds of a man's life? How can we know that a man has died
> without repenting? In the second place, most acts of suicide are
> committed in a state of inner compulsion or mental derangement
> which deprives the act of its full moral significance and blameworthi-
> ness. Few suicides are responsible or fully responsible for their act of
> killing themselves. For these reasons, it seems to me that while the

Church is right in holding in general that suicide is sinful, it is nevertheless wrong in withholding in general and as a matter of course from all suicides the right of Christian burial at one and the same time to mark the sinfulness of deliberate suicide and also able to commend to the loving mercy of God an erring Christian brother.

The report was a prelude to the Government's *Suicide Act, 1961* whereby suicide ceased to be a crime and there was criminal liability for complicity in another's suicide (imprisonment for a term not exceeding fourteen years).

One subject discussed at the 1958 Lambeth Conference required further exploration. How could a country like India ward off the threat of overpopulation unless there was family limitation which included the voluntary sterilisation of men and women? It was an ethical dilemma. In 1960 the Board for Social Responsibility formed a committee. The names are given as several of them will appear on future committees of which Ramsey is either a member or chairman.

The Bishop of Exeter (R.C. Mortimer) Chairman
Miss Josephine Barnes, MRCP, FRCS, FRCOG
Revd Dr Edward Carpenter, Canon of Westminster
R.M. Hare, Fellow of Balliol College, Oxford
Basil Mitchell, Fellow of Keble College, Oxford
The Worshipful Chancellor E. Garth Moore, Fellow of Corpus
    Christi College, Cambridge
Revd Canon Ian Ramsey
Revd G.R. Dunstan – Secretary

Sterilization – an ethical enquiry was published in 1962. The chief concern of this was with voluntary sterilisation as a means of population control. Therapeutic sterilisation, eugenic sterilisation, punitive sterilisation and compulsory sterilisation were mentioned but did not come under the committee's penetrating sights. The committee examined current practice and nothing was left to 'chance' or prejudice. Everything was examined which began with the word 'voluntary'. What thinking Ramsey 'caught' in these committees he made his own in addition to bringing a cascade of his own ideas. What was 'valid consent'? 'There is serious moral danger in any campaign or propaganda in favour of sterilisation, particularly when backed by monetary inducements, of hasty action without proper consideration, and without joint consent.' What of the special responsibility of doctors, and their medical ethics? The pastor may be in a position of both responsibility and difficulty. If the Church formally, in some synodical or other authoritative way, pronounced against sterilisation outright, the pastor's position would be eased. That is not the Anglican way. A paragraph from the report conveys the method of working and a way forward:

> We are not setting ourselves up as champions or advocates of sterilisation as the sovereign remedy for over-population; we are not suggesting either to governments or to people what they ought to do. We may feel convinced – as the Indian Government shows itself to be convinced – that sterilisation alone is no remedy for the existing problem, and that it will do nothing to alleviate the pressures of population without far-reaching social, educational and economic advances as well ... But faced as we are by a situation in which a responsible government is pursuing, together with other ameliorative measures, a policy of persuasion for voluntary sterilisation, and asked by Christian doctors and nurses involved in the carrying out of this policy for help in deciding for themselves how far they can co-operate, we are bound to conclude that we find no grounds on which to reply in terms of an absolute negative. The Church of England does not claim to be infallible, and it may err. But it does believe in progressive revelation under the guidance of the Holy Spirit. And we believe that light on this question is slowly dawning, and we are prepared tentatively to express the opinion that there are circumstances in which an operation for sterilisation may be legitimately employed. This conclusion obliges us to consider further the casuistry of the matter – to consider it as a patient or doctor would when deciding whether or not the operation would be legitimate.

Consideration of medical and social ethical subjects in the 1960s brought together Ian Ramsey and Robert Mortimer. They were by background, temperament, personality and churchmanship complete opposites yet by working together they achieved a number of remarkable achievements for the Church of England. Robert Cecil Mortimer (1902–1976) was Bishop of Exeter for twenty-four years from 1949. The previous twenty years had been spent in Oxford variously as lecturer, Canon of Christ Church Cathedral and Regius Professor of Moral and Pastoral Theology. There was always about him an air of intellectual power and aloofness, a person whose bite was worse than his bark. His style was the reflection of himself – clear, strong, fearless, never sentimental, verbose or ostentatious, yet he had a retiring, almost embarrassingly shy persona except in the company of a variety of close friends. His scorn for whatsoever was unreal or merely ostentatious added a cutting edge to many of his phrases. He was adept at disentangling fact from opinion and the proven from the plausible.

Robert Mortimer was an honest man, striking in gaitered appearance. 'Serious' is a word ascribed to him. He did not have the practical smile to warm, although he had a developed sense of humour. At a time when bishops were increasingly busy he gave an appearance of the opposite with boredom nudging his elbow. High intellect can be a troublesome companion. It is not light, only the wick of a lamp which must be fed constantly with the oil of compassion if its light is to shine before other people.

Mortimer was rooted in the Catholic tradition of the Church of England though perhaps more 'High Church' than 'Anglo-Catholic'. Michael Ramsey could also be so described. When the 1968 Lambeth Conference had a debate on the honours, customary addresses and style of living of bishops it was proposed that forms of address or adulation such as 'Your Grace' and 'My Lord' should fall into desuetude. Mortimer was one of only two bishops in the Anglican Communion who dissented. Was he the last of the Lord Bishops with more than a dash of patriarch and potentate? He would have made an interesting Prince Bishop though he was never an inaccessible proud prelate. Those with troubled consciences, suffering crises of faith, or deeply burdened with sin were never sent empty away. Moreover, he despatched his correspondence with alacrity either delegating a reply to others or responding by one, at most two, sentences on a postcard.

Two contrasts of the two bishops are illuminating. Firstly, sin is a word not greatly used today. For Mortimer sin, penitence and reconciliation were indivisible. Sacramental confession is intended to be difficult, not depressing. It is a tonic to strengthen the good in people and not merely the bromide to quieten the evil. It hurts, but it is the bracing hurt of returning health, the growing pains of restored grace in the soul. That is the requisite for reconciliation. He quoted words of Forbes Robinson, one time Dean of Christ's College, Cambridge, with approval, 'I never try as some people do, to classify and enter into details about my sins. I bring the whole contradictory, weary, and unintelligible mass of them to God, and leave them with Him. I am quite sure that I will never do better without Him. But I know that He believes in me, and will help me in spite of myself.'

Secondly, with his clarity of thought, precision, incisive use of logic, and his command of language, Mortimer was eminent – and trusted – in debates in Church Assembly, Convocation and the House of Lords, where there was no doubt of his power, impact and influence. Of his time there was no spiritual peer to match him. He changed minds and in some cases changed the direction of a debate. Mortimer was the antithesis of 'modern' and scorned popularity – no celebrity he! In 1955 his translation to London was effectively blocked by Archbishop Geoffrey Fisher, who having welcomed an episcopal canonist at Exeter thought, 'there is a real lack of something in him which would still be more evident in London'. Fisher had little understanding of Mortimer beyond his expertise in Canon Law and probably did not like him as a man, and definitely not his perceived churchmanship. Was it both the Church's and London's loss when Henry Montgomery-Campbell of Guildford, rather than Robert Mortimer, went to London?

Professor Basil Mitchell knew Mortimer and Ramsey. 'My memory is that, unlike Ian Ramsey, Mortimer was very much the regulative type of chairman who confined himself to monitoring the discussion which he did in an eminently fair-minded and clear-headed way and left it to the Secretary (Gordon Dunstan) to write the Report.'

Following Mortimer's speech at Church Assembly which opened this chapter, there was immediate action, namely the setting up of a group on Christian Ethics and Natural Law. Members were:

Ian Ramsey (Chairman)
Revd P.E. Coleman, Chaplain of King's College, London
Canon E. Le Grice, Sub-Dean of St Albans Cathedral
Revd J.S. Habgood, Rector of St John's, Jedburgh, Scotland
Canon D.J.B. Hawkins, Roman Catholic philosopher and parish
    priest at Godalming.

Dr R.F. Hobson, Consultant Psychiatrist, Bethlem and Maudsley Hospital

Revd E.L. Mascall, Professor of Historical Theology, King's College, London

Dom Illtyd Trethowan O.S.B., Downside Abbey

Revd H.A. Williams, Fellow and Dean of Chapel, Trinity College, Cambridge

Canon G.F. Woods, Fellow and Dean of Downing College, Cambridge

Canon G.B. Bentley, Canon of Windsor

Revd Fr Herbert McCabe O.P., Blackfriars, Oxford (replacing Dom Illtyd Trethowan)

Revd Gordon Dunstan (Secretary)

The first overnight meeting was held at Lambeth Palace (3–4 January 1964) at the invitation of the Archbishop of Canterbury, Michael Ramsey, and Mrs Ramsey, and three further of the eleven meetings were held at Lambeth during the period ending February 1967. It was suggested at the time that this was perhaps the first occasion since the Reformation when two Roman Catholic priests had been overnight guests at the Palace. The visit, too, gave Canon Hawkins the opportunity to celebrate his first and only Mass in St George's Roman Catholic Cathedral, Southwark, as a member of the cathedral body, for a week or two later he died suddenly, to the impoverishment of the whole field of scholarship of which he was a distinguished and enlivening contributor.

As an academic group no fault can be found. Papers were prepared and circulated in advance of each gathering. Texts were revised as a result of energetic discussion. However, the group cantered all over the place; ideas bubbled their way to the surface; the group did not recognise any boundary fences. A few of the papers were published in *Theology* and two of Ramsey's were published, 'Towards a Rehabilitation of Natural Law' in *Christian Ethics and Contemporary Philosophy* (1966) and, posthumously, 'Censorship' in *Theology* (January 1974).

Other completed papers were:

'Tax Avoidance' (Ian Ramsey)

'Homosexual Problems' (Peter Coleman)

'Family Responsibilities' (John Habgood and Edwin LeGrice)

'The Concept of Natural Law' (Eric Mascall)

'Chastity Problem' (Peter Coleman)

'Telling the Truth' (Herbert McCabe) and separately (Edwin Le Grice)

'Is Ethics a Science?' (John Habgood)

'Oaths and Promises' (Gordon Dunstan)

'Aquinas and a Science of Values' (R.F. Hobson)

'Some Aspects of the Psychology of Morals' (R.F. Hobson)

'Natural Law and Christian Ethics' (G.F. Woods)

'One Approach to Natural Law' (G.B. Bentley)

'A Natural Law Miscellany' (E.L. Mascall, D.J.B. Hawkins and Illtyd Trethowan)

'Forgiveness and Christian Virtue and Natural Necessity' (Gordon Dunstan)

'Censorship' (John Habgood)

Ultimately why was there so little to show to a wider public? In part it was a failure of chairmanship. In some ways the group could have lightened its task and shortened its labours, if it had been content to argue the relation of Christian ethics to natural law in the terms laid down by about two thousand years of developing tradition. This would have made a neat academic exercise. But the questions did not come before the group as an academic question. They came in terms of popularly debated, emotionally charged moral issues, of fears on the one side lest distinguished Christians and clergyman were publicly repudiating Christian morality, particularly in that part of it which concerned sexual relationships; and of fears on the other side lest the Church, through tenacity to the forms in which Christian morality had in earlier generations been expressed, was either refusing to face the implications of new knowledge, new freedoms, new obligations, in short, of a new society, or was unable to speak meaningfully, in terms of morals, to that society today. The group chose, therefore, to start its search from within some of those moral issues: to take particular cases of moral decision, to analyse the empirical factors involved, to discover what guidance could be given in terms of the Judaeo-Christian revelation, as contained in Holy Scripture and the tradition of the Church, and what indications there were of grounds for decision which might be said to derive from 'natural law'.

Would anything emerge from the group's deliberations other than isolated articles from individual members in theological periodicals? The group was overflowing with ideas and someone needed to call 'halt' and look at each idea in some form of sequence. Ramsey's generosity of spirit and his interest in each and every subject was an obstacle to exercising firm chairmanship. Although there were individual satisfactions the planned volume of essays was not published. This was regrettable.

Ramsey was at his most effective when working in small groups, as chairman or member, where there was a specific subject to be considered and when there was a core of continuing members. A supreme example of this approach resulted in a commanding report *Decisions About Life and Death. A Problem in Modern Medicine* (1965), which was reprinted many times. Mortimer was chairman and to the regular membership of Ian Ramsey, G.B. Bentley, R.M. Hare, Basil Mitchell, Garth Moore, and Gordon Dunstan, were added G.F. Abercrombie, a former President of the College of General Practitioners; and Lord Amulree, President of the British Geriatric Society. It cannot have been the intention of the group to provoke comment and accelerate readership by quotations from literature, but that was the effect as reviews in newspapers and periodicals used the words to preface their own observations:

> Vex not his ghost: O, let him pass! he hates him
> That would upon the rock of this tough world
> Stretch him out longer.
>
> (*King Lear*, v. iii)

We do not respect life the less for recognising the boon. There comes a moment, life being what it is, when it is good to die; and therefore good also to allow the other to go unvexed to death. But when is that moment? How is it recognised when it comes? Lear knew, with all the certainty of madness:

> I know when one is dead and when one lives
> She's dead as earth — Lend me a looking glass;
> If that her breath will mist or stain the stone,
> Why then, she lives.
>
> (*Ibid.*)

But Cordelia was dead.

What would a medical team to-day have done with that scene? What tests for life, what efforts to resuscitate, what apparatus, what choice of essences to inject into the vein! To Lear, stripped of his kingship, they might accord the prerogative of age, with licence there and then to die. But Cordelia, young, newly married, a victim of a treacherous assault, they would not have allowed to slip away so easily.

In short, the resources of knowledge, apparatus and skill which modern medicine can organise to combat death are now so formidable that they raise forcibly the question of the ethics of their use.

When Gordon Dunstan, by now Emeritus Professor of Moral and Social Theology in the University of London, gave the first Ian Ramsey Memorial Lecture in the Examinations Schools, Oxford on 2 December 1986, under the auspices of the Ian Ramsey Centre, he referred to the 1965 report:

The technology of intensive care has advanced since 1964, and the discussion of when to terminate life-support systems is a fading candidate for sensational television. Twenty years ago this was not so. Bishop Mortimer opened the discussion seriously with the quip from Clough, when the British Medical Association (BMA) invited him to address it at a meeting in his diocese, in Torquay. Then a lady from Bristol wrote to the Archbishop of Canterbury to ask whether her husband, whose comatose condition she described, were alive or dead. The Archbishop replied modestly that he didn't know; but the group was already at work on it. Its report, *Decisions about Life and Death* bears the stamp of Ramsey's mind. At the critical point two cases are argued, one 'utilitarian', by Hare, the other, 'traditional' by Bentley. Ramsey worked these around to a practical conclusion. The report had notable merits – short shrift, for instance, to the undisciplined use of the language of 'love' and of 'doing God's will'; a repudiation of a notional formula 'to give guidance in all cases'; a warning – ignored, alas, in the USA – of the awful consequences of being able to sue a doctor for not using every available resource for keeping a patient artificially alive against his better clinical judgment; an admonition to give serious attention to the emotional stress and troubled consciences of nurses, as well as to the potentially bereft; a clear statement that, while consultation is essential to the process of clinical judgement, 'society cannot take the duty of decision away from the physician'.

The report made its way in the medical literature, and it received the compliment of being plagiarised without acknowledgement. Another sequel was more important. We brought Lord Amulree, one of the founding fathers of modern geriatrics into the group, to our great benefit – and he enjoyed it too. When, at about that time, a clergyman named Edward Shotter came to talk over with me his vision of what was to become the London Medical Group and now the Institute of Medical Ethics, I told him firmly that he must have respected medical backing, for counsel and repute. He took the point and said, But whom? I sent him to Amulree. Their creation began to fulfill what Ian Ramsey knew ought to be done.

(Journal of Medical Ethics (1987))

The subject of euthanasia was not buried. The 1965 report was followed by a pamphlet and correspondence war. It appeared that the tide of opinion was moving in favour of change. In 1969 Lord Raglan, Labour peer, moved the second reading of the Voluntary Euthanasia Bill. Bishops Mortimer and Ramsey and Lord Amulree were expected to be in the House of Lords. There were those who wondered what would be Ramsey's approach after his liberal voting record on abortion. There was hatched a surreptitious plot. Gordon Dunstan was asked to take him down to St Christopher's Hospice to meet Dr Cicely Saunders. Dunstan has a vivid memory: 'If Ian was ever in doubt about how to meet the moral claim of a human being so miserable as to want to die, Dame Cicely, as she became, convinced him that there was a better way than to kill them; she gave Ian a vision of the moral obligation of enhancing terminal care.'

This is a pertinent and revealing observation. Ramsey's mind could be halted, changed or enhanced by a personal encounter. It may be a conversation in a taxi or in the street or at a parish bun-fight or in a question and answer session following a talk or lecture. He would go away and 'worry' a solution out or reach a modified or changed position. His fundamental direction rarely changed but the route his argument took him varied. This was in contrast to Robert Mortimer who formulated his principles and made his decisions sitting at his study table. Gordon Dunstan, as draftsman of reports, received from Ramsey sheaves of papers annotated, in a minute hand, in all four margins and on the reverse. From Mortimer there came a typical note, with wit encoded in the learning:

My dear Dunstan,
    Melior est conditio possidentis, I think, applies.
       Yours +R E

Lord Raglan moved the second reading of the Bill on 25 March 1969. The Bill would have empowered hospital doctors to administer euthanasia to incurably ill patients who had previously signed a declaration of assent. This declaration would have lasted three years, unless re-executed in the year preceding its expiry, when it would have remained in force for life. No doctor or nurse opposed to euthanasia would have been required to take part in its administration. Mortimer and Ramsey spoke. Ramsey's argument was that there was no single Christian view on euthanasia:

> In the context of pain the argument for euthanasia is much weakened because of the development of pharmacology and analgesic drugs, that something like euthanasia might well in principle be justified in the context of extraordinary means of keeping people alive; and it would be highly problematical in the case of mental distress and likely to be hazardous in the case of alleged social desirability.
>
> Part of the trouble of this Bill is that it tries to cover too many cases. But suppose we agreed, as I have done, that in some cases euthanasia might in principle be justified, suppose we hesitated in other words to have a universal moral negative, does a prior declaration which seems inevitable for euthanasia ever to become a recognised general practice in fact help? Or does it make present difficulties even worse?
>
> This is the crucial question which the Bill raises. Does a prior declaration which seems to be an administrative necessity if we wish to give individual moral decisions a statutory and legal context help us? My view is that the undoubted need for a declaration brings with it so many difficulties that the Bill turns out to be not for the benefit of humanity but to its detriment.

Ramsey held that it was obviously very difficult for people who were seriously ill to make a reasonable declaration of their intentions and desires. Once a declaration was made, it would subject doctors to all sorts of unfair pressure, which could well become intolerable. Relatives might well be unscrupulous, though they might well be equally insistent and pleading, determined by the possible risks that the Bill might bring in, say, the field of alleged social desirability. Ramsey said:

I am quite prepared to see that any moral advance brings with it risks and it would be a disastrous day when Christians give the impression that they will take no risks in reaching their moral decisions. For they will display a harsh, unyielding obscurantism, and even give the impression of knowing all the answers beforehand.

There is an obvious need to disseminate by teaching and practice recent knowledge about drugs and terminal illness. Further, we need to bring together those whose experience is of people dying in great pain and those who have found ways of enabling terminal illness, to have such relief as to leave the patient mentally alert and reasonably peaceful, to see how far the residual cases of pain and distress — sometimes given at present as fifteen per cent — could be reduced . . . Finally, if there is any doubt whatever about the legality of withdrawing artificial means of survival when a considered medical moral decision judges it to be right, no doubt this is something which needs seriously following up.

During the House of Lords debate Mortimer said that the Bill would increase fear and anxiety:

> so that they will spend the last years or months of their lives in a really distressing condition of fear, of never knowing, or never trusting those who look after them.
>
> So I think that the compassion which has inspired this Bill would be better replaced by compassion for the millions of elderly people who are already in some fear and anxiety, and that the true compassion is to press for further research into drugs and pain-controlling analgesics, and for more money to be spent to improve both the staffing and the conditions of geriatric homes and hospitals. That is the true expression of the compassion which we all feel for the old and the incurably ill: not to allow them, with the help of a doctor, to kill themselves, but to provide for them the conditions and the circumstances which will make their lives bearable, so that they may die in peace and in dignity. I think this Bill is altogether a wrong expression of the compassion which we all feel.

The Voluntary Euthanasia Bill was defeated by sixty-one votes to forty.

Such was the impact of *Decisions About Life and Death* that when a more precise study of the issues raised by euthanasia was needed another working party was set up, this time under Ramsey's chairmanship and whose members were Lord Amulree, R.M. Hare, Basil Mitchell, Garth Moore and Gordon Dunstan. To that number were added Dr Cicely Saunders, Medical Director of St Christopher's Hospice, Sydenham, London; Revd M.A.H. Melinsky, Chief Secretary of the Advisory Council for the Church's Ministry and Chairman of the Institute of Religion and Medicine. When Gordon Dunstan (then a full member) resigned, his place was taken by the Revd P. Baelz, Canon of Christ Church and Regius Professor of Moral and Pastoral Theology in the University of Oxford. When Ramsey died in 1972, Canon Melinsky acted as chairman. The new report, *On Dying Well. An Anglican Contribution to the Debate on Euthanasia* was published in 1975 with a second edition in 2000.

Abortion and divorce reform will be considered in a later chapter, 'Lord Spiritual'.

CHAPTER 3

Ian Dunelm:

I AN RAMSEY WAS IMMUNE TO that virulently contagious disease in the Church of England – prefermentitis. Once caught it is difficult to control, impossible to cure. It makes its presence felt by a constant nipping away at the interior self. A priest eagerly anticipates episcopal retirements and notes deaths of bishops, deans and archdeacons. His mental and emotional energies are swift to imagine himself filling a vacant diocesan or suffragan bishopric. If he is at a university, the opportunity of ascending to a plum professorship will rustle his imaginative longings. When he reads of the appointment of a peer or junior (in age and experience), he is deflated and discouraged. There is nothing that more effectually destroys pastoral efficiency or academic excellence than a divided mind and the restlessness of discontent.

An ambition to serve in a different and enlarged sphere of opportunity is not unhealthy. A priest should be realistically aware of his natural gifts, acquired skills, and sheer, solid, proven ability, without obliterating or overlooking any flaws of personality and weaknesses in his ministry. A wise friend or spiritual director should ensure that the ego will not lead to pastoral distraction and spiritual travail.

Hard-working parish priests are familiar with temptation and torment, of energetic striving and mental effort, back-breaking and heart-rending ministry, inflated by successes and coping with failures; of finding many souls and losing some; of endeavouring to be holy and good; of holding in almost impossible equipoise the family of God of the parish and his own wife and children. Consider a Nolloth Professor of the Philosophy of Christian Religion in the University of Oxford who stretches his restless mind to the utmost, endeavouring to construct a new and convincing apologetic for the Christian religion in an unfavourable climate. There is a mixture of engaging enthusiasm, rapid speech, subtle distinctions, popular illustrations and vocabulary, all informed by a warm personal faith, which seems able to survive the most devastating intellectual readjustments. A whirligig of academic activity, authorship, chairing or membership of innumerable Church of England working parties considering ethical problems of national significance, brings the professor wider notice. Criticism of aspects of his thought do not diminish the respect and affection in which he is held.

Ian Ramsey was unaware that the Bishop of Durham, Maurice Henry Harland, was retiring until he received a letter from Prime Minister Harold Wilson on 6 August 1966:

> I left home for College, knowing nothing of what awaited me there. Opening letters on my desk, I had read about half, when I noticed, amongst the circulars at the bottom of the pile, a large envelope, which seemed to me of better quality paper than its neighbours. Inquisitively, I drew it out and then noticed the words 'Prime Minister' on the outside.
>
> I opened it. 'The Bishopric of Durham will become vacant at the end of this month . . .' I gasped. The letter concluded: 'It is my hope that you will allow me to submit your name to The Queen for succession to the See of Durham.' It was a complete surprise and I was quite overwhelmed. The view from my window in Oriel College was suddenly changed into one of a Cathedral built on a rock, surrounded by a University, and set in a County which has had its full measure of both industrial pioneering and industrial distress. Nor on the Feast of the Transfiguration was I likely to suppose that there could ever be a transforming vision without its sequel in a call to exacting service.

No English bishopric is more interwoven with the nation's history. In history the Diocese of Durham must be pictured as a little kingdom, equipped with the complete machinery of government – courts, civil and criminal, sheriffs and other officers, parliament, mint, prisons and an army. The area between the Tweed, the Tyne and the Tees formed the immediate patrimony of St Cuthbert and was known throughout the Middle Ages and for long afterwards, not as the 'County of Durham' but simply as 'The Bishoprick'. (Today the tourist industry flaunts 'The Bishopric' in County Durham, now subtitled 'Land of the Prince Bishops' and there is 'The Prince Bishops' indoor shopping centre in the city.)

What were the factors which combined to create and maintain the extraordinary independence which the Palatine implied? There was the fame of St Cuthbert. Beyond question the origin of the Palatine Jurisdiction is religious. The history of saints often presents an insoluble problem. Why should such vast influence have been wielded by such persons? The problem is nowhere more intriguing than in the case of St Cuthbert. His life was one of asceticism rather than of labour. By far the larger part of it was devoted to the care of his own soul, and he was not remarkable either as a reformer of ecclesiastical order, nor as a preacher of the gospel. Yet the Church held him in extraordinary veneration. It is suggested that his fame reflected rather the interest of a Church than the merits of an individual. But of his immense popularity and lasting fame there is no question. Great grants of land were made to him by the kings and nobles of Northumbria. Legend has probably magnified the facts, but the facts are sufficient. The miracle-working body of the Saint was a magnet of pious gifts, and it created the famous sanctuary which for centuries hallowed the local independence, and filled the coffers of the Benedictine monastery.

The Palatine Bishoprick was in a strategic position. Yet the King exercised a dominating influence over episcopal appointments, and could make sure that the Bishop of Durham was the man of his choice. It did, indeed, sometimes happen that the Bishop disappointed his Royal patron's expectations. However, the Palatinate would not have persisted, had it not been for the circumstance that it was held and developed by a remarkable succession of strong palatine bishops. They included some of the most masterful and outstanding figures of the national history – Ranulf Flambard, Hugh de Pudsey, Anthony Bek, Thomas de Hatfield, Richard de Bury, Richard Fox, Thomas Ruthall, Cuthbert Tunstall, Thomas Morton, John Cosin. None of these figures was translated to York or Canterbury. It was mightier to be Bishop of Durham as rulers, builders, governors, diplomatists, statesmen, warriors, and scholars. All were exceedingly strong men capable of standing up against the enemy in the field, and the monarch in the council. They were Princes as well as Bishops. Such men as these were not likely to leave unused whatever powers they possessed, nor would they let slip any opportunity of increasing their prerogatives. On the whole they succeeded in maintaining their position with astonishing success. In the history of The Bishoprick to date only eight bishops were translated to York, and only two (Charles Thomas Longley and Michael Ramsey) from York to Canterbury.

It was inevitable that change would come with the despotic temper of Henry VIII, and with his compulsive centralising methods. The same logic which required the destruction of St Cuthbert's shrine, and the dissolution of the Abbey of Durham, required the abolition of the Palatinate's independency. Although the blow fell in 1536, stripping its substantial powers, the Palatine Jurisdiction survived, albeit in attenuated form, for no less than three hundred years save for its temporary suppression by the Puritans. It expired in 1836 with William van Mildert, the last of the bishops of Durham who possessed the rights and dignity of Earl Palatine. Van Mildert handed over Durham Castle to be the home of University College which he founded in 1832.

The Diocese of Durham covered the whole of the counties of Durham and Northumberland but following The Bishoprics Act 1878 new dioceses were established including Newcastle in 1882, when the parishes in Northumberland were severed from Durham.

Ian Ramsey was meticulous in accumulating and using statistics and sundry facts to aid and abet his ministry. On such a foundation he built pyramids of information as his knowledge of places and persons grew. It is of more than common interest that the following facts are here recorded to illustrate Ramsey's work ahead. Population figures are those for 1966. The total number of clergy was 360. There were two archdeaconries.

The Archdeaconry of Durham comprised 8 deaneries, 160 benefices with a population of 1,029,896:

a	Deanery of Chester-le-Street	20 Benefices	146,332 Population
b	Deanery of Durham	16 Benefices	61,934 Population
c	Deanery of Easington	22 Benefices	97,578 Population
d	Deanery of Gateshead	21 Benefices	154,261 Population
e	Deanery of Houghton-le-Spring	16 Benefices	90,140 Population
f	Deanery of Jarrow	23 Benefices	175,905 Population
g	Deanery of Lanchester	16 Benefices	75,390 Population
h	Deanery of Wearmouth	26 Benefices	228,356 Population

The Archdeaconry of Auckland comprised 6 deaneries, 100 benefices with a population of 484,105:

i	Deanery of Auckland	21 Benefices	84,486 Population
j	Deanery of Barnard Castle	11 Benefices	89,922 Population
k	Deanery of Darlington	19 Benefices	108,392 Population
l	Deanery of Hartlepool	14 Benefices	118,402 Population
m	Deanery of Stanhope	13 Benefices	23,525 Population
n	Deanery of Stockton	22 Benefices	130,378 Population

Amongst the twentieth-century bishops of Durham the name of Herbert Hensley Henson, 1920–1939, was and is historically pre-eminent. He was followed by Alwyn Terrell Petre Williams, who was translated to Winchester, his natural home, in 1952. Arthur Michael Ramsey was Canon Residentiary of Durham Cathedral and Professor of Divinity in the University of Durham for ten years before a very short sojourn as Regius Professor of Divinity in Cambridge, before returning to Durham to be acclaimed as its bishop. Many went from Durham to York Minster for his consecration on St Michael's Day 1952 and remember the thrill that ran through the Minster when the fourth verse of 'Stars of the Morning' came round according to the English Hymnal version 'Who like the Lord thunders Michael the Chief'. And in a sense that was that! Within two years he was translated to the archbishopric of York en route to Canterbury.

In 1954 an unanticipated appointment came with the translation of Maurice Henry Harland from Lincoln. Why sixty-year-old Harland whose best work was done as Bishop of Lincoln? He was in the mould of Archbishop Geoffrey Fisher who was the influence behind his nomination to Lincoln. Harland was a man of the 'establishment' and, again, like his Primate, detested clergy who rocked the boat. He was intelligent, not intellectual like Alwyn Williams or Michael Ramsey. When he went to Lincoln in 1947 there were people in the diocese who still remembered the 'saint', Edward King, with admiration and reverence (bishop from 1885–1910). Harland was as different as could be! He was a practical man capable of re-organising the diocese after the war. He succeeded in getting the precarious finances on to a sound and useful basis. The word 'quota' was dropped and 'tribute' took its place. He did not think a bishop should be too accessible to the clergy whereas he looked to influential laity in the diocese for support. However, unlike some diocesan bishops, his appointment of suffragan bishops and archdeacons did not provide mirror images of himself. There was collegiality but without any doubt who had the last word. He was a true countryman, liked riding and fishing and had fought in the First World War. However, none of these qualities pointed to experience or empathy with the industrial north of England. However, writing to this biographer he had these reflections to offer on his Durham episcopate:

> The parishes in Durham are huge and growing; a parish of 5,000 population is a small one in those parts and there were very few with populations under 1,000. Huge housing estates sprang up everywhere; church buildings and men to staff them had to be found. The shortage of men seeking ordination was not acute. Church life in Durham is very strong. Those good people do not do things by halves, but what they undertake they do with a will. It was the ambition of the majority of the clergy before ordination, to offer themselves for the Ministry, to be trained in their own county, to minister to their own people. This worried me at first. Durham has good schools, University and Theological Colleges, so could needs train its own clergy. I came to appreciate the great strength this brought, though I never ceased to hope men to go further afield for their training and initial experience and learn what the world outside their great County was like. Many followed my advice but nearly all soon returned.
>
> New housing areas with inevitable, make-shift buildings and equipment have their own exhilarations and challenges, but men can be very lonely in them and they have great spiritual strains. Something in the nature of group ministries and house-churches were needed. But how can a group ministry be created? Not, I am convinced, by orders from on high, or schemes worked out on paper, or by proposals from diocesan staff. A group ministry must, in my judgement, spring or emerge from the men who are able to compose the group and this is what actually happened. Near Sunderland, for instance, there was a number of new housing estate parishes contiguous with one another. I was able to find an assistant curate for each of them. The incumbencies came together and formed themselves into a team. They had regular staff meetings and worshipped together. They pooled their resources in gifts and talents. The parishes remained separate but were staffed by the clergy working together as a team. It was one of the most inspiring, thrilling ventures I have known. This sort of thing happens when the clergy are trusted and encouraged to

1. *Arthur Ramsey (father) as a GPO Telegraph Boy*

2. *May Cornthwaite (mother)*

3. Ian Ramsey at 3 years old – a card sent to his father during the First World War

4. Arthur and Ian (8 years old) on board Wyre Wyvern *from Fleetwood to Morecambe in 1923*

5. *Ian (8 years old) left of centre with sailor hat and glasses, looking at camera on a Whit Saturday walk, 1923*

6. *Ian at Graduation in Cambridge*

7. *Margaret McKay in August 1938*

8. *Arthur, May and Ian Ramsey at Ripon Hall, Oxford, 1939*

9. *Ian on Ordination Day in Christ Church Meadow*

10. *Ian and Margaret in snow and in love, Oxford 1942*

11. *Wedding Day group in front of Master's Lodge, Christ's College, with Canon Charles Reven, Master of Christ's, standing behind Ian and Margaret. Present: The Revd Rex Luckraft (Best Man), Arthur Ramsey, May Ramsey, Ian and Margaret, Mrs Spooncer, Mr Spooncer, Helen McKay – Margaret's sister*

12. *Margaret with Paul, Bishop Guy Vernon Smith of Leicester and Ian at 292B Hills Road, Cambridge, their home from 1947 to 1951*

13. Paul, Vivian and Ian enjoying the beach at Cromer, Norfolk in the early 1950s

14. Paul, Margaret and Vivian on board Cairngowan *in Liverpool Docks before their Christmas 1962 Atlantic journey*

15. Ian in his Rooms at Oriel College, Oxford, 1966. © Oxford Mail & Times

16. Bishop Maurice Harland and Ian on his first visit to Auckland Castle, 15 August 1966.
© courtesy of NCJ Media Limited

work out the problem of their own area with the full support of the bishop and his staff.

In a large diocese with more than one suffragan, I do think each should have a specified area under the diocesan. This was the case in Lincoln (with suffragans of Grantham and Grimsby). Where there is only one suffragan as in Durham, it is impracticable – in my view. We dealt with the problem by dividing the Diocese into two parts for Confirmations and so forth. To administer Confirmation is one of the chief occasions for the Bishop to 'get into' the parishes. It meant that Alec Hamilton (Harland's choice as Bishop Suffragan of Jarrow at the end of his Durham episcopate) and I spent alternate years in each half of the Diocese. It was not a hard and fast rule and each of us strayed over the other's boundaries as wished and by mutual consent. I am sure that too much is made of the heavy responsibilities laid upon bishops. Of course the job is too big for any man – so is the priesthood – most bishops learn how and where to devote their major energies and plan their work accordingly. There is no evidence that we are a short-lived lot. It is rare that a bishop dies of over-work. As regards efficiency, I think that working under the stimulus of pressure sharpens the faculties. We all tend to think we are over-worked and how much better we would do if we had more time and leisure to think and read and pray, but I wonder – when there is more time and leisure, there is the greater temptation to be so busy with other things we like doing as to leave no time for the uncongenial and the 'chores'. The exercise of particular gifts needs to be corrected by the discipline of the more mundane duties, or so I feel. Experience indicated that the jobs are best done by those already at the stretch, they seem to be the only folk who have time for the extras.

When the See of Norwich fell vacant in 1959, Archbishop Geoffrey Fisher thought a new bishop should be unobtrusive in churchmanship with the ability 'to lead the rather feudal and slow-going people of Norfolk, with a wife who understands that kind of life.' He approached several bishops including Maurice Harland having heard that 'you and the mining population have not clicked and that you are feeling your work there as a burden hard to be endured.' Harland's response was immediate intimating that he was 'entirely happy with the challenge which Durham provides.' (*Fisher Papers* cccxxi pp. 303, 322, 306. Lambeth Palace Library). Launcelot Fleming, a bachelor, who had been second on the archbishop's original list, was translated from Portsmouth to Norwich. It was an imaginative appointment of a bishop whose experience included being a rowing coach, geologist, Antarctic explorer, head of the Scott Polar Research Institute, pacifist and naval chaplain. He was a remarkably good bishop and after twelve years was appointed Dean of Windsor.

This historical note prompts an observation. If Harland had been translated to Norwich in 1959 it is unlikely that Ian Ramsey would ever have been nominated for Durham. At the time Harold Macmillan was Prime Minister and Michael Ramsey, Archbishop of York. There is no evidence that Ian Ramsey was ever on Archbishop Fisher's lists of could be/would be or possible/probable bishops!

What were the factors surrounding the nomination of a successor to Maurice Harland? Harold Wilson was Prime Minister and though well-informed and personally interested in appointments to bishoprics, he relied on a labyrinth of contacts reporting to him by stealth. However, he was personally responsible for the appointment of two former overseas bishops, Leslie Brown of Uganda to St Edmundsbury and Ipswich and Kenneth Skelton formerly of Matabeleland, then Assistant Bishop of Durham to Lichfield. He would have liked Trevor Huddleston to be an English diocesan bishop but there were reasons for that possibility failing to come to fruition. By 1966 there was another person in the ecclesiastical appointments pie, namely one particular Prime Minister's Patronage Secretary whose knowledge and influence was substantial, at times decisive. The records show that when it came to the Durham vacancy the most influential finger in the pie was that of John Hewitt, the P.M's Patronage Secretary from 1961 to 1973. He was the son of a clergyman, gifted, diplomatically perceptive and extremely thorough with his confidential enquiries. But there were two blemishes affecting his judgement, for good or ill. First, if there was the slightest whiff or rumour of moral turpitude, not least of a sexual nature, a name would be deleted from the list. Secondly, if any priest or bishop were in favour of modification or unravelling the established nature of the Church towards disestablishment, their name would not reach the Prime Minister's desk. The persuasive 'power' he accumulated to himself exceeded his brief. The Archbishop of Canterbury, Michael Ramsey, was uneasy at the accelerating influence of the Patronage Secretary on episcopal appointments. This was not a recent problem. Michael Ramsey's biographer, Owen Chadwick, had access to all relevant papers and saw a change developing during Prime Minister Clement Attlee's years. 'Then the work of the patronage secretary started to grow in importance as consultation was needed until that secretary became an extra weight in the choice of bishops which had to be taken into account; and although this was much to be admired for its conscientiousness, and for its occasional inspired nominations, it was not the right way for the Church's chief pastors to be chosen.' The Archbishop wrote, 'It belongs to the maturity and health of a Church that it should choose its own pastors . . . A Church without such powers is warped in its potentiality of growing, through whatever hazards and mistakes, in the practice of Christian wisdom.' John Hewitt was responsible for putting a block on Eric Kemp and Hugh Montefiore. After he retired, they became bishops of Chichester and Birmingham respectively.

Who for Durham under this tripartite method of appointment – Archbishop, Prime Minister and Patronage Secretary? Whatever the pressing local needs of the time, they should not be pre-eminent or the sole reason. A bishop of Durham automatically has a seat in the House of Lords so may have a distinctive voice in that chamber. A person of experience in the central councils of the Church (then, Church Assembly and Convocation), a northerner, already a bishop ripe for translation? Part of Durham's historic distinctiveness and strength is that it has not had a line of bishops who have been translated from other Sees. Neither have its bishops necessarily been previously prominent figures in the institutional church. They have been independently-minded people. In 1966 there were few scholars on the bench of bishops. Although both archbishops favoured an injection of intellect the 'who' and from 'where' were not easy to unite. It was well known that some of the outstanding professors of divinity, moral theology or ecclesiastical history were offered and declined bishoprics. When Ian Ramsey's name was made public, it appeared as an unforeseen and unrumoured appointment. It was received with everything ranging from surprise to acclaim and rapture. Here was a man of academic distinction, wide sympathies, pastoral sensitivity and personal probity. In the episcopal lineage the one with whom comparison came most quickly to mind was Joseph Butler, Bishop from 1750–1752. For Butler, like Ian Ramsey, found himself called upon to proclaim and defend Christian faith at a time when it was widely attacked and despised.

Ramsey had a contractual obligation to complete work at Oxford so could not be resident in the diocese until mid-December. The Consecration was fixed for All Saints' Day. Ramsey refers to the word 'Consecration' in *The Bishop's Letter* November 1966:

> 'Consecration' is not a word which I can bring myself to write or to utter very easily. Derived from the Latin word for 'holy', it always has for me an awesome character. But it does of course tell of a complete commitment and dedication to God in Christ. We may recall the hymn 'Take my life and let it be/Consecrated, Lord, to thee . . .' where 'consecration', uniting moments and days, is then spelt out in terms of hands, feet, voice, lips, possessions, intellect, will, heart and love. 'Who is sufficient for these things?' (II Cor. 2:16). It is indeed an awesome ideal, and the word 'consecration' would be utterly unpronounceable were it not for the assurance that 'our sufficiency is from God' (II Cor. 3:5).

We are invited to travel with Ian Ramsey on his journey to York Minster for Consecration:

> So as to go to the Consecration with my work and life in Durham foremost in my mind, I first travelled with my family to Bishop Auckland, where on the Sunday evening and Monday morning we worshipped in the Oratory and Chapel. Evensong in York Minster on the Monday was followed by the Confirmation of Election which I found surprisingly edifying and impressive, with the Litany set within a legal dialogue, and the whole representing a characteristic inter-weaving of Church and State, faith and society. Archaic? Certainly; where else would we use the verb 'porrect'? Needing to be reformed? Very likely. An empty formality? I was far from thinking it so. Not for the first time, too, was I grateful to have with me Dr Ferens (Legal Secretary to the Bishop), whom I have already come to associate with a rare combination of legality and humanity.
>
> All Saints' Day dawned crisp and clear. The meadows were covered with frost and there was a mist rising from the river as we went into the Chapel at Bishopthorpe to accept gratefully the gift of a new day and the trust of its hours. At Mass that morning in the Roman Catholic Chaplaincy at Oxford, appropriate biddings were made; friends as far apart as Buenos Aires and Helsinki were offering prayers;

in the Chapel of the group of Psychiatric Hospitals whose Management Committee I have chaired for many years, a service incorporating the Consecration Collect, Epistle and Gospel was held. I mention these as tokens of all those, near and far, and in all kinds of Churches, whose prayerful remembrance I shall never forget. I cannot express adequately my gratitude to all those who by their planning or participation, by their presence or by their messages, but above all by their prayers helped and sustained me on this great day.

(The Bishop's Letter December 1966)

The Service of Consecration was wholly magnificent and magnificently holy. At the centre was a little, tubby figure robed in 'magpie', as they call the black and white chimere and rochet. He was presented to the Archbishop of York (Donald Coggan), by the Bishops of Leicester (Ronald Williams), and Oxford (Harry Carpenter). It is the custom for the consecrand to choose the preacher. Ian Ramsey invited his first teacher in the philosophy of religion, by now Canon John S. Boys Smith, Master of St John's College, Cambridge. Here again we are fortunate in having Ramsey's own memories:

I see it as gathering together past and future in giving significance to the present, a present where God ever calls us as Canon Boys Smith so well reminded us in his sermon, not to blind and unquestioning obedience, but rather to 'see', to have eager, single-eyed discernment of the young child, the kind of devotion which can inform intellectual candour as well as all human toil, and in which the work of us all is equally fulfilled. Reminders of past years were my old Headmaster, and a Lancashire coal-miner, long retired, who once taught me in Sunday School; former colleagues from Cambridge, and many school friends. I was grateful for all who had joined us from the County and City of Durham representing to me as they did the future. Some I met by a delightful chance in the streets of York, including our indefatigable Diocesan Secretary, Miss Carter. The theological perspective – ranging again from past to future – looked back to our Lord's commission to Simon Peter, to the sending forth of Paul and Barnabas from Antioch; to the pastoral concern of St Paul for the Church at Ephesus; and forward to 'the latter day' when the 'chief Shepherd shall appear.' Here, then, in the Consecration Service was one of those moments between past and future where the Holy Spirit comes to inspire, and the grace of God comes to empower, when the past is fulfilled, and the future made possible. Phrases still echo in my ears:

'Take heed therefore unto yourselves, and to all the flock over which the Holy Ghost hath made you Overseers . . .'; 'the edifying and well-governing of the Church'; 'true understanding', 'wholesome Doctrine', 'faithful diligence', 'gentle, and . . . merciful for Christ's sake to poor and needy people, and to all strangers destitute of help'; 'authority . . ., not to destruction, but to salvation; not to hurt, but to help'; 'Be so merciful, that you be not remiss; so minister discipline, that you forget not mercy'.

Finally, the recessional hymn 'For all the saints . . .' As the Archbishop, with Ian Dunelm: (Ian Ramsey's official signature) on his right hand moved in procession 'Singing to Father, Son and Holy Ghost' there were many damp faces.

On 6 November Ramsey went to Buckingham Palace for the simple ceremony of doing homage to the Queen. Only the Home Secretary, Roy Jenkins, was present with the Queen when Ramsey was received to pay homage. He was accompanied by the Clerk of the Closet, the Bishop of Chichester, Roger Wilson, bearing an open Bible upon a cushion. Ramsey knelt, placing his hands between those of the Queen, repeating the homage sentence by sentence after the Home Secretary, and kissing the Bible at the conclusion.

On 6 December, Ramsey was introduced into the House of Lords by the bishops of Winchester (Falkner Allison) and Wakefield (John Ramsbotham, a former bishop suffragan of Jarrow). Ramsey's own wish was that an old friend, Lord Todd of Trumpington, Master of Christ's College, Cambridge, would be one of the introducers but there were insurmountable obstacles for a lay peer to act in that capacity for a spiritual peer.

Ramsey was a great respecter – even delightful indulger – in traditions, national or local. He used to explore and explain their meaning for contemporary usage. Thus on 14 December an ancient custom, unique to the bishops of Durham took place. Although the rights of the earl palatine reverted to the Crown in 1836, some traditions persisted, including the presentation of a mediaeval sword, the falchion, on arrival in the diocese. The ceremony of the bestowal of the falchion took place when Ramsey was greeted where the river Tees is spanned by Croft Bridge near Darlington, the gateway to the Diocese from the south. Ramsey commented, 'Some have written to tell me as a Lancastrian that the custom also symbolises my rescue from the clutches of Yorkshiremen!' The Town Council gave him a warm welcome and Civic Reception at Darlington.

Those clergy and laity who expected a radical and reforming bishop to lead them were surprised when their new bishop appeared in traditional episcopal dress. Gaiters, completed by a frock coat worn over a knee-length cassock, usually called an apron, was normal dress when bishops travelled in their dioceses by horseback. Gaitered Ramsey was appreciated by many clergy and parishioners, and young people revelled in his attire!

The Inthroning, Installing and Inducting of The Right Reverend Father in God Ian, Lord Bishop of Durham, took place in the Cathedral Church of Christ and the Blessed Virgin Mary at a quarter past two in the afternoon on Thursday, 15 December 1966. The Bishop's Throne at Durham is claimed to be the highest throne in Christendom, built over the tomb of a predecessor, Thomas Hatfield. One custom was overturned. When Ramsey arrived at the Cathedral, resplendent in cope and mitre (the mitre set in a coronet, the symbol of a Prince Bishop), he faced not a closed door on which he would thrice knock with his crozier for admittance, but an open door, a symbolic sign of the Bishop, clergy and people drawing closer together in devotion and service.

The thrust of his sermon, too long for instant digestion, endeavoured to distinguish between an authority in response to which people find their freedom and life, and an authoritarianism which is cramping and oppressive. Those – the majority – who were unfamiliar with Ramsey's language in lectures or writings, heard words and phrases which would thereafter recur and resonate in pulpits and on platforms. He mentioned a report which had just been published by the Northern Economic Planning Council under the chairmanship of T. Dan Smith – *Challenge of the Changing North*. He acknowledged that social blueprints and theology can be equally authoritarian and disastrously oppressive. 'Both need to be redeemed so that they can be expressive of a vision when each will then possess the kind of authority which all of us need to acknowledge if we are to find our fulfilment and our life. The alternative is not only social calamity; it is the loss of our very souls as well.' There was a moving conclusion which precisely illuminated the treasure in this particular earthen vessel.

I trust that the authority I exert will never be incongruous with the Gospel or with conscience or with reason, so that whether in its exercise or in its acknowledgment you and I – all of us – may, 'under authority', hear the word of Christ which can bring healing and newness of life to this county and diocese of Durham, whose traditions have been so gloriously set by so many distinguished predecessors into whose heritage I now enter. May we, in our own day, be found faithful. So help me God.

CHAPTER 4

The Institution

IN 1966 THE GOVERNANCE OF THE Church of England was under the umbrella of Parliament, Church Assembly and the Convocations of Canterbury and York. In 1970 'Government by Synod' was inaugurated. The liberating hopes of synodical government were short lived, partly dashed. It was little distinguished from the parliamentary model with its flawed procedures and combative confrontation. Synod was ever in danger of becoming self-important, bureaucratic and lopsidedly partisan, where friction and divisiveness became all too evident. There was a centralised curial tendency with an inflated and numerical increase at Church House, Westminster. As long as Michael Ramsey was Archbishop of Canterbury, he was the primary focus of Anglican identity. And Lambeth Palace remained relatively free of 'ideas above its station'. From the 1980s the House of Bishops began to have a centralising influence. The independence of bishops was less evident. The Northern Province lost something in this transition. The Convocation of York would have been a near-perfect forum for Ramsey. Reading the twentieth-century debates of the Upper House of only fourteen diocesan bishops is to encounter a rich mixture of intellect, forensic skills, doctrinal diversity, theological dexterity, independent thought and very plain speaking. On major issues each and every bishop contributed.

Would synodical government be the panacea for rectifying and renewing the Church's organisational failure? Ramsey was circumspect:

A new organisation by itself will effect no radical changes without changed attitudes on the part of us all, and I can hardly exaggerate the changes that are needed if we are to bring the Gospel to bear effectively on the life of our Church and society. In particular, the success of Synodical Government will depend very largely on the character of the Deanery Synod, which is the only fundamental change which Synodical Government brings to our institutional structures. If the Deanery Synod is to be, as it is intended to be, a focal point of our Church life, it will have to be a highly responsible and efficient body. This will mean in turn that there will have to be lay members who are active and well-informed, and clergy for whom co-operation with the laity is not just a catch phrase. Nothing that is done by way of organisation and resolutions will itself look after the qualities I have just mentioned. Yet without them Synodical Government will be but another of those time-consuming exercises, with which we are all painfully familiar, which take hours of thought and energy and then leave the Church precisely where she was half a century ago.

In the diocese a bishop inherits his senior staff – bishop suffragan, archdeacons and diocesan secretary. He may be fortunate with his inheritance but he will look forward to the possibility of bringing into the diocese fresh blood of his own choosing. It should not be overlooked that the ethereal presence of former bishops may be encouraging or hampering. Durham was full of clergy who had been ordained by Herbert Hensley Henson and Michael Ramsey, who had resonance and 'followings'. Fortunately Ian Ramsey had no jealousy in him and gloried in his inheritance.

What of his relations with the other members of the diocesan hierarchy who had been appointed by his predecessors? In prime place was Alexander ('Alec') Kenneth Hamilton, Bishop of Jarrow. Alec Hamilton's clerical genealogy stretched four generations. He was a product of a prep school; Malvern College; Trinity Hall, Cambridge, and Westcott House, Cambridge, the latter under the doyen of theological college principals. Hamilton has some pertinent reflections on Westcott House Principal, Canon B.K. Cunningham:

> I think that the influence he had on me was due to the kind of person he was rather than the teaching which he gave to us. He never gave the impression of being 'pious' but one did not have to be long in his company to realise that there was a man for whom God was a living reality and whose life was truly hid with Christ in God. I think it would be fair to say that his chief concern in the training he gave was to help the men in his care to grow and develop into the kind of people God intended them to be. The very last thing he wanted was to mould them into a pattern let alone a clerical pattern. Clericalism in any form was anathema to him. He realised how vital it was for a priest to remain fully human. In B.K's time it was not in any way a

'party' college. Anglo Catholics, Liberals and Evangelicals came to Westcott House and nearly all were happy to be there. Living as we did in a close-knit community, in which great stress was laid on the value of the 'common-life', we did not simply learn tolerance but were able to learn from one another, and so were able to gain an insight into the richness of our heritage in the Church of England. One lasting effect this had on me was to implant a determination never to join any group or society to which a 'party' label could be attached.

Hamilton was a tall, spare, serious-looking, ascetic figure. Once ordained, he served his second curacy under Kenneth Moir Carey at Whitworth with Spennymoor in the Durham diocese. Carey was a future principal of Westcott House and Bishop of Edinburgh. A curate needs to know what is expected of him, to know that his own ministry is valued and his gifts fostered and encouraged. When Hamilton was a parish priest he tried to put into practice the lessons he had learned from Carey. There was a lesson in self-knowledge too. 'Being a bachelor myself and having had a considerable experience of working with bachelors I do not think I always appreciated the particular needs of my married colleagues or tried to help them as much as I should to integrate the claims of both family and ministry.'

Hamilton was an effective naval chaplain, always better with men than women, before appointment as vicar of the essentially working-class parish of St Francis, Ashton Gate, Bedminster, Bristol. The main employer, in two large factories, was W.D. and H.O. Wills. It was in the early stages of the Parish and People Movement and Hamilton caught and practised its main tenets accompanied by a whiff of incense. He was High Church but the ceremonial he found or introduced was always unfussy. In manner 'Father' was straightforward with a no-nonsense school of thinking, without favourites. In his thirties he was already known as a good trainer of curates. He started with a parish hall whilst a new church was being built. His organisational ability enabled him to bring to fruition carefully planned initiatives, with lasting benefits. Everything stemmed from Hamilton's priesthood. He held that it was his duty and his privilege to be a person 'who stands on the Godward side in relation to man.' In all he said or did he strove to lead his people to God, to show them the love of God. He was a man of prayer with two small publications on prayer to his credit.

In 1958 Hamilton was invited to be vicar of the city centre church of St John the Baptist, close to Central Station, in Newcastle-upon-Tyne. Eight and a half centuries of life and worship can be traced in this building. Hamilton succeeded an extrovert priest who was a brilliant preacher and a hopeless administrator. Hamilton rapidly introduced his own routine, starting every day not later than 6.30 a.m. with his private prayers, followed by Matins and Mass. Lunchtime services were imperative for workers and attendances increased by his imaginative use of time. It was not the only High Church in Newcastle but it was the most significant, best attended and genuinely hospitable one. This was the priest who became Bishop of Jarrow. We have Hamilton's own account of his relations with Ramsey written to this biographer:

> It is essential for the well being of all concerned that the diocesan and the suffragan work happily together, particularly in dioceses where there is only one suffragan. I can truthfully say that I worked quite easily with all three diocesan bishops I served under. They were very different sorts of persons and the differences showed in the way they regarded me. To Maurice Harland I was a friend with whom it was a pleasure to work. To Ian Ramsey I was a colleague with whom the episcopal ministry in the diocese was to be shared. To John Habgood I was seen as a subordinate, though a valued and useful one. In fairness to John I think, though he would never have admitted it, that to start with he was rather nervous of me because I had been a bishop for a number of years and had an intimate knowledge of the diocese while he was new both to the job and the diocese. I ought also to add that he always listened to any advice I cared to give him and often reacted on it. In addition I think he learned from our relationship and the lessons he learned proved useful in his dealings with colleagues later on. The announcement of Ian Ramsey's appointment was, at least to me, not unexpected. Our paths had never previously crossed so that all I knew of Ian was that he was a distinguished theologian and academic. As I was away on holiday, playing golf, I did not meet him when he paid a visit to Durham. It was arranged that I should go to Oxford to meet him at his home just outside Oxford. We spent half a day together. He was a short tubby man who spoke with a slight Lancashire accent. We got on extremely well. He seemed to me a

warm hearted and friendly person whom I felt the people of County Durham would take to and with whom I would be able to work with.

There were no demarcation lines setting out what he should do and what I should do. It was in that sense a shared ministry but a ministry we each got on with in our own way. We met, of course, at staff meetings but in addition to that we met together on our own every month. There was no fixed agenda for these meetings so we both felt free to bring up any matter which we thought needed to be discussed or merited discussion. The subjects dealt with covered a wide and varied field. They included the needs, and sometimes the short-comings, of individual clergy; deployment of clergy; matters relating to parishes; diocesan administration; diocesan policy; the mission of the Church in the country as a whole and also in the diocese. On all these matters Ian had plenty of ideas, though the practical implications of his ideas had all too often not been fully worked out. However it was stimulating to listen to what Ian had to say and I learned a great deal about the way in which he regarded his own ministry. From the outset it became clear that he believed he had a responsibility not simply to minister to the Church – though he took this responsibility extremely seriously – but also to do all he could to improve the quality of life of the community at large. This led him to take a special interest in those sections of the community which had special problems and were in need of help. The pit villages where the colliery had closed and the raison d'être for the villages to continue to exist had largely disappeared was one of his concerns. Another was the housing estates surrounding most large centres of population and the New Towns.

Staff meetings under Maurice Harland, Ian Ramsey and John Habgood took much the same form. We commenced at 11.00 a.m., broke for lunch and continued in the afternoon until the business had been completed. But there were differences. The meetings presided over by Maurice and John were conducted in a business-like way and we stuck fairly rigidly to the agenda. The atmosphere of the meetings with Maurice was relaxed as he puffed his pipe and any member of the staff, when wishing, was free to smoke. John did not really approve of smoking but did not actually forbid it. This sort of attitude made the atmosphere of the meetings less free and easy.

With Ian Ramsey meetings were less business-like. He did not always keep to the agenda, introduced matters which were on his mind or thought of interest and all the way through talked endlessly, even though often interestingly. The result was that meetings tended to last very much longer. I remember on one occasion when I had a

Confirmation in a parish at the other end of the diocese on staff meeting day, I decided to put a suitcase with my robes in my car. It was just as well I did as I went straight from Auckland Castle to the parish concerned and got there just in time for the Confirmation service at 7 p.m.

Most serious of all was an underlying feeling of a looming omen by those close to Ramsey. From the outset it was evident that he had little discriminating power. If the 'buck' stopped with the bishop, it rarely went anywhere else. His activities outside the diocese were manifold and unsustainable, yet they increased. To begin with few people were aware of these activities because when he was at home he seemed to be here, there and everywhere and fitted in so many engagements that his absences were hardly noticed. There were no complaints. People from all sections of the community and all types of church congregations were glad to meet him and were stimulated by what he had to say.

Within six months of his enthronement Ramsey had this to say in his Presidential Address to the Diocesan Conference on 27 June 1967:

> I am distressed, not to say appalled, at the delays which inevitably occur at the moment to my correspondence, and I am clear that to deal with it adequately will necessitate a great deal of delegation. I know that members of the Diocese will understand if, on occasion, their letters to me are answered by someone other than myself. I can assure them that this is no endeavour to hide behind a barrage of correspondence; it is just part of the determined effort I must make to deal with that correspondence more efficiently, and therefore more satisfactorily for everyone concerned. As part of this policy I am hoping that many decisions can be made on my behalf by the Archdeacons and Rural Deans and, if this streamlining necessitates as it may well do, clerical assistance where clerical assistance has hitherto been absent, I should very much hope that the Diocesan Conference will be ready to approve expenditure in this direction, especially when it will have been examined along with other competing claims, by the kind of consultative group I have mentioned before, and therefore have the approval of the Board of Finance.

There was a large ingredient of self-delusion in these words. Ramsey did not delegate. His desire to deal with almost everything himself was implanted and strangely irremovable. He convinced himself that there was good reason why he should personally respond to this or that particular letter or query. The pending pile grew. However, something far more serious had occurred. On 22 March 1967 the archbishops of Canterbury and York announced the appointment of a Commission on Christian Doctrine, the first since 1922 which reported in 1938, and Ramsey had accepted an invitation to be chairman. In the same month it was also announced that the Church of England Board of Education and the National Society had set up an independent commission to inquire into religious education. Ramsey accepted the chairmanship. Moreover he not only chaired this commission but chaired one of the sub-groups. It was understandable why Ramsey was the 'perfect fit' for the Christian Doctrine chairmanship, but why did religious education need a bishop to chair the commission? Other chairmanships followed. His philosophy was that, if there was work to do, it should be done. He was unable to prioritise. He accepted any invitation offered by letter or by mouth, however trivial. He looked upon his diary not as an aid to memory but as a booklet which had to be filled up. It was a very attractive but literally fatal characteristic. He gave of himself beyond the utmost!

On one occasion Alec Hamilton had a lengthy and friendly conversation with Ian Ramsey during the course of which he gave him a piece of advice that he had first given to one of his former Newcastle curates – that his first duty was to do the work he was paid for and only then to undertake additional tasks. 'Needless to say,' notes Hamilton, 'my words had no effect whatever'. As this is such a deep embedded flaw, words of another bishop, written to this biographer, are salient and potent. Mervyn Charles Edwards was vicar of St Martin-in-the-Fields, London before he was nominated as Bishop of Worcester:

> In the end it is up to the individual bishop to realise that in any job there are always conflicting pressures and he must sort out his values and stick to them. My task and duty was to be a pastor, particularly to the clergy and their families. What the parish priest should be to his people, the bishop should be to his clergy. This sounds conceited but knowing how one failed, I say it in penitence. I tried as far as I could to mirror by thought, words and action Our Lord. A bishop should be a sacramental creature.

(And to any new bishop) The advice given to me at my consecration by the then Bishop of Pittsburgh, Dr Pardue, who preached the sermon. 'Grow but don't swell'. You must humbly accept the fact that you have been called to this office in spite of what you know are your failures and sins. Trust that He who has called you will give you the grace you need. Whatever the pressures, stick to your prayers. You will find the early morning is your only really free time. Make an annual retreat and have a wise friend who can tell you frankly where you get off! Love your people and make a real effort to cure any defects in your personality which makes it difficult for you to communicate with ordinary folk.

This is the nub of the problem. Ramsey ignored the advice and pleadings of 'wise friends' and did not have a spiritual director who would have confronted him with the consequences of his weaknesses which were also sins.

There were two archdeacons in the diocese, those of Durham and Auckland. By canon law, the office of archdeacon in the Church of England is styled by the bishop's eye. But he is also in hallowed practice the bishop's nose, poking it into all manner of parochial affairs to which curiosity attracts him. A good archdeacon combines his tidy habits and business-like approach to ecclesiastical affairs with a rich pastoral ministry, not necessarily a parochial one. How that ministry may be best undertaken varies according to the direction or whim of the diocesan bishop. But an archdeacon is unlikely to be effective if his ecclesiastical antennae are not ever alert to the clergy in his jurisdiction. He should be trusted by the clergy. Clergy in trouble do not rush to their bishop or confide and share their problems with rural deans or fellow clergy. They know the archdeacon is capable of stirring people from slumber and sloth to activity. But he is, or should be, a trusted adviser and an encourager too. He remains foremost a priest so when a brother priest confides in him he will be in a position to decide if and when a specific problem should be referred to the diocesan bishop.

Traditionally, the archdeacons of Durham and Auckland were also Residentiary Canons of the Cathedral, and lived in the College which is a grander version of the picturesque Cathedral Closes at Winchester, Salisbury, Lichfield and Norwich; the Precincts at Canterbury; the Minster Yard/Court at York and Lincoln; or the

Canons' rooms at Christ Church, Oxford. Was there something 'comfortable' and 'separate' about this accommodation? Although there were financial considerations for the arrangement was it right or sensible to have two pairs of archidiaconal gaiters in the College? Previously there was a wholly unsatisfactory arrangement whereby one of the archdeacons was also Bishop of Jarrow. Alec Hamilton refused to be a Canon and reside in the College. He lived in Melkridge House, about a mile from the cathedral. Although he had no official position at the cathedral he attended the daily Eucharist and was invited to celebrate twice a month. He had his own small chapel in his house and used it for his own daily offices and prayers, and for hearing Confessions.

Both archdeacons were in their sixties. John Oldcastle Cobham was appointed by his friend Michael Ramsey as Archdeacon of Durham in 1954, retiring in 1970. There were two strands in Cobham's background. At Corpus Christi College, Cambridge he was influenced by Fellow and Dean of Chapel, Revd Sir Edwyn Hoskyns, later writing his entry in the *Dictionary of National Biography*. Men and women went to Cambridge for the sake of Hoskyns' lectures on the theology and ethics of the New Testament which were exceptionally vivid, forceful, trenchant, and unexpected, delivered with a sustained enthusiasm and excitement. Hosykns held that no interpretation of the person and teaching of Jesus which failed to explain the faith of the primitive Church could be true history. That led Cobham to appreciate the thoughtfulness and sound judgement of the doctrine of the Church of England. The second strand was the emergence of the Parish and People Movement, of which Cobham was on the Council. He also served on the Church's Liturgical Commission.

Cobham's skills as a teacher, reformer and administrator united to make him a steady and sturdy Principal of Queen's Theological College, Birmingham from 1934 until his appointment as archdeacon. Reliability was another feature. Clergy trusted and heeded his word and accepted rebukes when necessary. On his retirement Ian Ramsey's tribute was accurate, 'Uniting scholarly interests with a patient pastoral concern, cautious and sensitive in manner yet shrewd and firm in judgement, he has benefited not only the Archdeaconry but the whole diocese, and indeed the whole Church of England by his ministry.'

The Archdeacon of Auckland from 1958 to 1973 was Charles James Stranks. His ministry covered twelve years in Japan, a parish priest in Morecambe, followed by the wardenship of Whalley Abbey (Blackburn) for seven years. He was not an obvious candidate for archdeacon but Maurice Harland thought otherwise. It proved a good choice. The robustness of northern life suited him and he it. He enjoyed scholarly pursuits without being an academic or totally absorbed in them. Religious education was a constant companion. He was keen to share his knowledge in small but not light publications and encouraged clergy and laity to devote time to studying the Christian faith and its implications. Stranks was a strong believer and advocate of the strength and importance of the parochial system. He made it his business to know what was happening in parishes and clergy learned to know that it was unwise to endeavour to pull the wool over his eyes.

Ramsey had only one major vacancy to fill during his time at Durham, the archdeaconry of Durham following Cobham's retirement in 1970. The appointment of thirty-six year old Michael Charles Perry tells us much about Ramsey. Ramsey trumpeted Perry into his archdeaconry with paeans of praise! Perry had a grammar school education, followed by first class honours in natural sciences and theology at Cambridge, a two-year curacy, appointed by Gordon Fallows as chaplain of Ripon Hall, Oxford, and, since 1963 Chief Assistant for Home Publishing at S.P.C.K. Perry's academic credentials were exemplary. His many short books reached an appreciative audience. He had worked closely with Ramsey on the Doctrine Commission – Perry was Secretary. Ramsey informed the diocese that Perry 'always shows a great readiness to grapple with problems whether biblical, doctrinal or pastoral (and most problems have all these three qualities at once), a concern for appropriate patterns of worship, and combines the clarity and incisiveness of a scientific attitude with humanity and sensitivity of a true pastoral care.'

That Michael Perry was one of the 'up and coming' clergy for promotion in the Church was clear. But had Ramsey been too quick to decide that Perry was the right and best person for this particular appointment? As archdeacon this young priest would be dealing with many senior and tough-minded clergy. His pastoral experience was limited in both time and scope. Working in a publishing environment, acquiring useful experience as official scribe to commissions and working parties, possessing a quick and adaptable mind suggested traits of personality that would find fuller expression in wider service. But were Ramsey's perceptions correct that Perry would grow into and in his new position? Did he have the kind of personality that would be at ease with or gain the trust of the majority of clergy in his jurisdiction? Perry was safe and acceptable as long as Ramsey was bishop, but when John Habgood arrived relations between bishop and archdeacon were cold. As a person and priest Perry had considerable skills which were not used to best effect as Archdeacon.

There was a further appointment of Ramsey's which needs space. Let the introduction come from the person himself. Kenneth John Fraser Skelton, was Bishop of Matabeleland in Rhodesia. In June 1970 he informed his diocese:

> I have been asked by the Bishop of Durham to be responsible for the implementation of the recommendations of a Commission which is at present engaged upon the re-organisation of the whole of the Church's work in Sunderland – a pioneering project involving the complete rethinking of the task of the Church in an urban situation and the reshaping of its institutions to cope with this. This is, I understand, the first time such a project has been attempted in England, and therefore it is a challenge and an opportunity of an unusually creative kind. For some time it has been clear to me that family responsibilities were forcing me to return to England; but I want you know that had it not been for the pressing nature of these responsibilities I should not have thought of relinquishing an episcopate which has brought me much joy and has also given me the challenge of occupying a 'key' position at a critical time. Every one of us has to balance his various conflicting responsibilities one against the other, and it has not been an easy decision for either my wife or myself to make, to leave a Diocese in which we have found so much friendship and so much opportunity in the service of God, his Church and his world.

Skelton's appointment was as Assistant Bishop of Durham, Rural Dean of Wearmouth and Rector of Bishopwearmouth. His central focus was to analyse the report *The Church in Sunderland* when it was published in 1971 and consider the practical outcome of its proposals, one of which was a proposal that there could or should be a bishop in Wearmouth, an innovative bishopric, neither diocesan nor suffragan but with links to the historic See of Durham.

Skelton's Matabeleland letter covers less than it reveals. He was a controversial figure in Ian Smith's Rhodesia. The Unilateral Declaration of Independence (U.D.I.) came in 1965, the middle point of Skelton's episcopate. He was known as 'Red Skelton' by the government and lived up to his reputation. Prior to his consecration he had been a parish priest for twelve years in two Lancashire parishes. In Rhodesia he was a relatively lone voice in condemning government legislation. He was in contact with the black population but not with their leaders who were in exile or gaol and would not reappear until the guerrilla war began in the 1970s. The black population was divided on old tribal lines. The Zimbabwe African National Union (ZANU) included the Shona Kingdom and was led by Robert Mugabe. The Zimbabwe African People's Union (ZAPU) – the former African National Congress – included the Ndebele Kingdom with Joshua Nkomo at the helm. There were two Anglican dioceses: Mashonaland, primarily 'Shona', and Matabeleland, primarily 'Ndebele'.

Skelton applied pressure on the government and was the subject of parliamentary debates. It was the kind of pressure which irritated, caused offence, attracted vicious diatribes and implied threats. There were three views about this seeming mild-mannered bishop. The overwhelming white Rhodesian population thought he should keep his mouth shut and his pen in its holder. They were waiting and hoping for his expulsion. For other people there was an ambivalence in their attitude. They liked the man and mistrusted the bishop. The overwhelming black population looked on Skelton as their leader. He fed the British Government with confidential reports of the deteriorating situation in Rhodesia, wrote forthright and disturbing newspaper articles, some of them, for example in *The Guardian* published anonymously. After his return to England it became known that he had been briefed as a 'spy' by Maurice Oldfield of MI6. He got under the skin of Government ministers and many white clergy and laity, because of his uncompromising stand and his way of expressing his convictions in the starkest of ways. He was renowned for gathering facts and proof of iniquities before speaking. He was a divine disturber, God's gadfly. However, Durham and Sunderland were not receiving a warrior or flamboyant leader in the mould of Trevor Huddleston or Joost de Blank. There was no exuberance about him. He was nearer Ambrose Reeves. Essentially, he was very plain speaking and straightforward in his dealings with people. Theologically he was radical and his double first from Cambridge served him well. This honest man was not physically striking although rather dapper in appearance. We will appraise his relationship with Ramsey and discover if he was able to make an impact on Sunderland.

When Ramsey arrived, the Diocesan Office was in the College, Durham. Since the 1920s the diocesan secretary came from one family. John Pearson Carter effectively 'ran' the diocese being secretary of six diocesan Boards. In 1952 he was succeeded by his daughter, Miss Phyllis Carter, who left office in 1979. The Bishop's Secretary and Registrar of the Diocese was Henry Cecil Ferens, was likewise an 'old hand' and still there when Ramsey became Bishop. Unusually, all three people were also representatives of the House of Laity of Church Assembly. To a considerable extent the Carters had a grip or stranglehold on the way the diocese functioned and became too much a law unto themselves. J.P. Carter was wholly dedicated to and consumed by the diocese as Secretary to the Diocesan Conference, and the Boards of Finance, Training and Ministry; Church Building; Dilapidations; Care of Churches, and edited the Diocesan Calendar. Ferens was a very different character – solicitor, councillor for Durham City, justice of the peace and Diocesan Reader, prominent in the Church Lads' Brigade, with active sporting interests – cricket, hockey, fives, golf and swimming. By the time of Ramsey's appointment the administration of the diocese was a ramshackle affair. Phyllis Carter was well-meaning, over-worked and stressed, supported by a couple of clerks. The way the administration had developed through numerous committees and subcommittees was peopled by clergy who thought there was a cachet or status in membership and as meetings were usually on weekday afternoons only leisured laity with a free afternoon attended. There was the luxury of avoiding ultimate responsibility with consequences for the decisions they made. Miss Carter knew and served with Bishops Williams, Michael Ramsey, Harland, Ian Ramsey and Habgood. She was left largely undisturbed during the 'fiefdom' of Williams and Harland. Like her father her word and work were unquestioned.

There is always a temptation for public servants of ability and influence to extend their role and exercise some power. In Durham that depended on the bishop. In the episcopates of Ramsey and Habgood she was seen typing minutes of a meeting that had yet to take place!

Before turning to diocesan and national work we consider Ian Ramsey in his home at Auckland Castle.

CHAPTER 5

Auckland Castle

HISTORICALLY THE BISHOP OF DURHAM had two houses. One was Durham Castle, which the nineteenth century Bishop William van Mildert, the last of the bishops who possessed the dignity of Earl Palatine, handed over to the newly constituted University of Durham. He ensured that his successors had rooms and rights in the Castle. The other was Auckland Castle, twelve miles from Durham, originally the bishop's country residence. From the twelfth century onwards, the town of Bishop Auckland grew up round a market at its gates. An 800-acre park was a place for episcopal perambulations. Auckland Castle began as a Norman manor house and was castellated about 1300. It is the large chapel of St Peter which remains an architectural treasure. It owes its origin to Bishop John Cosin, the restorer of The Bishoprick (1660–1672) who converted the medi-aeval banqueting hall into the finest episcopal chapel in England. Auckland Castle itself has memorable State Rooms, the product of the eighteenth century, which have remained intact with their valuable furniture, ornaments and the best collection of pictures in any episcopal house. The main State Room is 40 feet long, a huge dining room and fifteen bedrooms gave a mistaken impression for bishops in the last half of the twentieth century whose accommodation was limited and style of life modest.

Nothing can remove Ramsey's excitement at living in Auckland Castle. He loved it and history pressed itself on him: King John occupied the Castle as his own during the vacancy of the See in 1216; King Edward III was entertained by the great scholar bishop, Richard de Bury, in 1333; King Charles I, with Archbishop William Laud, stayed there as Bishop Thomas Morton's guest, and Queen Victoria, as a young Princess, slept in the great State Room in the north wing on a tour of the north.

Ian Ramsey lived there with his wife, Margaret, and their two sons, Paul and Vivian, when they were home from university and school. A flat in Auckland Castle had already been prepared for his ageing parents so when his father died on 28 February 1967 it was inevitable that his mother should move into the Castle.

The transition from their Oxford home to Auckland Castle was difficult for Margaret Ramsey. Suddenly she lived with two people – the husband she had married and the person who had been consecrated bishop. There was no one to prepare her for being a bishop's wife. No help with being set apart, perceived to be different, when she didn't feel different and didn't want to be different. No help with the reality of the fishbowl aspect of life. No encouragement to find support beyond the Church. No preparedness for the 'disconnectedness' of her role, or the isolation in Auckland Castle. No parish community. No children at home except in vacations. No elastoplast to cover inner wounds.

The Revd Tony Hart was domestic chaplain to Maurice Harland and remained through the interregnum into Ramsey's episcopate. Bishops hand-pick their chaplains so it is rarely easy to continue serving with a new bishop. In Harland's time there were only four people living in the Castle – the bishop, Mrs Harland, the chaplain and the cook. The Harlands treated Tony Hart as one of the family, and had considerable influence on him. 'I learned a great deal from their example of how to lead a busy life in the service of others and still remain human, sane and more or less happy.'

Hart has reflections which cast light on his 'new employer' at home and at work in the Castle:

I found myself accepted to a degree which I had never expected and certainly felt I didn't deserve. He asked me to stay on as chaplain. This, as I later found out, was typical of him, to expect and then to get the best out of people by trusting them, almost beyond their merits and, apparently, without having checked up on them much in advance. The Bishop's office had its own way of working. The Secretary, Mrs Maud Harrison (also inherited), and I knew that there were probably much better ways of running things, but we had a number of routines which had served us well. We expected some changes. Again we found that we were well treated and as long as we were able to produce what he wanted the new Bishop was for a while content. Doubtless the administration did not compare well with the university bodies and hospital management bodies with which he was familiar, but he had a courteous respect for what was to him in many ways a strange new world. We were careful not to refer overmuch to the previous regime in the Bishop's hearing. By ourselves we could not help making comparisons especially as they affected the office. The new Bishop's capacity for work was infinitely greater, but right from the start his secretary and I were disturbed to notice the things which were given priority. The morning's letters could go without a proper answer while he finished an article for a learned journal. A journey to London to fulfil an engagement made in Oxford days could take up another day. Letters would soon accumulate, and even taking them with him on car and train journeys and occasional long sessions with the Dictaphone at weekends never succeeded in reducing the pile or the delays which could be as long as six weeks. Unfortunately the piles of papers stayed in his study which made it difficult for Mrs Harrison to get at them and sort out at least the urgent ones and, even more unfortunately, many of the letters which had to wait for an answer were those from the parish clergy. When the reply did come it was always sympathetic and often lengthy, but the delay had been damaging. My own explanation of this was that, certainly in his first year, the Bishop had not sufficiently realised that, although the subject of a clergyman's letter might not be vital, certainly not in comparison with other things which the Bishop had in hand, writing to his bishop is a fairly momentous thing for a parish priest and an acknowledgement of the relationship which exists between them. A prompt reply confirms that bond, but a delay inevitably weakens it. There was an apparent inconsistency here, because at the same time he was always willing to see his clergy and would respond as generously as possible with his time and interest to appeals for help and advice. I think the Bishop was simply trying to do everything which came to hand and misjudging the relative importance of some of his newest responsibilities. The daily sessions which Mrs Harrison and I had with Bishop Harland first thing in the morning, between us dealing with the day's letters and engagements, were a thing of the past and we could not at that stage see a better system to replace them.

Home life in the Castle was equally friendly and pleasant for me, although it seemed to lack something of the confidence and regularity of the Harlands. We sat over our meals for a very long time. I imagine that the usually busy father was content with this to make up for his absences from his family at other times of the day. The evening meal was infinitely variable, and was sometimes in its size and timing made to depend too much on the promised refreshments at the Bishop's evening engagements. In the early months this caused a lot of amusement when the Bishop discovered that the term 'refreshments' in a parish priest's letter could mean anything from tea and a biscuit in the parish hall to a four course sit-down dinner in the vicarage.

Mrs Ramsey had had a pleasant breakfast room-cum-kitchen for herself made out of the old butler's pantry and this tended to become the family's centre of communications. It was that in another sense as well, because it had two telephones. One of the changes which the new Bishop did require in advance was more telephones. Instead of one phone with, as far as I can remember, three extensions, we were now to have a complicated system of ten extensions operable from each receiver plus an entirely new line with two further extensions. Auckland is not an enormous house and phones galore in adjacent rooms and two phones in Mrs Ramsey's kitchen seemed at first ridiculous. In some ways (not only physically but sometimes, as it seemed to me, mentally as well) the Bishop was unwilling to move very far. He would use the phone rather than take a few steps; he would use the official car and chauffeur for very short distances. One incident which I remember well was when the late Michael Farey, a mild and gentle member of the Church Commissioners' architects' department, was visiting the castle to check up on various works. There had been an error in the installation of the new oil-fired central heating boilers, the fault of the heating engineers or the plumbers. The Bishop, Mr Farey and I had crossed each other's paths in the castle entrance hall, and Mr Farey explained what had gone wrong. It was complicated, the Bishop wanted to know more, and was extremely indignant at all the inefficiency. In fact, he delivered himself of a considerable expostulation to the innocent architect. All the time the boilers themselves, the plumbers and the engineers were a few feet away, but it never seemed to occur to him that the whole business could be grasped and settled in a moment by taking a walk into the boiler house. (I noticed in other matters this unwillingness to encounter the things itself, but rather to find more to say and more to do a few steps away from it.) Another amusing occasion of much ado about not very much was on Boxing Day when the Bishop announced a walk for the family in the afternoon. Everybody's compliance was secured and a time was fixed. I think the weather was discussed as well. My notion of an episcopal walk was Bishop Harland's who, whenever he could, at a moment's notice, would collect Mrs Harland, the dogs and a stick after lunch, and be halfway up the park before you realised they had gone. On this occasion, however, the Ramseys eventually set off and to my amazement they were back in a quarter of an hour. The walk had been once round the Bowling Green.

Auckland has two chapels. The large one is glorious but arctic. The other one was made by Michael Ramsey out of Bishop Cosin's book room and is small, warm and convenient. Bishop Harland's arrangement had been to say Mattins daily with his chaplain, and to have Holy Communion regularly on two weekdays, every holy day, and Sundays when possible. We never attempted to say Evening Prayer together. I used to say it before tea or dinner; he himself would always go into the oratory (as we called the small chapel) last thing at night. Bishop Ramsey was obviously concerned to establish a household timetable of worship. We would certainly have Mattins every morning, and Holy Communion on Sundays. I waited for some mention of a weekday Holy Communion, but it never came. Eventually we had a celebration on certain holy days. For a while we attempted Evensong or Compline depending on the day's timetable, but it never worked out and had to be abandoned. The Bishop was a great amender of the liturgy, putting his own bits in and taking others out. Personally I found this painful and irritating, but it was obviously done from the highest motives of devotion so that it was easier to bear.

After one year Tony Hart, greatly appreciated by Ramsey for 'his friendliness, his thoroughness and his reliability', moved to a parish in Hartlepool and then became Team Rector of South Shields then to Durham Cathedral as Canon Residentiary and finally to Easingwold in the Archdiocese of York. Ramsey appointed Richard Ferguson, who had spent a year in industrial work at Coventry before ordination, and was fortunate to serve his title at Stretford, Manchester, under the pastoral oversight of Frank Wright. Unfortunately he had a medical condition which required monitoring at hospital so he left after a year to move to Newcastle. In May 1969 Ramsey announced that his chaplain was to be the Revd Harry McClatchey, aged forty-nine. He would also be Vicar of Escomb and Vicar of Witton Park. Ramsey knew McClatchey and the appointment appeared to be an inspired and much needed one. Educated at Merchant Taylors' School in Liverpool and Brasenose College, Oxford, where he read theology, he served in the Navy during the war. After graduation he became appointments' secretary of the University Appointments Board in Oxford, thence to Trinity College, Dublin, to found an appointments office there. This was followed by employment with Shell in Lagos, Jakarta and London. After Shell he prepared for the priesthood and served his title at St Mary the Less, Lambeth. He was already earmarked for Durham and, following preliminary visits, he returned with a car laden with fruit and vegetables from the Auckland Castle garden. Harry was married to Diana who played a leading role in the campaign that led to the Church of England accepting women into the priesthood. She had read history at Lady Margaret Hall and completed a D.Phil. (later published) on the Oxford clergy 1771–1859. She had an analytical mind and was enormously respected for her skill in debate. She was ordained a deaconess (using the Form and Manner of Making of Deacons) and hoped to be ordained priest but by the time General Synod voted in favour of women priests, Harry had had a series of strokes and she needed to care for him.

Harry McClatchey was able to wrest papers from Ramsey in a way that a younger and inexperienced chaplain could not have done. He was adept at handling typescripts, checking proofs of publications, and providing Ramsey with background material for sermons, lectures and House of Lords speeches. There was mutual respect. In 1974 he moved to Worcester as Chaplain to the bishops, first Robin Woods, then Philip Goodrich, and was a greatly loved and effective Rector of Hartlebury.

There is a big 'BUT'. Ian Ramsey still insisted on dealing with much of his correspondence and the piles on his desk grew and grew, mounds of correspondence, some growing whiskers, awaiting replies. Entries in his diary are despairingly frequent – 'a day dictating letters' . . . 'I still dig away at the mountain of correspondence' . . . 'Still plodding through shoals of correspondence' . . . 'Spent 9½ hours dictating' . . . 'So much to do – so little time.' A letter from a child needs a reply in his own hand; an out of work miner would like to see him when he is next 'in the area'; a local authority councillor needs advice on some plans; a clergy wife is going through a tough time . . . these have to be put to one side for a reply 'as soon as possible'. His domestic chaplains knew how difficult it was to prise him away from an after service bun-fight or discussion group. There was always just one more person with whom he must have a word – and another, and another. A note made on something he would follow up, a telephone call to be made, an appointment to be arranged, very little to be delegated! Was not this the ministry of a pastor? Noticing the unnoticed, like the Samaritan in the parable and Jesus' own alertness to a blind man's cry in the crowd; celebrating the non-celebrities – the party in Matthew's house after his conversion, the woman who put her last farthing in the collecting box; questioning the un-questioned – the questions Jesus asked about the Sabbath Day, about paying the special tax, and his challenge to the use of the Temple for exchange and sale of livestock; empowering the powerless – Jesus' training of twelve working men to become leaders of a new movement that could challenge the old theology and contemporary practice. His dealings with the man born blind and with the woman who was a sinner; putting in touch the out-of-touch – Jesus' reinstatement of Zacchaeus, his dialogue with the Samaritan woman at the well and with the Gentile woman of Syro-Phoenicia. And who can cast a stone at Ramsey for giving people advice, reassurance, optimism and hope? Was it not also a form of evangelism? He recognised an immediate need of the Church was for lay apostles, men and women who believed the Faith and understood it, who were eager to bear their witness, and willing to learn how to do it. He encouraged parishes to 'teach' in order that those who will 'go forth' were not being asked merely to assent to a set of ideas but were being called to enter upon a life, and a life which would have to be lived among all the human imperfections of the Church. For Ramsey, evangelism was not an invitation to become one of a spiritual elite for one's own spiritual satisfaction. How often he emphasised that Christianity is not a prescriptive religion with rules and regulations and directions for daily life, so clear, so precise, and so sufficient, that there will be no need for thought, reflection, consultation and arrangement.

Ramsey was located and found in the common flow of life, not in great events. He did not portray the God of big things. Virginia Woolf, in her novel *To the Lighthouse* says, 'the great revelation had never come. The great revelation, perhaps, never would come. Instead there were little daily miracles, illuminations, matches struck unexpectedly in the dark.' Once a bishop becomes more interested in campaigns, causes and committees than in people he may gain the futile applause of worldly authority but he loses his true authority. The bishop is vulnerable if he takes a towel to each pair of feet.

A lady tourist visited Auckland Castle to look at its treasures. A bustling little man appeared in a clerical collar and immediately asked who she was, where had she come from and proceeded to point out some of the glories of the castle. Ramsey was merely passing by, but he paused. He introduced himself. She was a lapsed churchgoer. They talked and he left. He had served.

Geddes MacGregor, Emeritus Professor of Philosophy at the University of Southern California, included Ian Ramsey in his book *Apostles Extraordinary. A Celebration of Saints and Sinners* (1986); others included were Martin D'Arcy S.J., Austin Farrer, Charles Laing Warr and René Le Senne. MacGregor recalled:

> Even in the midst of his extremely busy life he found time, while I was a guest at Auckland Castle on three occasions, to talk, if only in a few minutes snatched between pressing duties, as we had talked in the past of the great moral and theological issues that were never really out of his mind. The Castle was a busy place as well as a peaceful haven . . . During one of my visits Margaret suggested a trip to a local market, saying that Ian would be too busy to join us. But he suddenly appeared with that curious, almost laughable and very characteristic raising of the eyebrows in a look of expectancy. Join us he did. And in that market, old men and women, young lads and lasses, greeted him as spontaneously as they would have greeted a friend in a neighbouring cottage, yet with an affection and respect that they would have bestowed on hardly anyone else. In his presence they always looked as though they were breathing in fresh air. Nor did any such obvious admiration ever seem to affect his easy friendliness. Ian was fundamentally unspoilable. Much of his charm lay in his never having quite grown up. He was a kind of ecclesiastical Peter Pan with a prodigious mind.

CHAPTER 6

Doors of Opportunity

THE 'SERIOUSNESS' OF PRIESTHOOD was always evident in Ramsey. For him priesthood 'must always have a Godward and a manward aspect'. He lectured to groups of clergy throughout the country on the Theology of Priesthood: for example, to the Bath and Wells Clergy School at Keble College, Oxford in 1969 and stressed:

> We see the priest as engaged broadly in an endeavour to witness to and to express the faith dimension, the Godward aspect of human life and existence, the love and grace and power which was in Christ. He will do this by being a crystallisation point between different disciplines, skills, traditions, patterns of self-sacrifice and service. In this way the priest becomes a secular 'representative' in virtue of his sacred office. He is a secular presbyter with a divine priestliness . . . The priest is one who is a representative person, holy, i.e. especially related to God, in particular by actively offering things as sacrifices, encouraging self-sacrifice, and offering all to God to create wholeness, soundness and so to lead to perfection.

Ramsey had also this to say:

> Indelibility must not be taken metaphysically, as some metaphysical characterising attribute, but related to the depth of commitment to God . . . That absolution is not an exclusively priestly function, sacerdotal in that sense, but a representative declaration . . . We must be cautious against too monolithic a view of priesthood, or of setting the context in too inexplicable a discourse. The concept of priest-hood, as I elucidate it, would have as its practical implications the priest as enabler, a crystallisation point made between God and man.

Does this explain how his episcopal ministry developed? Wherever there were opportunities for fresh vision, enabling, innovating and bridge-building, we discover a response of spontaneity, action, theological synthesis, and pastoral warmth from Ramsey. What was it like to be on the receiving end of Ramsey's pastorate? A few examples follow as written by clergy who served with Ramsey as

73

their bishop. The date in brackets is the one when the incumbent arrived in the diocese; the named incumbency is that provided in the Durham Diocesan Directory (1969).

The Revd Hilary Jackson (1951), Vicar of Heighington:

> I remember ITR as a man 'fizzing with enthusiasm' especially intellectually, always exploring the meaning of words, 'Unpacking the portmanteau' (his words). He attempted to start an open discussion circle with any of the clergy who cared to attend, monthly in Auckland Castle. I attended once, and it was the most stimulating and enjoyable intellectual experience I have ever enjoyed. Sitting informally round the fireplace, he threw out a word, an idea, a question, and it quickly became a 'free for all'. He would listen to other people, pick up one of their words, explore its meanings briefly, and throw one of them back. It was fast and furious, like intellectual 'rugger'. He was criticised in the diocese because in his enthusiasm he created burdens for the clergy. We seemed always to be receiving letters, reports, discussion documents from him about every contemporary issue facing the Church. It contrasted sharply with earlier, more leisurely, regimes.

One priest has a specific memory:

> Pastorally I found ITR immediately accessible in a time of crisis, when in obedience to the homily in the Book of Common Prayer (Holy Communion), I felt bound to bar a member of my own family from Communion, and to offer my own resignation to the Bishop. Dear Ian gently talked me down to earth, counselled me to reconcile the offender and live with failure and disappointment alongside my ideals. I realise this episode betrays more about me than ITR, who was immediately pastorally effective.

The Revd Ian Zass-Ogilvie was ordained priest by Ramsey in 1967, serving as a curate in Washington and as Bishop's Social and Industrial Adviser for North Durham. He first encountered his future bishop at King's College, London where Ramsey gave a sparkling series of lectures on philosophy:

> His enthusiastic delivery in a delightfully broad Lancashire accent, interspersed with his characteristic throat clearing, was refreshing indeed after the standard Anglican BBC-speak of others. He generated within us a new awareness of 'disclosure situations' when 'pennies

dropped' and 'ice broke' . . . invariably illustrated with some strikingly homely frames of reference. He carried this same iridescent teaching style into his episcopal ministry, never far from common reach and imagination and gently seasoned with shafts of captivating humour. I remember one of his contributions to a Diocesan conference with children at Bede College, where he was illustrating the relative value of time . . ., asking the age of the youngest present and then citing his own age (as the eldest) and noticing the difference to be but some forty odd years and then asking 'just what is that when compared to the age of the universe?' Again at the Durham Miners' Association Hall, where he was giving a series of lectures for the Workers Educational Association, he delighted his hearers with an illustration of our perceptions of identity – he had in the summer of 1963 been caught speeding (unwittingly) on a highway in mid-west USA and the speed-cop issuing an on-the-spot fine had asked him who he was. His reply, he said, now could have been 'Well, I'm the Bishop of Durham' (he was dressed in shorts and open-necked shirt). This could elicit the response, 'Yeah, and I'm President Roosevelt'. He was a brilliant academic who brought both vitality and quest to his wide-ranging work as Bishop of Durham. His energy and imagination were infectious and many of the more impressionable young clergy found their early ministerial style influenced accordingly. His unassuming and enabling style of leadership (at least as perceived by those working at arm's length, as I was, on his behalf) was particularly timely for the North East and for the Diocese.

Washington, where I served my title with Peter Croft and saw the beginnings of the New Town, typified the changes that swept through County Durham in the sixties and seventies. It was very much a mining community centred around three pits (the Glebe, Washington and Usworth) plus a large chemical works down by the River Wear, each having its own community of work, housing, shops and Working Men's Social Clubs. The whole was then under the governance of Washington Urban District Council with which the Washington New Town Development Corporation eventually developed a creative working relationship. Much of the necessary cultural change within the community was generated by the sensitive direction of Joan Demmers (Chief Community Development Officer of the Corporation) and her team. For this I observed at first hand the benefits of facilitating change in such manner that it could be genuinely owned and managed to a degree by those most affected. It was a delicate exercise in the transference of power and in affirmation of the emerged community. The Church also swiftly adapted itself to the new circumstances, in the formation of a Group Ministry, in ecumenical endeavour and community ministry. In this, it was the vision of Peter Croft (Rector of Holy Trinity, Washington) that pioneered the way, not least in the publication of a monthly town-wide freebie. Peter allowed me, as curate, to be linked to Industrial Mission and to be appointed as chaplain to Glebe Colliery. I was National Coal Board trained for work underground and spent the foreshift on Mondays on any one of the working faces – an amazing and formative experience!

I mention this in some detail as this was not untypical of Durham parish ministry in those days, when church attendance was tolerably high, baptism commonplace, Sunday Schools large and there remained a strong sense of the place of the Church in community. Despite some inevitable cultural alienation, residual community loyalty and goodwill made ministry well-defined – although never unquestioned or uncriticised. Ian Ramsey was an inspiration for such a time – affirming traditional patterns of ministry where they worked effectively and enlivening the Church with a spirit of enquiry and dialogue with the secular. With hindsight, it was as if he had almost foreseen the decline in formal Christian allegiance we have witnessed in Britain during the last twenty-five years and so was seeking a pre-emptive strategy. His parish visitations made early in his episcopate were thorough and far-reaching. In the case of Washington, although most interested to meet the church community, he was just as anxious to be introduced to the nodal interactive points between church and local community and industry. His was a truly catholic vision, ever apparently in enquiry mode, his questions and observations were such as gave due value to those to whom he was speaking. He was a man with no personal agenda other than to seek truth with humanity and it was interesting to note that he won both respect and affection in some of the least likely quarters. Never a favourite with some of the more conservative readers of the *Daily Telegraph* he found a special place in the hearts of the people of Durham – having a common touch and patently seeing things more from the viewpoint of the working man. This was perceived as something of a radical change from that which had typified some of his predecessors in office. With Ian Ramsey's support, in the early 1970s at a time of rapidly rising unemployment (particularly of the young), we established the Durham Environment Group (DEG). This included people such as David Bellamy, then lecturing at Durham University. The primary objective was work creation, linked with environmental and conservation projects. Durham in those days was a county littered with evidence of its labours down the years — derelict pit heaps, sheds, yards and workshops, river banks denuded of planting and used as dumping grounds etc. The DEG proposal, with Ian's imprimatur, which sought substantial government funding, elicited and received the formal support of all the relevant local authorities in Co. Durham, as well as that of significant Trades Unions. Ian Ramsey enthusiastically propelled this forward and requested a specially convened meeting of the Northern Group of MPs in the House of Commons. I was asked to meet him just five minutes beforehand for a swift re-briefing, which transpired to be considerably less (literally just hurrying down the corridor together) . . . but, as ever, his gift for grasping issues was only exceeded by his ability to explain and commend them to others. The initiative resulted in the government launching the *Special Environmental Assistance Scheme* — one which began the greening of Durham and other industrial areas in the 1970s.

A framed photograph of Ian Ramsey hangs yet in my study in Edinburgh. It looks as if it was taken in his study in Oxford. Surrounded by books and evidently in the midst of reading one, looking up as if he is about to respond to a question. I look at that still, if stuck with a sermon, a difficult letter, or a challenging phone call. So the memory of Ian Ramsey inspires and encourages me still. Others can write his epitaph better than I, but I shall always be deeply grateful for the fact that he was my bishop, and in a sense amongst the company of the saints still is, since he was quite the best and most inspiring under whom I have since had the privilege to serve.

The Revd Sam Burrows (1958) curate-in-charge of the Conventional District of Leam Lane Estate, Gateshead:

(I) first saw Ian Ramsey as the tip of a mitre as he processed into the cathedral behind the shoulders, head and mitre of Alexander Hamilton. It very quickly became obvious as he began his ministry in the diocese that we had a man of stature amongst us and as our Father in God. Very soon after his arrival he arranged to make a tour of the new estates and new towns in the diocese. Incumbents were to meet him at a chosen point of entry in their parish or district. In my case — Leam Lane Estate. I waited at the top of the hill near the then Leam Lane Secondary Modern School. The bishop arrived in his chauffeur-driven car and I was invited to sit with him, and to describe the estate and its people and the way the Church was working to make a useful contribution and to be a Christian presence and to preach the Gospel in this place. We talked and moved on through the estate – stopped at the church – walked around the shopping centre – noted the Roman Catholic and Methodist churches which are also in the centre. We drove to the lower part of the estate and at the boundary I got out of the car and he moved onto his next visit. He called me Sam, and that was an immediate contrast to Bishop Maurice Harland who called me Burrows (as the custom then was). He was friendly, interested, positive and open. I felt good about the whole experience. Bishop Ian was good in the pulpit – simple and profound, and at Confirmations his preaching was actually heard and commented upon afterwards – by the candidates. Indeed, he excelled on such occasions, being sure to speak to everyone – candidates, their families, church-wardens, servers, choir. He never seemed to be in a hurry. He always went personally to the kitchen to thank those who had made the refreshments. Once at the end of a visit as I escorted him to his car he put his arm round my shoulders and said, 'Sam, you're doing a good job here'. You may imagine how that put a new spring in the step.

The Revd Peter Moss (1961) was responsible for building the brand new church of St Bede on the Town End Farm Estate in Sunderland:

It was up to Bishop Ian to open and consecrate the building. The work was shared ecumenically with the Methodists, and so I proposed and Bishop Ian agreed that we would spread the ceremony over two evenings, since the particular Methodists we worked with would not have felt comfortable with consecrations of altar and font and with the splendid liturgical vestments which we had.

In typical fashion he decided to come both days himself. In equally typical fashion, I remember him trotting along to a reception at a local school chatting to me en route about Bradley and Idealist Philosophy (about which I was and am almost entirely ignorant). He took a most detailed interest in the orders of service, and he dressed (at my suggestion) in his plainest black chimere when he and the Superintendent Minister (in a dark suit) walked side by side from our home to the new church.

The Consecration itself could have been an ecclesiastical and liturgical disaster! Peter Moss was the first priest-in-charge on Town End Farm. However, the estate fell within the parish of St Margaret,

Castletown, but that was on the other side of a busy road and clearly separate. The vicar of Castletown was Father Peter Spargo – notorious for his extreme Anglo-Catholic practices and had been placed under a ban by Bishop Maurice Harland. Many people wondered what action Ramsey would take with this Romanising rebel. He visited Fr Spargo on his first tour of Sunderland, genuflected in the church, pretended not to notice a statue of Pope Pius X, and won Spargo's heart. St Bede's was one of the most original and well-thought-out churches in the diocese. After the consecration ceremonies an attractive booklet was published covering first the simple ceremony and then the liturgical one – the latter with Ramsey in chasuble and mitre, flanked by the two Peter's – Moss and Spargo, and full Catholic ritual. One of the photographs shows the Bishop in procession, thoroughly at ease, blessing the people.

Canon Keith Woodhouse (1958) was vicar of Peterlee – appointed by Maurice Harland and continuing in the same parish throughout the episcopates of Ian Ramsey, John Habgood, David Jenkins and into Michael Turnbull's. St Cuthbert's, Peterlee was another new church for a new town. Canon Woodhouse was also appointed Rural Dean by Ramsey:

> As Rural Dean I frequently had reports of 'drop-in' visits by the Bishop, to enquire, extend sympathy in bereavement, in times of sickness and need by the clergy, and he always knew you as well as your name.
>
> Ian Ramsey (our 'Diddy Bishop' as the people called him) was a great support. He made a number of visits to Peterlee notably the televising of the Parish Eucharist (15 October 1967) on Tyne Tees Television when he presided and preached. The visits to the Durham New Towns (Newton Aycliffe, Washington, Peterlee) led to another initiative by Ramsey, namely the establishment of the New Towns Advisory Committee. The support given by the Bishop was invaluable in a situation that was in many ways quite 'isolated' and in need of much 'encouragement' during those exciting pioneer days.

Wherever Ramsey travelled in the diocese he was meeting and conversing with new people from the ordinary to the influential. As a result initiatives tumbled from his ever fertile mind. When he saw opportunities for advance he acted. When he noticed gaps he proceeded to fill them. This did not always result in significant developments but more often than not they did. An example is contained in a letter from Ramsey to Canon Woodhouse (18 December 1970):

> On various occasions I have discussed with Mr A.V. Williams, General Manager of Peterlee Development Corporation, the development of the Science Centre at Peterlee, and in this context the proposal for a centre for the Arts and Humanities. I am myself very pleased that the Corporation considers that this latter Centre is of major importance, and an essential corollary to the first. I know that the Corporation has had discussions with a number of people and agencies about the Arts and Humanities Centre; further, it is generally recognised that it will be necessarily slow to develop. I have, however, suggested to the Corporation that in this development I hope that the wider sociological problems will be considered in depth. I think it is essential to have the same standards of excellence and knowledge, which will be applied to the research institutes, applying to the humanities as well. There are in this field multi-variable problems deserving of inter-disciplinary investigation, and I think a close specialist study of the liberal arts would pay dividends. It is in this context that I have agreed to arrange an informal discussion, and I think it would be extremely valuable if you could possibly come to talk over the whole matter with myself and the other people (or their representatives) shown on the attached list. I do hope you will be able to attend, or be represented at such a meeting. If so, perhaps you will kindly let me have one or two dates and times which would be convenient, and which would obviously be well into the New Year.

Such was Ramsey's reputation that he had no difficulty attracting the best 'top' people for the task in hand. On this occasion they were:

Sir Derman Christopherson, Vice-Chancellor, University of Durham
Dr Henry Miller, Vice-Chancellor, University of Newcastle
D.H. Curry, Deputy Director of Education, Durham
David Dougan, Director, Northern Arts Association
Dr C.J. Bell, I.B.M. Science Centre
L.E. Watts, Principal, Easington Technical College
Representatives of Peterlee Church

The Revd Bert Galloway (1964) was a curate in Darlington before moving to Teesside as Industrial Chaplain:

> My appointment to the team on Teesside was subject to the qualification that I should work in industry for a twelve-month period. The reason for this was that I had no long-term experience of the world of work. My only experience had been working during university and theological college vacations. It was arranged that I should earn my living as an engineering labourer with a firm of underground mining machinery makers at Newton Aycliffe. In order to fully experience the world at work it was decided that my identity as a priest should be kept secret and that my livelihood should be supported only by my earnings with the firm. I ought to mention that I imagined that a labourer's earnings would have exceeded those of a curate and therefore I was not too worried in agreeing to this. It was only after the year was completed that I discovered there was a gap between what I had earned and what I might have expected as a full-time employee of the Church. Somehow Bishop Ian heard of this. I was very agreeably surprised to receive a cheque from him drawn, I think, on discretionary funds. My experience since of the support of Bishops for industrial mission has been, to say the least, very mixed. I am glad that my memory of Bishop Ian is of very real and tangible support.

(Canon) Richard Davison was ordained priest by Ramsey in 1967 to a curacy at Cockerton in Darlington. He recalls the Bishop's setting up of the 'Unbeneficed Clergy Council':

> This was not a council of those who had been removed from or had lost their benefices, but of clergy who had never to that point held a benefice – mainly newly ordained curates. The formation of the Council arose out of murmurs and complaints among the junior clergy in the 1960s – the time when 'doing our own thing' meant to many 'doing better than the older generation'. The Council was a channel for ideas and criticisms to be fed 'upwards, and it put forward members to act as observers' at the various diocesan committees. I suspect that the idea bemused or even irritated some of the older clergy, and the Council and its observers did not last very long. It is difficult to see what it achieved apart from allowing some 'blowing off of steam' – but perhaps that was what Ian Ramsey intended.

> In a different vein, I remember Ian Ramsey telling a story about his clash with the then Chairman of the National Coal Board (Lord

Robens); the Chairman had referred to the 'diddy bishop' and had been far from friendly in his attitude and comments, and some bitterness had crept in. The two of them then found themselves together in the back of the same car going to a BBC interview, and Ramsey commented that it seemed much more difficult to keep up a bitter argument when placed in such close proximity to one another.

I served an interregnum in both of my curacies; at the end of the second the churchwarden asked Ramsey for permission to pay me 'extra for the responsibility of the interregnum'. He not only agreed but also ensured that I and my family were among those receiving special holiday grants that year. On another occasion when I had to leave a meeting early he too left it for a few moments as he saw me going, to give me his sympathy and the assurance of his prayers on the death of my mother.

Ramsey encouraged his clergy to write to him on any subject concerning them or their ministry. He delighted in receiving comments on contemporary theological or philosophical issues. He liked to have 'feedback' on lectures and sermons they had heard by him or others. For example, here is a response to the Revd Philip Wright (1957) vicar of Tanfield (7 January 1972):

I was greatly interested in the letter you sent me as a result of Professor Nineham's lectures. As you may have gathered from my comments, I go along with you in your reflections, I entirely agree that the gospel cannot be completely transferred to twentieth century categories. Christianity is an historical religion and we cannot cut ourselves off from the historical roots without fundamental loss. But as I took it, some of the points Professor Nineham was making were:

(a) We must not suppose that these roots are more visible or more accessible than in fact they are, and the New Testament is rather like a collection of different views of a landscape in which what matters are the roots of the various trees.

(b) We must always be anxious (in the words of your own metaphor) to travel constantly on the journey from moon to earth and back again so as to keep in touch with both the basis of the gospel and the contemporary scene. In fact, it is part of the doctrine of the Holy Spirit as it is part of the rationale of the ministry of us all, that we must be capable of making this journey constantly ourselves in a way that finds expression, one way or the other, in sermons, addresses, conversation and action.

One clergyman received a telephone call to enquire if he would be available the next day for a visit by the Bishop. With a slight feeling of alarm he said, 'Yes', knowing that he had written to Ramsey concerning some theological statements which were worrying him. Ian Ramsey arrived and plunged into a long discussion on the matters troubling the priest. After two hours he left, leaving behind an enthralled and encouraged priest. Ramsey did not wipe the troubles away, but helped to create a larger space in which one man could begin to explore and allow theology to grow rather than stifle his thinking in a cramped space. For that particular person it was liberation and he became something of a student-scholar!

The Revd Noel Swinburne (1953), Vicar of Chilton Moor has a point to make:

> One was aware of 'murmurings' of criticism. The newly-growing charismatic group and fundamentalist wings of Catholic or Evangelical clergy felt threatened. There were the usual complaints of some Durham clergy about the imposition of another academic out of touch with the parish situation. To some extent the sheer dynamic enthusiasm of Bishop Ian and the way he threw himself straight into what he saw as the essential issues of Ministry was disturbing to some. Also, while he could be wonderfully patient and encouraging with those who genuinely disagreed with him, it was clear that he had, literally, little time for irrational argument.
>
> For some, including myself, however, it was a great relief to learn from a new bishop, by his example and words, of the essential teaching role of the clergy; that they were not there to defend entrenched positions and proclaim from on high literal interpretations of traditions and formularies, but, with the incentives and evidence of our own Anglican, Christian experience, to encourage the exploration of the grounds of faith, and of ways of expressing that faith in language which accords most truthfully with our general human experience and rationality.
>
> Bishop Ian spent a great deal of his time and energies engaging with people in the local community and in local affairs. I remember, for example, him becoming involved with local pop groups and hosting a local radio presentation with them, among many other varied enterprises. Some church leaders may undertake such works for PR reasons, or to 'wave the flag', or, more justifiably, as a gesture of goodwill and concern on behalf of the Church. For Bishop Ian, I

believe it meant even more than this. I'm sure that he saw every outreach as an exercise in practical theology; . . . recognising a universal God whose affairs were to be known and understood within the situations and converse of everyday life.

Ramsey placed great emphasis on the 'parish'. It is not a God-given structure. It is the recognition of a pattern of natural community. His arrival in Durham coincided with a time of shifting population and an accelerating number of pit closures and businesses. Those who were initially critical of an 'academic' bishop were quickly silenced when they saw a 'Father in God' in action, listening, sensitive, caring, hard-working. One was rebuked when Ramsey saw a note in the parish magazine – 'The vicar is available for interview between 5 p.m. and 7 p.m'. Indeed, those clergy who sent their bishop copies of the monthly parish magazine or paper – alas now an almost vanished form of communication – knew they would be read. On train journeys if Ramsey was not preparing a lecture or sermon or reading a report, out would come a parish magazine for his delight.

Ramsey took great trouble to find the best text or phrase to illustrate a theme of his choosing for a sermon or address. Words from Isaiah (32:2) are relevant to his view of the place of the parish church, its value in human society, the ideal which it represents, the claim which it has on the affection of the parishioners, to whom in a most true sense it belongs. 'As rivers of water in a dry place, as the shadow of a great rock in a weary land'. The church stands in the midst of the community of the parish as the witness and symbol of that unearthly, superhuman, everlasting reality, towards which with yearning and hope, people in trouble and perplexity may turn. The parish may be a tiny village, cottages clustering round the village church which stands among them in unchallenged supremacy, giving them a name on the map and distinctiveness on the landscape. Or the parish may be a vast assemblage of shops, factories, public buildings and houses which mark a modern community, though some of the buildings depicted a former glory. Or the parish may be a tightly-knit colliery village with a church more likely to be glorious within than the ugly bit of Victorian Gothic without. Or it may be a place where people had been re-housed, following slum clearance, into high rise flats, a vast series of connected blocks, a thousand houses of different sizes, like four streets built one on top of the other in the air. Or a New Town struggling to establish community.

The times were difficult for clergy with conflicting claims of parish and family. Some wives were heroic in putting up with it (Margaret Ramsey for one!), others, understandably, complained that they saw so little of their husbands, and that when they did, their husbands were so exhausted that they were either in a bad mood or fell asleep the moment they dropped in a chair. Some parishes took every waking hour of a parson's time if he let them. When an exhausted priest was brought to Ramsey's notice, he ensured that action was taken to arrest further deterioration. If there were mental or psychological problems he was able to recommend psychiatrists or professional counsellors. However, there are no short-cuts to pastoral care. Bishops have so to master time that they have time for their clergy, time to listen, time to consider, time to pray with them, not merely for them, and the capacity to be hurt by what hurts them. What greater hurt can any bishop suffer than to be told by a priest in difficulty that he was thought to be too busy to listen to him? Bishop Alec Hamilton was a great help with the few discipline cases during Ramsey's time.

Durham had something of everything: fifty-five parishes, each with a population of under 2,000, had a single incumbent. The parishes of Beamish, Chester-le-Street, Barton, Hedworth, Owton Manor, Pennywell and Winlaton had populations of over 15,000 served by a vicar and at least one curate. The large towns were:

	Population 1961	Parishes 1969	Total clergy 1969
Bishopwearmouth	94,340	14	24
Bishop Auckland	23,957	3	6
Darlington	65,702	8	12
Durham	22,927	5	9
			(exc. Cathedral)
Gateshead	84,473	11	13
Hartlepool	72,350	8	9
Jarrow	22,182	4	6
South Shields	62,305	10	10
Stockton-on-Tees	63,012	8	12
Billingham	30,251	2	5

One place is missing from this list – Sunderland! By 1971 the population of the then County Borough of Sunderland was 220,000 (in 1992 it became a metropolitan district and is now of city status). Sunderland grew out of three settlements – Wearmouth, Monkwearmouth and Bishopwearmouth. Sunderland was a ship-building and coal-exporting town for centuries but it was the Industrial Revolution of the nineteenth century which brought rapid growth and booming trade with new docks, the railway, the development of marine engines and the erection of many undistinguished public buildings. In the twentieth century other industries developed and prospered such as glass making, crane manufacturing and pottery. One of the biggest cast-iron bridges was built with a span of 236 ft. Housing estates spawned anywhere and everywhere around the town, leaving the centre dingy, ugly and neglected. The working-class attributes of neighbourliness, comradeship and community were strong and solid. The rate of progress and prosperity had ignored the landscape which was grim and when industries retracted or disappeared and poverty replaced prosperity in a sizeable proportion of Sunderland's homes the community was a safeguard against organised agitation.

In Ramsey's time there was evidence of change chiefly in the accelerating spate of new building – offices, shops, car parks and educational establishments. Nonetheless, no amount of new building and concrete could disguise or diminish the high level of unemployment and the acute problems surfacing in its wake. Sunderland boasted that it held the country's record in the provision of municipal housing; almost half the population were tenants of the County Borough. A visitor may have wondered if it also held the record for the number of working men's clubs and bingo halls.

In religious terms the name 'Sunderland' masks one of the most exciting places in the history of Christianity in England. There is Monkwearmouth which brings together the greatest names of a distant epoch, when English Christianity was in the fresh energies of its youth. St Aidan and St Oswald, St Wilfrid and St Theodore, Benedict Biscop and Coelfrid, St Cuthbert and the Venerable Bede, St Chad and St Hilda, all have their place in the historical picture which the very name Monkwearmouth brings before the mind's eye. In 1969 the Church of England alone had twenty-three parishes and four conventional districts with 10,884 on the electoral rolls, and forty-three full-time priests.

Ramsey established a commission to enquire into the place of the Church in Sunderland. It was chaired by Dame Enid Russell-Smith, formerly Deputy Secretary of the Ministry of Health and Principal of St Aidan's College, Durham. There were five members and two consultants (Bishop Kenneth Skelton and Archdeacon Michael Perry). In support there were six local committees to concern themselves with such spheres as civic life, social services, hospitals, industry and education as well as church buildings, parochial boundaries, and deanery organisations. Ecumenical participation was encouraged. A welcome departure from past relations was the co-operation from the Roman Catholic Auxiliary Bishop of Hexham and Newcastle, Hugh Lindsay, who was always very friendly towards Ramsey, and Kenneth Skelton's first visitor on his doorstep when he arrived in Bishopwearmouth. The local Roman Catholic priests were more lukewarm, due perhaps to the presence in the town of two former priests who had converted to the Church of England.

After twenty full meetings of the commission and many informal consultations, the report *The Church in Sunderland* (fifty-five pages) together with the committee reports (128 pages) with a preface by Ramsey was published in September 1971. In her letter accompanying the report to Ramsey, Dame Enid Russell-Smith wrote:

> Our main recommendations, of the organisation of the Church in Sunderland, follow lines accepted as sound in other fields of organisation: they seek to establish an area large enough to enable those concerned locally to see local problems as a whole, and to give local people a much larger measure of responsibility for the development of available resources. From the administrative point of view, I am sure this is right and should give considerable impetus to local thinking and initiative. Most of the laymen and women playing a significant part in the life of the town are accustomed to think in units larger than a parish.

The recommendations were wide-ranging but the one which hit hard was that Sunderland should become a single team ministry:

> There is a leader called the rector, and his colleagues who are called vicars are to be regarded as of the same status as vicar with his own

benefice and parish. The rector holds the benefice but the vicars share in the cure of souls. A vicar could have the cure of a special area which might be a parish, or he could have a special task over the whole area such as youth or industrial work, or he could hold a chaplaincy in an institution, or he could share generally in the rector's cure. There could also be assistant curates or lay workers, but they would not be members of the team; they could be invited to be present at chapter meetings. A rector in a team ministry may have a freehold or hold his benefice for a term of years. Vicars in team ministries always hold office for a term of years.

This was potent brew. The rector would not be the pinnacle of a mountain but the centre of a circle with 'seven groups' within it as proposed by the Commission. Kenneth Skelton has memories:

> The Sunderland Commission upset some of the clergy because they had been promised that all of them would serve on one or other of the committees: but then it was realised that there were other Christians in Sunderland than Anglicans (how typical of the C of E . . .) and that room would have to be made for their representatives; so some of the clergy had to give place. And Suspension of Presentation, which Ian (Ramsey) applied immediately, was a new and threatening idea. The Romanist Vicar of Castletown stated that if anyone tried to dispossess him he would take up his position with a machine-gun on the roof of his Presbytery – he didn't call it a vicarage. We did take the first steps in the formulation of a city-wide team, but there was no chance of all the clergy yielding up their freeholds to facilitate the process. But the Deanery Synod, which met every six weeks (not monthly), really did work as the meeting-place and 'engine' of the Church in Sunderland, even if there was not as much ecumenical participation as I might have hoped.

Some clergy and laity clung to the old certainties and their buildings like limpets. There were six exemplary tests of criteria to be applied when making decisions about the future of buildings. They are worth quoting as they are even more relevant today throughout the Church of England. In brief:

1. Every church must ask itself whether, in the light of those priorities which we learn from the Gospel, the percentage of total expenditure spent on its buildings can be considered tolerable.

2. Every church must ask itself whether or not the number of hours for which buildings are used justifies their existence.

3. Each church must ask itself whether the purposes for which buildings exist are important or necessary purposes.

4. Along with these criteria, the objective needs of the parish must be judged. On the basis of cost and usage alone, the wealthier parishes would be favoured at the expense of the poorer ones. We must beware of saying, 'You can only have a church or a hall if you can afford it'. If we said this, buildings might become a middle–class ecclesiastical luxury . . . The same problem, in a more serious form, arises over the employment of assistant clergy. We must recognise with slender resources of manpower and money, if matters are left to the 'workings of the market', there could be a suburban captivity of the churches in England.

5. The quality of a building must be taken into consideration. Philistine utilitarianism must not be allowed to exclude questions of beauty and architectural merit . . . In an area which possessed few buildings of architectural merit, we believe that Christians have a positive duty to preserve, as far as they are able, churches of such merit.

6. The role of a church as a place of private prayer must be considered. Church buildings have developed from being places for liturgical and corporate worship, into being also houses of prayer and meditation used by individuals.

What of a bishop in Wearmouth? In many places in the Church of England there was a concern that a bishop should have a manageable area in which he should act as Father in God. This concern existed in the north-east where the historic seniority of The Bishoprick of Durham was recognised but where many felt that social developments had made further re-organisation of episcopal care desirable, to supplement the creation of the diocese of Newcastle in 1882. The growth of Teesside provided one example, and Sunderland provided another:

> The fact that the present Rector of Bishopwearmouth is in Episcopal orders lends additional force to this suggestion, although our conclusion does not depend on personalities. We hope that it will be possible to make permanent the principles in the present

arrangements. Under these the stipend of the holder of this office is derived partly from the 'benefice' income (i.e. as a parish priest) and partly from the general funds of the Church Commissioners (i.e. as an Assistant Bishop in the diocese of Durham). The success of the proposal would obviously depend on a supply in the years to come of men willing and able to work as bishops in this new, local style . . . It would also be necessary to provide adequate secretarial help for the Bishop . . .

We urge strongly that, under a bishop in Wearmouth, the Church in Sunderland should be allowed to make the decisions as to the proper use of its own resources and manpower. While the links with the Bishop and Diocese of Durham will obviously remain, the authorities of the Diocese of Durham should work out agreements, whether legally binding or informal in the first instance, in order to give the Church in Sunderland its own life and liberty. We have in mind such matters as the choice of incumbents of parishes of which the Bishop of Durham is patron; the licensing of priests to non-parochial ministries and of assistant curates of parishes; the conduct of confirmations and institutions; expenditure of the Diocesan Stipends' Fund and other funds relevant to Sunderland; special responsibilities within the work of the Diocesan Board of Finance and the Diocesan Pastoral Committee and pastoral care in general.

The Commission was emphatically against a separate Diocese of Sunderland. 'A modern Anglican diocese has to be sustained by an administration which Sunderland clearly could not afford. We do, however, recommend that Sunderland should become a special area in the Diocese of Durham.' Here there was a missed opportunity for the possibility of a new kind of diocese in the Church of England which had not really been contemplated. In a lengthy article for *Church Times* (1 October 1971), David Edwards commented that whilst the Commission claimed that their proposals did not depend on personalities – 'but obviously the existence of one personality has given a good start to such ideas of close co-operation and substantial independence for Sunderland's parishes. This is the personality of Bishop Kenneth Skelton. Clearly the Christian life of Sunderland now has a strong leader, and the problem is how to develop this leadership into the third quarter of the twentieth-century.'

Ian Ramsey was enthralled and excited about the Sunderland proposals. He had provided the vision and fuel. He closed his Preface to the report with words which were so typical of his episcopate. You can 'feel' the vibrations as he writes, 'The Wear that links the Cathedral of Durham and the shipyards of Sunderland, Weardale, Auckland Castle and the North Sea, is never still but constantly moves into the oceans of the world. It is to be explorers, whether in Sunderland or elsewhere, and this Report can help us to be more faithful to our calling.'

Ramsey was faithful to his calling. Then the tragedy occurred. Within a year of the report's appearance Ramsey died and so effectively did radical realism for the Church in Sunderland and a Bishop in Wearmouth. The proposals, pregnant with possibilities would never come to birth although a number of the report's recommendations bore fruit in subsequent years. John Habgood had other ideas for the re-structuring of the diocese.

CHAPTER 7

The Kernel and the Husk

IN 1922 THE ARCHBISHOPS OF CANTERBURY (Randall Davidson) and York (Cosmo Lang) appointed a Commission on Christian Doctrine whose report *Doctrine in the Church of England* did not appear until 1938. There had been a gathering momentum for action to be taken following numerous events, for example, the furore over the nomination of Herbert Hensley Henson to the Bishopric of Hereford in 1918; the Anglo-Catholic Congress 1920; and the Conference of Modern Churchmen 1921. The Archbishop of Canterbury, whilst being an exponent of the comprehensiveness and strength of the Church of England, was reluctant to be embroiled in another conflict. However a group of churchmen, many of them young, under the expansive umbrella of the Bishop of Oxford, Hubert Murray Burge, wrote an official letter to the Archbishop in January 1922, co-signed by a broad sweep of twenty-six people, thoroughly representative of all sections of the Church, who the Archbishop could not ignore. After correspondence and consultation with the Archbishop of York and other bishops he agreed to a Commission with the following terms of reference:

> To consider the nature and grounds of Christian Doctrine with a view to demonstrating the extent of existing agreement within the Church of England and with a view to investigating how far it is possible to remove or diminish existing differences.

At the outset of their labours, the Commission adopted a skeleton programme which appeared to include all the main heads of doctrine with which they were called upon to deal and during the long period of their sessions they worked steadily through the programme which they had set themselves. The free interchange of ideas was characteristic of all discussions. The real and lasting regret was the too lengthy period from conception to birth. When the report was published in 1938, William Temple, Archbishop of York, who had succeeded Burge as Chairman, recognised the changed theological climate since the inception of the Commission. It was unjustly battered in the Convocations. The report promoted the coherence and stability of the Church of England by demonstrating the large area of unforced consent among people of different schools and at the same time allowed for the sufficient elucidation of divergent views where divergence arose. By this time the Church's mind was focused elsewhere as war was no longer on the horizon. Its prospect had moved to near-distance.

By the time the war was over nation and Church were changed for ever. William Temple was dead and his successor, Geoffrey Fisher, was concerned with canon law not theology. The Doctrine Report was effectively dead, but when the twenty-first century opened it has never been replaced or superseded! With the coming of a theologian to St Augustine's Chair in 1961 prospects for theological consolidation and advance seemed probable. Michael Ramsey turned his mind to another doctrine commission. If there was going to be a commission who should chair it? In March 1967 it was announced that the Archbishops of Canterbury and York (Donald Coggan) had appointed Ian Ramsey as Chairman of a new Doctrine Commission. He informed his diocese in these words:

This, unlike the Commission of 1922, is a permanent commission representing the Church's constant concern to think through its belief. Its broad purpose will be to discover precisely what and where is the apparent lack of theological coherence today, to try to remove some of the great bewilderment, not to say despair, which characterises contemporary theology, and to alert to contemporary thought, both its constructive suggestions as well as its critical challenges. As many of you will have heard me say in Confirmation addresses, 'edification' has always been a feature of the Anglican tradition, and the *Doctrine Commission* will be devoted to understanding as best it can, and so helping others to understand better, how to speak more reliably rather than less of that mystery which is God and the Gospel of his life in Jesus Christ.

The membership of the Commission was impressive:

Revds A.M. Allchin (Librarian of Pusey House, Oxford); J.A. Baker (Fellow, Chaplain and Lecturer in Divinity, Corpus Christi College, Oxford); Henry Chadwick (Regius Professor of Divinity in the University of Oxford); C.F. Evans (Professor of New Testament

Studies, University of London, King's College); E.M.B. Green (Registrar, the London College of Divinity); D.E. Jenkins (Fellow, Chaplain, and Praelector in Theology, The Queen's College, Oxford); C.P.M. Jones (Principal of Chichester Theological College); Hugh Montefiore (Vicar of Great St Mary's, Cambridge); D.E. Nineham (Regius Professor of Divinity, University of Cambridge and subsequently Warden of Keble College, Oxford); J.I. Packer (Warden of Latimer House, Oxford); H.E. Root (Professor of Theology in the University of Southampton); E.J. Tinsley (Professor of Theology in the University of Leeds); H.E.W. Turner (Van Mildert Professor of Theology in the University of Durham); M.F. Wiles (Professor of Christian Doctrine, University of London, King's College); and Messrs J.R. Lucas (Fellow and Tutor in Philosophy, Merton College, Oxford); and Ninian Smart (Professor of Religious Studies in the University of Lancaster). The Revd M.C. Perry, Chief Assistant for Home Publishing, the Society for Promoting Christian Knowledge, was Secretary. Membership varied as some members died or left. Others were invited including Revds J.T. Macquarrie (Lady Margaret Professor of Divinity, Oxford); A.R. Peacocke (Fellow of St Peter's College, Oxford) and J.G. Davies (H.G. Wood Professor of Divinity, University of Birmingham). In his Memoir of Ian Ramsey, David Edwards makes a salient and worrying observation that:

> To some the salvation of theology seemed to lie in a humbler apprehension of a great tradition going back to the Bible, to others, in a humbler encounter with contemporary knowledge and experience, to more, in both directions. In several ways the group was untypical of the Church of England as a whole. It contained no one who despised theology, no one wedded to the conventional, and no one unwilling to listen and learn. More lamentably, the only parish priest was the vicar of the university church at Cambridge.

And one further major omission – no other bishop.

Michael Perry writes of the way the Commission worked:

> Meetings began at lunch time. I had to protest in order to get discussion stopped for a tea-break – until then, tea was passed round as things went on. Break for supper; start again; go on till 10.30 or 11.00. Next morning, off at 9.30, coffee break if we were lucky, lunch break and discussion till tea-time. The secretary was frenetic with

activity, because he didn't have shorthand, and the chairman wanted a record of the minutes with a blow-by-blow account of the way the argument had gone. Overnight there would be a session to redraft any significant formula that might have come up during the day; and the conversation as he shaved the next morning would often be about the work laid down a few hours before. And the draft minutes would be extensively annotated by him, for purely stylistic reasons.

The first task laid upon the Commission was to consider the place of the Thirty-Nine Articles in the Anglican tradition and the question of Subscription and Assent to them. Every clergyman of the Church of England at his Ordination, and when he is admitted to office, whether as a stipendiary curate, or as an incumbent, is legally required to declare his 'assent' to the Thirty-Nine Articles. The actual formula was provided by the *Clerical Subscription Act of 1865*. By the mid-twentieth century the prevailing discontent with the Articles threatened to drive them into total neglect. Their disappearance would have been unfortunate as some Anglican confession is clearly indispensable. Revision was essential which would remove from the Articles whatever could be fairly shown to be superfluous, inaccurate, and obsolete, and retain only what was vital and demonstrably true.

Ramsey was a lifelong member of the Modern Churchman's Union which had always and consistently questioned the Thirty-Nine Articles. Like the Union he was convinced of the need for radical revision. As chairman of the Commission he found the task far from easy and less congenial than he anticipated. Although care had been taken to set up the Commission in such a way that all aspects of the Church of England were represented, they were not! This supposed representative strength was a stone of stumbling as the members were unable to agree on anything theological. How do you please both those who treasure the Articles and those who despise them? Any agreement depended on finding an acceptable formula and the Commission was fortunate in having John Baker, later Bishop of Salisbury, as one of its members. He was patient and persuasive, adaptable and trusted, finding words to match seeming contradictory views.

The report *Subscription and Assent to the Thirty-nine Articles* was published in 1968 in time for the Lambeth Conference. A new declaration and Form of Assent was recommended which, possibly, provides the only occasion when lay people hear of the sources of authority for the Church of England:

> (Preface) The Church of England is part of the Church of God, having faith in God the Father, who through Jesus Christ our only Lord and Saviour calls us into the fellowship of the Holy Spirit. This faith, uniquely shown forth in the Holy Scriptures, and proclaimed in the catholic Creeds, she shares with other Christians throughout the world. She has been led by the Holy Spirit to bear a witness of her own to Christian truth in her historic formularies – the Thirty-nine Articles of Religion, the Book of Common Prayer, and the Ordering of Bishops, Priests, and Deacons. Now, as before, she has a responsibility to maintain this witness through her preaching and worship, the writings of her scholars and teachers, the lives of her saints and confessors, and the utterances of her councils.
>
> In the profession you are about to make, will you affirm your loyalty to this inheritance of faith as your inspiration and direction, under God, for bringing to light the truth of Christ and making him known to this generation?
>
> Form of Assent: I, *A.B.*, profess my firm and sincere belief in the faith set forth in the Scriptures and in the catholic Creeds, and my allegiance to the doctrine of the Church of England.

Although the report was well-argued and each proposition was supported by adequate evidence, in the end the Commission was against partial or complete revision of the Articles. Why? Among other things there was the fear that the challenge of the Articles would be watered down or synthesised; that any changes by way of a light revision would produce a 'hybrid' form which was neither of the sixteenth century, nor that of the twentieth century; and that because of ecumenical doubts, any new form in which the Articles might appear would rapidly become out of date.

When the *Thirty-nine Articles* came before the 1968 Lambeth Conference the Lambeth Fathers seemed intent on disposing of them. The Bishop of California, James Pike, spoke for many when he lumped them with the doctrine of the Trinity and other credal beliefs as 'excess baggage' that were stumbling blocks for people who might otherwise embrace the Church. The historical setting of them tended to be overlooked. *The Thirty-nine Articles, a revision of Archbishop*

Cranmer's Forty-two Articles of 1553 as finally amended by Convocation in 1571, reflected sixteenth century anti-Roman thinking coloured by Calvinistic theology. They appeared in most Anglican prayer books except for Scotland, India, South Africa, East Africa, Japan and the Arabic version used by the archbishopric of Jerusalem. In East Africa the Articles were printed in the Swahili and English versions but not in most vernaculars. Ian Ramsey spoke in the Conference and claimed that he did not believe that the retention of the Articles was a hindrance to unity since 'the anti-Roman feeling is anti-Roman only to Rome of 1571'. A news conference ended in laughter when Ramsey commented, 'We do not want to sweep the Thirty-nine Articles under the carpet but to send them to a stately home in England where we can visit them from time to time.' Revived interest in the Articles was a reminder of the Englishness of the word which once referred to a chamber pot. Archbishop Geoffrey Fisher complained to Winston Churchill that there was insufficient furniture for the many bedrooms at Lambeth Palace. 'Well,' replied Churchill, 'you have Thirty-nine Articles!'

The Lambeth bishops accepted the main conclusion of the Commission's report, and in furtherance of its recommendation (Resolution 43):

(a) suggests that each Church of our communion consider whether the Articles need to be bound up with the Prayer Book;

(b) suggests to the Churches of the Anglican Communion that assent to the Thirty-nine Articles be no longer required of ordinands;

(c) suggests that, when subscription is required to the Articles or other elements in the Anglican tradition, it should be required, and given, only in the context of a statement which gives the full range of our inheritance of faith and sets the Articles in their historical context.

Ramsey underestimated the dissatisfaction of one constituency. At the Conference the Archbishop of Cape Town, Robert Selby Taylor, demanded a count of votes. This disclosed thirty-seven dissenters, of which English evangelical bishops were predominant. The total number of bishops present was 462.

In the Commission's report there was ambiguity and a flaw in the recommended formula. This was noted by Professor Stephen Sykes, a future Bishop of Ely and Chairman of the Doctrine Commission:

> The faith is said to be uniquely revealed in the Holy Scriptures and set forth in the catholic Creeds, but this does not affirm that everything in the Creeds must therefore be declared to be true. The statement requires, so far as the Thirty-Nine Articles, Book of Common Prayer and Ordinal are concerned, 'loyalty to this inheritance of faith as your inspiration and direction under God in bringing the grace and truth of Christ to this generation'. 'Inspiration' and 'direction' (subsequently the word 'direction' was replaced by 'guidance') is not the same as affirming the theology in these documents. It is compatible with such affirmations but it does not include it.
>
> (*The Integrity of Anglicanism* (1978))

The next report from the Doctrine Commission was self-evidently controversial before one turned to its pages. *Prayer and the Departed* (January 1971) contained a discussion of the arguments for and against praying for the dead. Within the Church of England there are those who regularly pray for the faithful departed in some such terms as, 'May the souls of the faithful, in the mercy of God, rest in peace.' But others believe that the soul's fate is fixed at death and that to pray for the departed is a denial of the Gospel. The Liturgical Commission had put forward proposals for a new burial service but they were blocked in Church Assembly because of the lack of agreement that explicit prayer for the departed could legitimately appear – even as an experimental option – in any service published by Anglican authority. The Doctrine Commission's task was to find something which was acceptable to all major points of view within the Church. Hugh Montefiore, by now Bishop Suffragan of Kingston-upon-Thames, captures a little of the mood and content of the meetings:

> Ian Ramsey was brilliant in keeping all sides together, but his trouble was that he had such a sophisticated mind that his qualifications almost meant that black became white. The report was useful because of its appendices on the evidence of psychic research and what the Anglican Fathers said, but its actual conclusions were an evident non-starter: 'May God in His infinite mercy bring the whole Church, living and departed in the Lord Jesus, to a joyful resurrection and the fulfilment of His eternal kingdom.' It was too long-winded, and did not

apparently pray for the dead but the evangelicals would not agree, although they were forced to concede that one would pray for the Church which includes the dead! We were allowed to commend individuals to God, including, incidentally, non-Christians, but that is hardly praying for them.

Concurrently with the publication of *Prayer and the Departed* came the first of a series of Occasional Papers from the Commission, *Our Understanding of Prayer* by I.T. Ramsey. Its genealogy is interesting as it explains and reflects his working practice. In reports of working parties where his contribution was large and vital, almost every paragraph had a history. An original draft was interpolated, amended, combined with matter from another hand. Occasionally it lost its freshness in the process. Yet there was an unmistakable Ramsey input and style in all the published products. Ramsey provides the background of *Our Understanding of Prayer*. It originated from an address given to the Oxford Mission of 1969. Then, in Ramsey's words:

> it was later given in a much revised form to an international Methodist Institute of Theological Studies in America. This draft was then further revised by the Commission, and in particular it benefited from a general discussion on the problems of prayer which the Commission was able to have during a meeting at Rugby with a group of lay people convened by the Rugby Council of Churches. Thereafter, it was circulated privately to a number of groups in parishes and colleges, with which members of the Commission were informally associated, and in the light of their comments there was a further radical revision and reconstruction.

Ultimately the lively style of writing is that of Ramsey. The paper was very well received by people who struggled with the whole concept of prayer, and in particular with the practice of intercession. An extract is worthy of space and contemplation:

> We cannot be too cautious about over-easy talking of God in relation to our prayer, whether in the words used in the prayers themselves, or in what we say about God's action or apparent inaction. It is futile if not near-blasphemous to speculate on the details of God's ways of working. That is not to say that there will be no response on God's part only that it is profitless for us to speculate about its detailed

character. To put the point in another way: suffice it that in prayer we
have given (if we may so phrase it) opportunity to God to locate His
activity in a particular direction, and opportunity particular enough
(and here is the rub) to include ourselves. If those conditions hold, we
are more likely to pray with integrity than if we think of the answer
of God as the message of an answering machine, or the kind of
message which comes out of a slot-machine which tells us our weight
and our fortune. We shall be content to know that the answer will be
an answer of love, and that it will be an answer which entails our
self-involvement.

A time of prayer can be like the Christian life in miniature. It can
be a point at which our whole life focuses on a speech-act, a small
pattern of words, images, behaviour and behaviour possibilities, which
we hope will be a centre where God discloses Himself and His loving
power in Christ. The details and full extent of this activity we properly
leave to God; but at least we can expect that from this moment we
ourselves shall turn empowered and renewed to grapple with the full
pattern of our whole Christian life and work in the world. God's
sovereign life, His redemption, His life-giving spirit, will activate us
as we realise what response He wills to give to the situation we are
laying before Him. When we ourselves then come alive in a total
commitment, our prayer will be fulfilled in inspired action. In this
way, intercessory prayer should follow from adoration, and lead to
dedication.

Intercessory prayer, therefore, cannot be wholly segregated from
other forms, and (potentially, at least) is a demanding occupation. It is
quite improper to have prayers for (say) a war in Indo-China, for sick
people, for the parishes of a diocese, or for the dioceses and areas
particularised day by day in the worldwide survey contained in the
Cycle of Prayer for Anglican Use, and so on, unless the actual
problems in some way or another form part of our lives – whether by
work or gifts or protest marches or by some other imaginative concern
or inner identification. There must be a willingness in principle to be
involved. This is obviously not to condemn the contemplatives, who
pray because it is their life's dedication to engage in prayer, nor the
many others, such as the housebound and infirm, who pray knowing
that for them any very practical action on the basis of prayer is
impossible. Both these cases are very different from that of the person
who goes through the motions of prayer and yet refuses to engage, or
never thinks of engaging, in any action open to him which harmonises
with the intention of the prayer. The information we have about the

subjects of our prayers should not only guide our intercessions and in this way be the springboard from which our prayer may arise, but also for that reason be the basis on which appropriate action may be taken.

There is an old phrase often used in appeal brochures, 'We want your prayers and your money'. This phrase, while making a point, can be very misleading. For in this context prayers would not be prayers unless the gift of money was part of the one action, and a gift of money is no Christian dedication unless it is an outreach pointing back to a moment of vision in prayer. To suggest, therefore, that praying and Christian giving can be thought of as two separable activities is to misunderstand both. But to see them as inextricably linked is the way in which secularity and spirituality come together as one. For prayer without any practical support or secular expression is empty, as secularity without prayer is unredeemed. Action and prayer are two expressions of one situation; in praying and doing, each fulfils the other. The deepest spirituality and the most active participation are one.

When the *Series III Holy Communion Service* had been issued it was discovered that there was no provision for 're-consecrating' if the bread and wine ran out. What should happen? Should a prayer be offered? Or should wine be added and more bread set apart in silence? In the end the Doctrine Commission decided on the latter course, and then found out that, as in Rites A and B, their advice had not been followed. Discussion on this single point meant that the whole of Eucharistic theology had to be considered. The result was a symposium on different aspects of it, resulting in a set of individual papers by J.R. Lucas, A.R. Peacocke, John Austin Baker, C.F. Evans, Hugh Montefiore, J.L. Houlden, H.E.W. Turner and M.F. Wiles. They were published as *Thinking about the Eucharist* (1972). Ramsey read the papers and wrote a preface.

A contentious subject on Eucharistic doctrine was Reservation of the Blessed Sacrament and devotional practices such as Adoration and Benediction, Exposition and processions at Corpus Christi-tide. These were considered by the Commission. Ramsey prepared a paper (unpublished) reflecting the Commission's position. There had been some parishes in the diocese of Durham which, whilst not under a formal ban, were not visited by his predecessor, Maurice Harland. But Durham had very few 'extremist' parishes, either Anglo-Catholic or conservative-evangelical. Many of the 'High' churches were well attended and had an outreach into the community they served. Nevertheless a number of clergy felt frozen out. The temperature changed on Ramsey's arrival and an immediate thaw came when he visited those parishes. The fact that no label was ever attached to Ramsey in terms of churchmanship was a great advantage. In his paper Ramsey wrote on the subject of devotional practices associated with the Eucharistic elements:

> On the one hand, some will think primarily of the theological risks, not to say the dangers to faith, which eucharistic devotions bring with them, and some of the ideas and the language which reservation has encouraged are not such as anyone with concern for reason as well as reverence, understanding as well as mystery, can gladly contemplate. For instance, it cannot be too often emphasised that devotion is not to the Blessed Sacrament but to God in Christ. The elements themselves must not be the object of devotion. They must be symbols and tokens leading us to God and to the redeeming love He shows in Christ in particular.
>
> At the same time, others readily granting the need for theological circumspection, will argue that eucharistic devotions, so long as there are suitable safeguards, may well provide another route by which the givenness of God in Christ can be realised and acknowledged in prayer and reverence, and that the devotion arising in this kind of context has a descriptive value which would be altogether lost if the practice were prohibited. On this view, it would be readily granted that no devotion would be justified, which took the elements away from the eucharistic action or in any other way redefined or over-valued them as objective objects. It would be theologically important that any devotional act which arose around the elements should have explicit links with the Eucharist from which the elements emerged, as well as with the use to which they will in due course be put in terms of some future communicants.
>
> In short, some would be conscious of the difficulties which the practice may bring with it; others of the enriched devotion which the practice, as a major source of spirituality, makes possible. No one would wish to encourage downright theological errors nor, however, to prohibit what may be to some a source of Christian spirituality. In giving due weight to both approaches to this devotional practice the Commission was agreed that the practice of such devotions should not

be prohibited, but that a critical eye should be kept, by those who value these practices, on the theology which the devotion explicitly or implicitly incorporates, as indeed it ought to be kept on all our devotions in general. For Bishop John Cosin 'In prece assidua' and 'In doctrana sana' embody complementary insights, and in the Anglican tradition both should be matched.

By 1972 the Doctrine Commission was settling down and some serious and solid work was contemplated. Ramsey's personal stock could not have been higher though there were criticisms of his style of chairmanship. What became increasingly evident were the fruits of his own pilgrimage. Gordon Fallows, one time Principal of Ripon Hall, Oxford, later Bishop of Sheffield, was a friend and fellow 'Modern Churchman'. In recalling Ramsey he said, 'In his search for truth he eschewed facile conclusions. These were days, as he once put it, when "the Church must learn to live with the builder's men always in the house".' In such a situation when the builder's men were knocking the house sideways it was good to hear above the clash of hammers the firm, steady, though always enthusiastic, voice of Ian Ramsey articulating Christian hope and faith for a new age in a new or reconstructed building. Shortly before his death Ramsey prepared a private paper for the Commission, 'A Personal Credo', in which he declared two features as definitive of his approach to the Christian faith:

1. The notion of disclosure situations which impress and haunt; moments of vision, flashes of insight, contextualised silences.
2. The notion of theological exploration both in discourse and community structure. Authority belongs primarily to the vision; and when it is translated into discourse, interpretations, community structures and so on these cannot have the givenness of God, the finality of the controlling vision itself. We must then distinguish between the norm which is decisive for our commitment and derivative norms of which there is a multiplicity and which need to be brought together in any particular Christian judgement, whether in doctrine or morality. It is for this reason that I relish the Anglican concept of a multiple Authority whose only unity and coherence is in the activity of God in Christ, which eludes any and all of the multiple expressions. Hence the Anglican

tradition can properly combine discipline and freedom, order and liberty, dogma and reason, discipline and good conscience.

Another of Ramsey's perspectives is illustrated in a section of his 'Credo' on the Conciliar Creeds:

> I see the great historical movements in Christianity as indispensable in so far as they were emphasising elements which had been overlooked and forgotten; tragedies in so far as by the circumstances of their emergence they were unlikely to be unsympathetic to alternative views. I therefore see, for example, the Reformation, Methodism and the Oxford Movement as indispensable tragedies; indispensable negatively in criticising certain contemporary attitudes, and positively in re-asserting what has been forgotten or denied; but tragedies in so far as, speaking generally, supporters of all these movements supposed their opponents to be advocates of pure error, and themselves to be witnesses to the clear truth. On the contrary, I do not deplore Christian disagreements provided that those who disagree constantly explore with each other the basis of their assertions and the possibility of creating a more comprehensive and coherent map. In this context, we may say that it is only certainties which divide; disagreements can create a sense of unity.

It has been said that 'a Creed should be a signpost, and not a ring fence'. Ramsey's life was devoted to attempting to find a perspective in which the re-statement of Christian doctrine could be articulated in his own time. Yet theology is in perpetual flux, in spite of the natural reluctance of devout and committed Christians to admit the fact, and in spite of the tremendous efforts made by ecclesiastical authorities to avoid theological innovation. A retrospect of Christian experience is the best prophylactic against the fears of an irrational conservatism and the infection of fanaticism. It is strictly true to say that a theological statement begins to become obsolete as soon as it has been formulated, for it sums up and marks the triumph of a movement of opinion, which begins at once, almost with the regularity of the tides, to recede from its 'high-water mark'. In claiming a freedom of continuous self-rectification, Ramsey placed theology on a level with the rest of science. All the sciences have their postulates, which are unalterable, and theology is no exception; but all have to apply those postulates in every varying circumstance, with reference to an ever-enlarging accumulation of knowledge, and again theology is no exception. Ramsey's successor as chairman of the Doctrine Commission was Maurice Wiles, Regius Professor of Divinity in the University of Oxford who recalls, 'I do not think I have ever met anyone more ready to give of his time, genuine attention, and interest to those who wanted and needed it. I think that his approach to religious thought and language (though in later years too easily and quickly applied) has a real validity. The combination of such personal, intellectual, and social concern in so human a frame is for me ample evidence of a real spiritual greatness.'

Away from the cloistered milieus of philosophy and theology many people found Ramsey's expositions difficult to comprehend. This is the 'lot' of philosophers and theologians. They may portray Christianity as a thesis to be argued, not a religion to be preached; a principle to be enunciated not a practice to be extended; a tradition to be maintained, not a passion to be communicated. And what of religious 'psychology' whose workings are intricate, intimate and unverifiable? We may look at a thoroughly good man, as fearless and upright as any man, a respected figure among scholars, a leader of the Church with a very able and sincere personality, who has thrown the whole weight of all he has to give on the side of Christianity, but who, for some reason, in spite of all his hard work and unquestionable seriousness does not convey the imperative and attractiveness of Christ. This did not apply to Ramsey. Even if people could not always understand his language, they knew he brought to the Christian religion his faith and his discipleship.

Ramsey's chairmanship of the Doctrine Commission revealed a most ardent Anglican. It is impossible to think of him as belonging to any other Christian community – Methodist, Baptist or Roman Catholic. For Ramsey, the Church of England's genius was to seek to bring out of its treasure things new and old – the new standing on the shoulders of the old, the old affording precedent for the guiding of the new – and both fusing together in a body of truth and practice which had both the virtues of gratitude to the past and attentiveness to present and future. Ramsey's watchword for the Church of England was development, with its ruling passion for truth, and its governing conviction that God fulfils Himself in many ways and that the Holy Spirit had still new avenues of truth down which to lead him.

There was nothing magisterial about the chairman of the Doctrine Commission. There was a modesty about Ian Ramsey whose personal religion was in a real sense 'simple' and his characteristic 'humble'. When Pamela Hansford Johnson (the wife of C.P. Snow) was writing *The Humbler Creation* (1959) she turned to Ramsey for help when portraying a vicar of a London parish. In her novel she beautifully conveyed the striving, frustration and love of a man who, perhaps more than those following any other calling, must keep his personal life free from all hint of corruption, but who, after all, is a man like other men. In *Barchester Towers*, Anthony Trollope described the Revd Septimus Harding 'as a good man without guile, believing humbly in the religion which he has striven to teach and guided by the precepts which he has striven to learn.' Remove Harding's imperceptible pace and apply the words to Ian Ramsey as 'a good man, without guile' and add 'an edifying man!'

17. *With Archbishop of York, the Most Revd Donald Coggan after Ian's Consecration on 1 November 1966*

18. *Ian and Margaret in conversation with a lady in York on the afternoon of 1 November 1966*

19. Being welcomed by the Lord Lieutenant of Durham, Sir James Duff into County Durham at Croft Bridge, south of Darlington on 14 December 1966. Photograph by Derrick Penman

20. Ian visiting Wolsingham Steel works in Weardale in September 1970

21. *Ian and Margaret clearly enjoying the Childrens' Harvest Gift Service at St Andrew's Parish Church in Jamaica. Photograph from Mrs Elaine Burke*

22. *Consecration of the new church of St Bede's, Town End Farm, Sunderland with Ian blessing the people in procession*

23. *Ian with Dean of Durham, Very Revd John Wild at the Cathedral. Courtesy of Tyne Tees Television*

24. *Ian in front of House of Lords. With kind permission of* Radio Times

25. *Dedication of Bishop Auckland General Hospital Chapel*

26. *Ian with other Lambeth Conference Bishops and his chaplain, Revd Richard Ferguson at Auckland Castle, 1968*

27. *Ian with young people at night club in Newcastle. Photo by Fietscher*

28. *Ian with Revd Harry McClatchey, his Chaplain in procession*

29. *Ian leading a demonstration against poverty in Durham. Courtesy of North of England Newspapers*

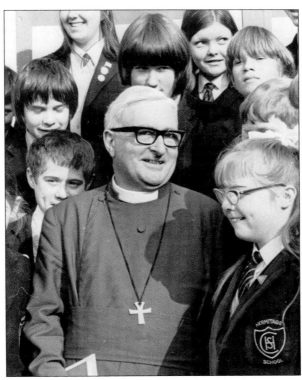

30. *Ian looking fit with children at Hermitage School, Chester-le-Street on 4 October 1972.*
© courtesy of NCJ Media Limited

31. With Sister Haykin in Bishop Auckland General Hospital, Ward 14 in April 1972

*32. Ian on ATCO mower, with Margaret and Mr Hedley, the gardener,
while convalescing in summer 1972*

CHAPTER 8

Bridge-builder

I N HIS UNPUBLISHED PAPER ON *The Bishop*, Ian Ramsey referred to an image for the office and work of a bishop, which 'perhaps in our own day . . . is even more apt than that of shepherds':

> This is the image of Bishop as Pontifex — bridge-builder. In no sense does this conflict with the image of the shepherd. For a bridge-builder today must guide rather than order and must act rather than dictate. A bishop must endeavour to be a bridge-builder in contemporary thought when, at the present time, we are reaping a harvest of centuries of neglect. For some centuries now we have, by and large, just not bothered to maintain or to re-establish communication between the world of scientific thinking on the one hand, and the world of theological thinking on the other. We need bridge-builders in society, between its fragmented groups. We need bridge-builders in the field of pastoral care so that the wisdom and skill and expertise of the many can come together in a common concern for those they serve. We need bridge-builders in a fragmented Church. We need bridge-builders in our political life. People may and do claim that I may aggravate some and stir others to abuse, which led a correspondent to conclude a recent letter to me with the phrase 'your would-be assassin'. But still a bishop must try to bridge-build, to express the authority of the Gospel to create trust.

What did this mean in practice as Ramsey constantly directed his attention and that of others to wide and broad issues of thought and action, doing what he could to hold together the faith and life and work not only of the people in his diocese, but the people of the wider world? That is why he welcomed such appointments, for instance, as his membership of the Council of Radio Durham, President of the Northumbrian Tourist Board, member of the Council of the Institute of Religion and Medicine, Chairman of the Central Religious Advisory Committee (BBC and ITV), member of the Executive Committee of the Social Morality Council (Christians, Jews and Humanists), Chairman of the Governors of William Temple

College, and chairman or member of a miscellany of national or informal organisations, bridging gaps and reconciling groups. He allied himself with a number of 'protests' such as that to protest against the supply of arms to South Africa. He acknowledged that he saw his main centre for work, other than the Diocese of Durham, was London, not least in the House of Lords! There was a smile on his face in saying, 'It is not surprising that I am well-known to the Refreshment Car attendants on the London trains.' Not only well-known but also 'well-loved'. He was never satisfied at being merely a name on a letterhead. Everything he did involved reading and commenting on minutes of meetings, correspondence and preparing for another meeting, submitting papers, a mighty engagement of his mind and time. His travels to Canada and Jamaica were further examples of ministerial bridge-building in the Church overseas.

Was Ramsey temperamentally suited for the work of a bridge-builder? He was strenuously in favour of Christian unity. The year before he became bishop fourteen rural deaneries in the Durham diocese indicated that the Anglican-Methodist Service of Reconciliation was a major point on which delay and further debate between the two Churches was desired. In eight deaneries there were strong complaints about the general apathy of the laity to the whole issue. For all the talk of The Bishoprick, the fact that Durham had a strong Methodist tradition, formed more by Primitive and Independent Methodists than by Wesleyans, led to a great deal of historic hostility between the Churches. There was a febrile and brittle atmosphere between contending Anglican partisans. Ramsey had the task of bringing order into cross-purposed talking:

> So we shall only honestly contemplate schemes for unity when –
> (a) There is some agreement on Christian doctrines which go beyond the Creeds we all share.
> (b) We are energetic and thorough in bringing the residual differences not only out for an airing, but out for a gruelling . . .
> But for none of us, Anglican or otherwise, could there ever be honesty in pretended agreement erected on ambiguities, or in disagreement ignored for comfort's sake.

It was clear Ramsey was well-versed with every side of the 'pro' and 'con' argument. He read all the available literature particularly that emanating from Evangelical and Anglo-Catholic organisations. In a paper on the Anglican-Methodist Proposals ('*The Bishoprick*' November 1968) he gave prominence to the Bishop of Willesden, Graham Leonard, whose publication *to every man's conscience* (1968) was a maypole around which opponents gathered. The central difficulty surrounded the Service of Reconciliation. For Ramsey the primary question to ask about this service was whether it was seen as leading by God's grace to a more effective ministry than was presently exercised either in the Anglican or the Methodist Churches. Was it a public act to give some sort of mutual recognition to each other's ministry? But, it might be asked, recognition of what? What did people suppose happens at the service? His response was as follows:

> The Anglican priest or Bishop will believe that he has something to give to the Methodist ministry, though what it is he would gladly leave to God: 'Send upon each of these Thy servants, according to his need, Thy Holy Spirit . . .' From the other side and speaking only for myself, I would say that I am ready to receive whatever God thinks necessary for me to have and may give me in this way so that I may minister in the wider community: 'Pour out upon each of these Thy Holy Spirit for a fresh dedication to Thy service in the coming together of the Methodist Church and the Church of England'.
>
> Now I grant that all that may seem very vague, and which some people at some time might well have denied. What I have said implies first that the Methodist ministry is in some way or other a bearer of God's grace. Secondly, what I have said, vague though it be, implies that the ministers of the Anglican Church are not already by themselves entirely sufficient, i.e. that their ministries do not already include what the Service of Reconciliation can give. It seems to me that to take part in this service (for which the use of the word 'Reconciliation' is open to some criticism) a man must believe that after this public act a unity is created that is not present before, and that in and through this new fellowship God's will is the more made evident and expressed, and so His grace more effectively mediated.

Ramsey dealt with anomalies in the overall scheme which needed further examination – in the Methodist Church there was occasional lay administration of the Holy Communion; unfermented wine was used at the celebration of Holy Communion; it recognised the ministry and sacraments of the non-episcopal Free Churches; and it was left to a minister to decide, in consultation with the Chairman of his district, whether to hold a public service for those who contracted a civil marriage while the former partner of either was still living.

Ramsey did not prescribe a way that clergy and laity should vote, albeit there was no doubt about his voting intentions. Many waverers followed the lead of their bishop. When the Joint Convocations met in London on 8 July 1969 Ramsey knew that whatever the result 'some are going to be grievously disappointed, others keenly delighted'. The result?

> Sixty-nine per cent. The figure came at the end of a hot day which had begun with a celebration of Holy Communion in St Margaret's, Westminster, and had continued with speeches in Church House until 6.30 p.m. Then had come half an hour of silence until at 7 p.m. the television arc-lights were turned on and the vote was taken. The bishops rose to be counted; the clergy filed through appropriate doors. The result was awaited with tense expectation and when it seemed to delay the tension mounted. Then came the historic announcement. In the Convocation of York the resolution had received 78% support from the Bishops (11–3, Carlisle, Ripon and Sheffield); and 68% support from the clergy (71–34): in the Convocation of Canterbury 93% support from the bishops (27–2, Leicester and Peterborough) and 67% from the clergy (150–77). The resolution had failed by 6% to get the 75% majority which the Convocations had agreed to be necessary. There was a stunned hush as the result made its impact on the crowded House – then all of a sudden a vigorous round of applause from the gallery, to be met immediately with saddened cries of 'shame.' The Archbishop of Canterbury commented that silence would have been more appropriate. The Archbishop of York led us in final prayers. We filed out and then within minutes came the news of the Methodist vote: 524–153, a majority for the scheme of 77.4%. It was on any view a 'Hard Day's Night,' and I do not apologise for the source of this singularly apt phrase.

Ramsey admitted, 'The question which had haunted me throughout the day was: How do I act responsibly whether to the majority (if the resolution fails) or to the minority (if it passes)?' He was sensitive to all parties and consulted with the Methodist chairmen of the Darlington and Newcastle Districts. With the coming of the General Synod there was another vote on 3 May 1972, this time including the House of Laity. The total vote 'for' was 65.8%. The scheme had failed again. In effect Christian Reunion between Churches was dead and Christian Unity has struggled ever since whatever overtures between the churches of Christendom have been made. Ramsey never relaxed in his strenuous efforts at conciliation and bridge-building at local level and his hand of ecumenical friendship was never withdrawn with anyone he met. With his own clergy, whatever their convictions on the issue, they knew there would never be recriminations for each was a member of a family of which Ramsey was always their bishop and Father in God.

There are three major qualities of a bridge which should never be underestimated as it constantly bears the weight of massive loads passing over it. It bears, it endures, and it connects. Ramsey was well aware of E.M. Forster's phrase, 'Only connect'. Was he better at connecting than bearing and enduring? Once asked when he felt most being and acting as a bishop, he responded:

> My answer would point to occasions when I grapple with deep human problems, whether of clergy or laity, whether of parishes or the country at large, and when I am helping people, if I can, to struggle and understand better the meaning and significance of their religious convictions. It is in this kind of context that I set the various meetings I attend, or the meetings with people who come here to Auckland Castle – those whose marriages are breaking up, churchwardens anxious about the next incumbent, schoolboys wanting comments on controversial issues, parties wanting to be shown around the Chapel and the State Rooms. In this context, I also put my openings of schools, my visits to works and factories and business houses, my visits to Rotary Clubs, presenting prizes, talking at dinners. It is not often that I spoke two successive nights at dinners to engineers, and to doctors and lawyers respectively. I have been glad to be guest speaker at professional dinners for bankers, architects, estate agents, engineers and others.

At one event above all others, Ramsey felt honoured by being asked to speak at the Miners' Gala on Saturday 17 July 1971. An extract from his diary:

> After a dull beginning it became a bracing sunny day & one I shall long remember – the Miners' Gala with the address I give on the

Racecourse. V. drives me in & I walk behind the crush barriers to the County Hotel. Meet Will Lowther & the Yugoslavian ambassador & his wife. We then group and line up with Mary Wilson & Jennie Lee & Vic Feather with the police escort. The proceedings begin with the Gresford band playing by & v. moving. What an epitome of humanity! Perhaps my talk was too much like a lecture than a political speech – but the crowd was wonderfully patient & encouraging.

In his address there was a lengthy historical opening, typical of his approach to major events. He continued by paying tribute to the miners in the north-east region where coal was the biggest business, with more than 50,000 men employed. He thought miners were undervalued – and undervalued themselves ('Oh! I'm just a miner'):

> He works under most difficult conditions of light, and noise, and dust. Further, he has to work as a member of a team, every man's job is interlocked with so many others. He still needs to be physically strong, even if in many directions machines have taken over the work. He needs courage for work which is arduous and still has its dangers . . . When I hear of the radio-controlled Eickhoff shearer at work in Dawdon Colliery, of high-speed man-riding facilities at Easington, when I think of this kind of equipment and the kind of qualities needed for this work, it occurred to me that if, so to say, miners could wear white coats their prestige would be enormous. It is I fear true, that being underground they are not only overlooked, but the significance of their work is often under-estimated.

Ramsey knew of the horrible effects of unemployment in the region because he met unemployed people on his ecclesiastical rounds. More significant, he was familiar with the inside of working men's clubs. He wished governments would enable a diversification of industry in the region. He praised the mining industry for its 'magnificent record of good industrial relations'. The miners knew he had objected to the Industrial Relations Bill as too narrow in its concept and too backward looking:

> Your Mining Union is far ahead of what is now being put forward as a code of practice . . . For in present negotiations and consultations in industry generally there is always the feeling that in the last resort there is an in-balance of power, that the management are always bound in the long run to win, not least when the management is in a

nationalised industry, be it the Post Office or even the Coal Board, though as other industries increase in size the conclusion in the private sector is much the same . . . For all industries a parity of control at the highest level. There must be balanced participation. There must be true partnership.

He ended his address with a typical Ramsey flourish:

The image I would leave with you as a symbol with which to face the future is the image of the pioneer, inspired by an ideal – the kind of image which I have of miners and their leaders in the past, tough and rugged men who never lost their faith in humanity. That is what we must be in the present if the future is to take us closer to what the Gospel – the good news – speaks of as having life more abundantly. In the words of Browning quoted in Fynes' *History of Northumberland and Durham Miners*:

One who never turned his back but marched breast forward;
Never doubted clouds would break; never dreamed though right
 was worsted
Wrong would triumph;
Held we fall to rise – are baffled to fight better –
Sleep to wake . . . The pioneer.

If we go forward with faith and the vision, the hope and the confidence of pioneers the future will be as different from the present, as the present, thank God, is different from the past. Not tyranny, but freedom; not oppression, but fulfilment. With that vision and in that struggle, we go forward together.

Building bridges: going forward together! It was no matter whether the miners only partially understood Ian Ramsey's message. His language could appear 'high-falutin' but the man was down-to-earth. As one of them said, 'We liked "our bishop". He had our interests at heart and fought for us.' This extended to the older and revered stalwarts of Durham miners. 'Whenever I see Baroness Lee in the House of Lords I generally see not far from her my old friends Lord Blyton, Lord Shinwell and Lord Slater of Ferryhill.'

By the time of the tenth Lambeth Conference in 1968, Ramsey's stock could not have been higher. There were rumoured expectations that he was a possible or probable candidate to succeed Archbishop Michael Ramsey at Canterbury, although people could not know that it would be six years before there was a vacancy by which time Ian Ramsey had died.

However, the eyes of many bishops watched Ian Ramsey in action with particular interest and it was noticeable that when he rose to speak the Archbishop was eager and particularly attentive. Ian Ramsey was immediately respected as a leader with his theological grasp and ability to articulate his thoughts and, for overseas bishops who may have heard of him but never met him, his sheer humanity appealed. One African bishop was surprised to meet an English bishop who was ordinary and approachable. A series of interviews of fifty-one bishops from the worldwide Anglican Communion, was commendably and carefully collated in a book – *All One Body* (1968) for the Lambeth Conference. Unsurprisingly, the longest and perhaps most sparkling and informative interview was with Ian Ramsey. The work of the Conference was set against a background of grim events in Vietnam, West Africa, and Czechoslovakia, and of mounting protests against social injustice throughout the world. The major theme of the Conference was 'The Renewal of the Church' divided into three sections – in Faith; in Ministry; in Unity. Ian Ramsey was assigned to 'Faith' as Vice-Chairman. The Chairman was the Archbishop of Rupert's Land and Primate of Canada, Howard Clark, with the Bishop of Llandaff, Glyn Simon, as Secretary. The Archbishop of Canterbury said that this section would be dealing with 'perplexities of the modern world' and hoped it would 'be able to say things that are strong and reassuring as well as things about the difficulties of faith.' It was a forlorn hope with thirteen subcommittees covering most subjects under the sun and a few beyond – from urbanisation, technological society, international morality, to the finality of Christ, the debate about God, and the nature of theological language. Ramsey could have chaired any of the subcommittees.

A number of official observers at the Conference criticised the Lambeth fathers in the 'Faith Section'. Professor John Macquarrie accused them of falling into an old trap, a dichotomy in their thinking and language about, 'matters theological and those that refer to the secular society. It is symptomatic of the state of the Church . . . If God is only a piece of metaphysical furniture, then perhaps it doesn't mean very much whether there is a God.' A popular and illustrated account of the Conference – *Faith Alert* (1968) – was edited by Ian

Ramsey, assisted by Michael Perry which went into hands that the official Report would never reach. The Conference *Message on Faith*, was somewhat impenetrable and written in officialese. Ramsey's article in *Faith Alert* was a healthy corrective, a record of his personal opinion and impressions, conveying encouragement with a challenge:

We need renewal in faith if we are to have that increased sensitivity without which we shall almost certainly misunderstand the language of theology. We also need renewal in faith if we are to make a balanced appraisal of new knowledge, not least those insights in psychology which are critical of well-established theological views about human behaviour.

Again, may we not see the 'debate about God', whatever misunderstandings and confusions it has created, and however much it may have suggested to many ordinary people that 'God is no more', as evidence of a theological humility, and see it with the eyes of faith as a liberating and renewing influence on religious thought? Further, it was agreed that we need a renewal of faith if we are to make sure that our urbanised, technological society, which gives us unprecedented opportunities of which our predecessors could never have dreamed, brings in fact true prosperity to the common man in this age which is characteristically his.

It is as and when we are renewed in faith, a faith which reckons with the possibilities and problems of the world around us, that we are able to see our age as an age of creative travail in which the purposeful activity of God is at work. We then find in the upheavals a cause for hope rather than alarm.

In this way a renewal in faith brings hope and confidence; it is also the only adequate and satisfying answer to those who regard the Church as 'a static institution, backward-looking, concerned chiefly with its own survival'. A renewal in faith enables us to 'combine Christian assurance with a bold exploration of theology and society'; to 'unite Christian confidence and intellectual and social risk'. The preamble to the Section report 5 recalls that 'these are characteristics that belong to the pilgrim and the pioneer', and rightly concludes that 'it is as pilgrims and pioneers that we shall show ourselves members of a Church renewed in faith.'

How shall we ourselves be pioneers? Some of the problems to which that question breaks down, and which are raised by this Section, are: What in our church organisations would be different if we were renewed in faith? What kind of renewal is needed if the

Church organises itself for mission to the contemporary world? What should be the Church's attitude to the revolt of youth? Can we discern in their protests 'an authentic note of criticism recalling Christians to obedience to the Gospel'?

In political and social matters do we pay 'excessive deference' to 'conventional wisdom and outdated institutions'? What can we do by way of 'bolder experiment in adapting local and familiar art-forms and prayer-forms, as well as modern forms of expression, in the development of the Church's teaching and liturgy'?

How can we be pioneers in prayer? In so far as modern ideas about God and man 'emphasise the way in which God goes beyond all that we know, and yet is to be recognised as present in the midst of the creative process', do they help us to pray better?

Does man fail in his stewardship of God's creation, 'in his pollution of air, soil, and ocean, and his scant regard for the balance of nature, or the needs of future generations, and his tendency, without disciplined restraint, to use the animal creation for his own ends'? How can we best witness to the Christian truth about race, world poverty and war? What ought to be our attitude to revolution, and non-violent protests?

These are but some of the questions that our Section faced as we considered the implications of a renewal in faith, and a faith alert. Now, over to you!

There was buoyancy and infectious enthusiasm in Ramsey that created a feeling that if everyone could be brought into a big and all-embracing Christian tent of his own design the Anglican Communion would go forward in good heart. His genius consisted in his humanity. He may also have been aware of looming tragedy in Anthony Trollope's remark, 'The Apostle of Christianity and the infidel can meet without the chance of a quarrel; but it is never safe to bring together two men who differ about a saint or a surplice.'

More strenuous and more effective than the Lambeth Conference were Ramsey's skills of building and crossing bridges overseas. For twenty years he was an active participant in the Anglo-Scandinavian conferences between the Church of England and the Lutheran Churches of Norway, Sweden, Denmark and Finland. In August 1957 he was in Sweden, in 1965 he was in Denmark, in 1969 he was in Finland and in August 1971 had the great satisfaction of welcoming the Scandinavian Churches to Durham. In May 1970 he went on a hectic preaching and lecture tour to Canada, in the dioceses of New Westminster, British Columbia, Cariboo, Kootenay, Caledonia and Yukon. From 26 November till 11 December 1970 he was in Jamaica for the centenary of the independence of the Church in Jamaica. He was in Canada again in June 1971 lecturing in Clergy Schools. His idea of regular clergy exchanges between Durham and Canada and Jamaica took root. He always returned from these visits bristling with new ideas, wondering how they could be implemented in the Church of England or more locally in his diocese. And, as always, a shoal of new contacts, people with whom he will keep in touch, and another avalanche of paper will descend on his desk. He planned to lead a pilgrimage to the Holy Land in May 1972, his first experience of the biblical places, and other overseas engagements were also planned, but heart attacks and sudden death prevented their fulfilment.

In a preface to a book on bridges the author, Shirley Smith, wrote, 'Standing on the bank of the river and looking over the broad brimming width to be bridged, one feels extraordinarily insignificant in the face of its challenge and the unknown obstacles which may well be encountered. I have tried here to impart something of the thrill of achievement as one by one the difficulties emerge and are overcome, and slowly the bridge takes shape, the piers rise above the waters and the spans stretch over from shore to shore.' In a nutshell these words encapsulate Ramsey's life and work. His questing and questioning mind was insatiable. It was ever thus. On 21 October 1930 he had given a lecture at Farnworth Grammar School on 'Weather and Weather Forecasting' with an explanation of the weather elements and their formation, and the section on weather forecasting contained hints for the would-be weather expert. This was not the pretentiousness of youth but a searching, probing analysis after reading and research. He was never superficial. When, as an adult, he undertook a lecture or speech it was full, often overfull, of background reading and evidence to substantiate his conviction on any given topic. This included his familiarity with Plato, Aristotle, Demosthenes, Homer and Thucydides and other thinkers throughout the ages.

Nowhere was his approach to any subject more evident than when he gave the Trueman Ward Lecture on 'The Influence of Technology on the Social Structure' to the Royal Society of Arts (more precisely the Royal Society for the Encouragement of Arts, Manufactures and Commerce, founded in 1754) on 24 March 1971. Ramsey followed in the wake of luminaries – Lord Adrian, Sir Mortimer Wheeler, Sir Bernard Lovell, Sir John Cockroft, Dr Ernst Chain, Sir Solly Zuckerman and Sir Peter Scott, in itself a tribute to another bridge-builder who was held in the highest esteem by his peers. In his packed rather than paced lecture Ramsey recalled some of the founders of the R.S.A., Joshua Reynolds, Samuel Johnson, William Hogarth, Thomas Chippendale, Robert Chippendale. And so eventually to technology 'which can bring about social changes which release humanity, or alternatively social changes which oppress humanity . . . Never has a society like the Royal Society of Arts been more needed than today, true to its original concern for the unity of culture and the cohesion of society, seeking to unite science and usefulness by a common ethos and moral concerns.' He was critical of the aloofness of citing Newman's conviction that it was the business of a university not to teach 'some temporal calling, or some mechanical art, or some physical secret' but to train gentlemen. One aspect of his much lauded lecture is the theme of this chapter. Ramsey said:

> The ship and the bridge make use of pure science – the principle of Archimedes, the theory of structures, and so on. But it is man's need to communicate with his fellow men and the moral significance of human fellowship as well as the inspiration of form and beauty which should apply the driving force to relate these scientific principles and this scientific knowledge to such materials as are necessary for the building of a ship or a bridge.

Without question Ramsey 'connected' with people and drew them together. It is the 'bearing' and 'enduring' which is less easy to confirm. Another aspect surfaces: surprising until explored and excavated. For all his outgoingness, friendship, and ability to bring divergent ideas and people together, was he a 'one-man show'? Strange it may be but more than an impression it is, that there was little collegial blood running in his veins, not at Cambridge, not at Oxford, not at Durham. He was **everybody's** bishop – which we now pursue.

CHAPTER 9

Everybody's Bishop

W AS IAN RAMSEY A 'one-man show'? He did not recognise boundary fences. He gave himself unsparingly to the people of Durham but also to everyone else. His academic pursuits continued and his apparent compulsion to respond to the calls of the wider Church was pursued without discrimination or discernment. Other invitations from non-religious organisations and groups were unceasing and received an immediate response with gusto. Narrower calls on his time were not declined, with the result that the most persistent and least urgent, often the latest, won! This was Ramsey. If he had listened and heeded the cautionary voices, particularly that of his doctor, would he have slowed down or changed direction? No! And if perchance he had changed it would have involved stepping completely outside his character.

The Revd Harold Saxby, a priest in the diocese since 1941 and Rector of St Paul, Jarrow, from 1964, puts his finger on an observable hesitation in approving his bishop:

> He was a kind-hearted little man with a superb intellect, but it would have been better for him to have remained a university professor because he found it difficult to distinguish the really important from the trivial in life so that he spent his energies using the sledge hammer of his intelligence on cracking walnuts. I think Michael Ramsey realised this when he said after his death, 'We must not do that again.' In 1973 we were due to celebrate the 1300th anniversary of the Venerable Bede and in contrast to a certain lack of interest in the rest of the Diocese and the Cathedral, in 1972 Bishop Ian called together the notables of the county to a meeting to plan the event and mark it of some significance in the North of England. Unfortunately, in spite of his enthusiasm and vision, it was felt it was too late to do what was necessary to prepare for such an event and little came of it.

There are countless examples of Ramsey's initiatives undertaken with zeal and a flourish, but, once his hand was off that tiller, when he moved to the next innovation elsewhere, interest evaporated. He would have been unsuccessful in a relay as the baton would have remained in his hand.

Nonetheless, during his short episcopate he was the focus of leadership. The 'common touch' was an authentic natural gift and recognised as such. In his cassock and cloak – the latter a favourite for wear outdoors – he could walk into a shop and chat to shop assistants in mini-skirts, walk into a bingo hall or club and engage people in conversation. It was not Episcopal patter but questions were asked and views obtained on current concerns – the pill, government benefits, unemployment. There is a lovely story told by Humphrey Carpenter in his biography of Archbishop Robert Runcie. It relates to Runcie's Consecration as Bishop of St Albans in Westminster Abbey on 24 February 1970:

> I (Runcie) asked Harry Williams to preach, and he preached at what he describes in his autobiography as 'sadistic length'. It was forty-one or forty-two minutes, and I remember Michael Ramsey, at the end of practically every paragraph after the first quarter of an hour, picking up his mitre – and then putting it down again! And Ian Ramsey of Durham, the most relevant and lovely of bishops, was off to a meeting at (puts on an accent) the Boony Cloob.' 'The Bunny Club?' I repeated unbelievingly. 'Yes,' explained Runcie, 'it had just opened, and Ian, who was never one for turning down an invitation, which would perhaps enable him to communicate a sort of penny-dropping disclosure of God, was going to some meeting there. And I remember him rushing into the reception and pocketing a number of sausage rolls, and saying, 'In case I don't get anything at the Boony Club. I told them I was having loonch here. But I didn't expect that sermon.' And somebody said to George Reindorp (Bishop of Guildford), 'That sermon should be published', and he said, 'Yes, as a book!'

Ramsey had no sooner placed a mitre on his head when the Church of England Board of Education and the National Society invited him to chair an independent commission to inquire into religious education. On this occasion his acceptance was not a foregone conclusion as it came in the same month as he had given the Archbishop of Canterbury an affirmative reply to chair the Doctrine Commission. The membership of the Commission was too large, though its network of subcommittees essential on Theology; Morals; Education; Independent Schools; Church. Why does it not seem surprising that in addition to his heavy load of work as Chairman, Ramsey also chaired the Theology subcommittee? The following full list of members of the subcommittee includes many already familiar to Ramsey:

> The Revd Professor P.R. Ackroyd, Samuel Davidson Professor of Old Testament Studies University of London, King's College
> The Revd J. Bowker, Fellow of Corpus Christi College, Cambridge
> Canon F.W. Dillistone, Fellow of Oriel College, Oxford
> Dr W.P. Kent, Dr Lee's Reader in Chemistry, Christ Church, Oxford
> Professor B.G. Mitchell, Nolloth Professor of the Philosophy of the Christian Religion, University of Oxford
> The Revd S.W. Sykes, Dean of St John's College, Cambridge
> The Revd Professor E.J. Tinsley, Professor of Theology, University of Leeds
> The Revd A.C. Wedderspoon (Secretary)

There were co-opted members: Revd Professor G.W.H. Lampe, Ely Professor of Divinity, University of Cambridge; Professor H.D. Lewis, Department of the History and Philosophy of Religion, King's College, London; Professor W.R. Niblett, Professor of Higher Education, University of London Institute of Education.

Ramsey, Bowker, Dillistone and Sykes contributed to the initial drafting. The whole Commission was exceedingly fortunate in its admirable secretary, Alexander Wedderspoon, then Education Adviser to the Church of England Schools Council, later Canon Residentiary of Winchester Cathedral and Dean of Guildford from 1987 to 2002. His contribution to David Edwards' *A Memoir* of Ramsey carried salient information and invaluable insights as an 'insider', some of which are now repeated:

> Ian Ramsey later told us that he had resolved to refuse the chairmanship because of his existing commitments. But he decided to at least come and see us. It was a dismally wet evening and he arrived in our offices in Westminster wearing a long raincoat which he removed to reveal full Episcopal dress, including gaiters. He had just come from an official occasion in the House of Lords and wryly apologised for his appearance. In a short time we were in the midst

of a discussion which quickly kindled into an excitement. He accepted the chairmanship and began at once to make plans for the first meeting. The thirty members were made up of teachers in schools, colleges of education and universities, together with educational administrators and advisers. It was obvious from the start that they all had minds of their own and were certainly not going to be rushed into easy agreement. Most of the basic work was done in subcommittees, each with several co-opted consultant specialists. Bishop Ramsey took the chair at all meetings of the full Commission and of the theological subcommittee. Between 1967 and 1969 this involved him in twenty conferences of two or three days each and regular background reading and negotiation. He was also involved in the final approval of each section of the report.

Perhaps the most outstanding feature of his chairmanship was his sheer intellectual grasp of the subjects under discussion. He was, of course, completely at ease with the most complex argument in theology, philosophy, or ethics. But he also had a sufficient fund of psychology, sociology and common sense to be able to discern when a specifically educational discussion was becoming precious or absurd. He could demolish an argument with force and clarity, but his rejoinder would usually include some homely and hilarious anecdote which would reduce the Commission to prolonged laughter – in which any bruised feelings were at once forgiven.

It is scarcely surprising that he found it difficult to enthuse over the complex problems associated with the administration of church schools. The muddled tale of denominational bickering and reluctant compromise was, for him, a constant source of incredulity: 'it makes you wonder what they thought they were at'. He made it clear that it was his view the church schools should be allowed to continue only if good educational and pastoral reasons could be shown to justify the expense. He made it equally clear that it was not the Commission's duty to manufacture reasons for the preservation of the status quo. This was regarded in some Church circles outside the Commission as a doctrine both startling and seditious, but his insistence upon a rigorously objective enquiry was fully justified.

The Fourth R.: the Durham Report on Religious Education was published in June 1970. The report was weighty in the best sense. With Ramsey in the chair and an abundance of the brightest minds of the educational firmament as members how could it be otherwise? It was also hefty, 368 pages plus bibliography and index; 577 numbered paragraphs led to forty-seven recommendations. Fifty of its included pages of evidence could have been omitted. There were three major recommended changes. First, the repeal of the provisions of the 1944 Act in relation to religious instruction and school worship and the abandonment of the machinery for making agreed syllabuses – 'a relic of the ecclesiastical era in religious education'. A measure of statutory obligation was essential but schools must have a wide measure of flexibility. Secondly, the term 'religious instruction' should be replaced by 'religious education', which 'should form part of the general education received by all school pupils', acknowledged on educational grounds and not by making it alone of all subjects legally compulsory. Thirdly, the Commission urged that the dual system should not be perpetuated for 'denominational advantage', but only to enable the Church 'to express its concern for the general education of the young people of the nation'. The whole tenor of the report with its 'flexibility' and 'openness' (after all Ramsey was chairman) was a retreat (though some said an 'advance') from the clarity and definiteness of the 1944 Act. The Durham Report immediately had high sales and was well received for its educational justification for teaching religion in schools. Ramsey presided over a crowded and lively press conference and he made several successful broadcasts and television appearances.

Robert Beloe, a former headmaster, Chief Education Officer for Surrey, and then Secretary to the Archbishop of Canterbury, reviewed *The Fourth R* in *Theology* (October 1970). He wrote for others in justly finding that the chapter on Theology and Education (forty-four pages) was probably unique in a Church report on religious education, 'The theologian shares a place with the psychologist, economist, sociologist, historian, politician, parent, teacher, educationalist, journalist . . .: the theologian will be granted no place of privilege'. This is the secret of Ramsey's approach to every subject he was invited to examine. Somehow it subsumes constraint and boldness. It is a special gift. Few of his contemporaries brought together such a variety of erudite, often warring educationalists and produced genuine agreed statements:

> The Christian contribution to modern education is an account of the individual and his potentialities which, as we have sought to argue, is

more true to life than its alternatives, and offers society a more
satisfactory basis from which its educational procedures can set out. Its
special advantage is that it offers for each pupil's consideration criteria
by which a critical assessment of his own role in society and the world
at large can be made, and by which he may be able to stand over
against this society, if need be. It points to an education leading to
personal fulfillment and characterised by a critical freedom.

In 1968 another theologian and friend persuaded Ramsey to join the
Social Morality Council. It had developed and largely replaced the
Public Morality Council which concerned itself almost exclusively
with sex. When Joost de Blank, Canon of Westminster Abbey, and
a former Archbishop of Cape Town, became President of the new
Council, supported by an energetic, forward-looking and underestimated imaginative Secretary, Edward Oliver, a Roman Catholic
layman, complete transformation of direction took place. Christians,
Jews and Humanists collaborated in the promotion of responsible
citizenship. The scope of its activities included such matters as
disarmament and overseas aid. The 'persuader' of Ramsey was Bishop
C. Butler, Auxiliary Bishop to the Cardinal Archbishop of Westminster, a former Abbot of Downside and one of the principal
progressive participants in the Second Vatican Council, who many
hoped would himself have gone to Westminster in 1963 in preference
to John Heenan! Butler succeeded de Blank as President. Harold J.
Blackham, former Director of the British Humanist Association,
chaired the Council. Once again Ramsey was in his element,
extending his vision with another range of people.

There was always time to further the work of the William Temple
College of which he was Chairman of Governors. In 1966, Len
Tyler, Archdeacon of Rochdale, was appointed Principal. It was a
college where unions and management met, dropping their defensive
attitudes, and lay people, women in particular, were welcomed to
study theology and sociology. And all the time Ramsey was
encouraging, provoking, conciliating, stretching minds – and himself
– as if it were his major concern. Len Tyler recalled how they met
in curious places:

after a late meeting at the House of Lords; before an interview at the
BBC; for breakfast in the Athenaeum; in a railway cafeteria –

times and places which in themselves speak of the total commitment which he brought to high episcopal office and which he adorned not only with superb intellectual gifts, which made him an international scholar, but with a simplicity of lifestyle which made him so admired by people who recognised intuitively real greatness – that greatness which God inspires in those who seek His face. Here was a man for whom truth and love and justice mattered – when occasion demanded, he accepted controversy and public conflict, but he always brought to the debate, as his speeches and writing reveal, both integrity of mind and compassion of heart.

When the Rugby buildings were sold, the College came under the umbrella of Manchester University. In 1972 Tyler moved to a parish but just before he died Ramsey was able to ensure that his friend David Jenkins was appointed Director of the William Temple Foundation in Manchester.

The Institute of Religion and Medicine was founded in 1964 to seek greater knowledge of the principles on which health, in its widest spiritual, mental and physical sense, is based, and to promote a better understanding and co-operation between all people of whatever creed or discipline, who are concerned with the care of the sick and the health of the community. Ramsey was a founding member, became the vice-chairman of its council in 1966 and its chairman in 1971. It was another 'priority'. Whilst at Oxford he served as Chairman of the Warneford Hospital Management Committee at a critical period of the hospital's history. Earlier, in 1953, he was a member of the Archbishops' Commission on *The Church's Ministry of Healing*, the title of its report published in 1958. The Bishop of Durham, Maurice Harland, was chairman. Surgeons, medical practitioners and psychologists shared membership with bishops, clergy and philosopher-theologians. They traced the history of healing in the New Testament, evidence of healing, and cooperation between the clergy and the medical and nursing professions. Ramsey was drawn to considering some common misconceptions – that healing inevitably follows faith; that suffering is always contrary to God's will; that sickness is caused by sin; that modern medicine has superseded the Church's ministry of healing; that only the specially gifted can practise the Church's ministry of healing; that the Church's ministry of healing is separate from its other work, that physical healing is all that matters; that the Communion of the sick and Unction are part of the 'last rites' only; that a medically unexplained healing is more wonderful than one brought by medical means. They considered that misconceptions about medical factors in healing arise from (a) ignorance of the natural history of illness; (b) the supposition that if some change follows a spiritual ministration, then that ministration is necessarily its cause; (c) the belief that doctors frequently and confidently pronounce a sentence of imminent death; and (d) the supposition that doctors have a vested interest in sickness.

Within the Commission Ramsey was able to speak of his own experience when, as a student, he realised the importance of the clergy's approach to the sick in hospital. At Durham he visited clergy who were ill at home or in hospital, less as a bishop more as a priest, encouraging the patient's hope and to enable them to offer their suffering and life, in union with Christ's all sufficient sacrifice to the loving and redemptive will of God.

Ramsey was a regular visitor and speaker to groups. He had a special affinity to the Sunderland-Tyneside Field group of the Institute of Religion and Medicine. In November 1969 he gave the Third Margaret Allan Memorial Lecture in Edinburgh to the Scottish Pastoral Association. His title was 'On Not Being Judgemental'. He contrasted 'judgement' and 'acceptance' from the point of view of a caseworker who 'is suspicious of the judgemental attitude because of the shallow and superficial understanding of human nature which it often implies' and 'because it uses methods or concepts which, whether because of implied hostility otherwise, inhibit response and oppress the spirit of man by being embodied in some authoritarian judgement. The judgemental attitude often names or condemns a situation, or both, rather than reacts creatively to it.'

Ramsey had something interesting to say about the matter of absolution:

Now undoubtedly absolution can describe an activity which is as empirically naïve as it is ritually stereotyped and theologically suspect. Undoubtedly it can, it may, tempt a priest to play the God role and in this way to pretend to an infallibility, an omnipotence and a divine status which, since they are given to no finite person, are inevitably and necessarily parodied and contorted. That needs to be said. But another interpretation altogether can be given to the act of absolution. In relation to sin and wrongdoing, it can in principle occur as an expression of the Gospel, just as in relation to a community the Church occurs as an expression of the Gospel, and as in relation to written words the Bible occurs as an expression of the Gospel, and just as in relation to food, the Lord's Supper, the Holy Communion occurs as an expression of the Gospel. What I am saying is that in relation to sin and wrongdoing absolution may occur as one of many legitimate expressions of the Gospel, the Gospel of God's redeeming love. In this sense absolution can be a feature of the reconciled community which in this way shares through its spokesmen in the unsearchable riches of Christ. This I believe to be the true interpretation of verses 19–23 of the twentieth chapter of St John's Gospel viz. that absolution is a characteristic feature of the forgiven, reconciled community, reminding its members of the redeeming love of God in which they constantly live. Absolution may in its rite and ceremony, and when justified always will, mediate His redeeming reconciling love in a disclosure.

Ramsey was honoured in being asked to give the inaugural lecture at the British Medical Association Conference in Cyprus, in April 1972 on 'Moral Problems facing the Medical Profession at the Present Time'. The lecture was prepared but, as Ramsey was ill in hospital, it was read for him. Controversy ensued as he referred to the moral problems which arise, for example, around the medical prolongation of human life by artificial means; around the development of transplant surgery; around developments in pharmacology and in the vast increase in the number and use of new drugs; around developments in endocrinology or neurosurgery, where medical treatment, like many physical illnesses, can effect far-reaching personality changes; around the possibilities of genetic engineering; around experiments to do with fertilisation of the human ovum outside the body which could result in the fertilised egg from one woman being allowed to grow in the uterus of another and perhaps in circumstances where the identity of the father might be in doubt.

Those present in Cyprus who neither knew Ian Ramsey nor were familiar with his work were spellbound and astonished. They felt the force of the lecturer even in absentia, not a bishop pontificating, but someone with amazing technical knowledge of the subjects and power to expand and explain moral problems – an imperative – in contemporary medicine. No whisper of simple decisions or facile solutions. His uninhibited probing of questions and problems which beset BMA members was profound for them and troubling for black and white moralists back home when reports appeared in newspapers.

No speech or lecture by Ramsey was devoid of Christian content. On this occasion his observations on the significance of death are especially poignant as five months later he would be dead himself:

> Must death always be regarded as a failure for medicine? From a Christian standpoint in particular, is death a failure? The Christian has a very complicated context for death. There is within the Christian tradition a sense of the propriety of a man desiring to consummate his life on earth in what an old prayer calls 'a perfect end'. To make the same point from another direction, we may say that death is of all events that one in which the grace of God is to be found. In all the stark loneliness of death, confronted by the abyss of death, we are to prove pre-eminently God's transforming power. In this sense death is the gate to Life Eternal. Now if that is, even in outline, anything like the attitude which the Christian takes towards death, death on this view is certainly not something to be avoided by any and every possible means for as long as possible. Death is rather something natural and inevitable for which not only can we but must we prepare, the gateway through which we are to move to that fruition, that fulfilment which is God's purpose for us. All this lies behind the familiar maxim: 'Disce mori' – learn to die. It is also supported from the side by the medical insight embodied in the well-known aphorism that 'Life is a disease with a mortality rate of one hundred per cent.' In short, Christian belief in personal survival, while it readily acknowledges the natural inevitability of death, takes away from death any threat of annihilation . . .
>
> If we think that death does annihilate us and bring us to an end good and all for ever, then we might well want to exercise the principle to 'keep alive at all costs' because the alternative is precisely nothing.

In 1970 the Bishop of Bristol, Oliver Tomkins, resigned as Chairman of the Central Religious Advisory Committee (CRAC). These were strenuous and difficult times for religious broadcasting, and the BBC and the Independent Television (now Broadcasting) Authority knew they must have someone of outstanding quality who would make this a central plank of his interest and effort. Penry Jones, the Head of Religious Broadcasting made an informal approach to Ramsey. It was not long before the Chairman of the BBC, Lord Hill, was confirming the appointment! In his response to Lord Hill, Ramsey wrote, 'I must shed what I can of what has less priority'. That he was incapable of doing, and on 18 March 1971 he attended his first meeting of CRAC and thrust himself with vigour into new responsibilities.

Of whom was it written, 'In mind he never grew old. He welcomed every new development, if only he was persuaded it was true development, and he waited for more. The Divine Spirit he believed in was a living Spirit, speaking and moving in the Church today, and he trusted every fresh age to add to the glory of God's revelation. And he expected God still to send messages through Samuel to Eli, "You must see visions"?' Ian Ramsey? The words were a perfect description of him. They were in fact used of one of his predecessors at Durham, Brooke Foss Westcott.

CHAPTER 10

Lord Spiritual

IAN RAMSEY WAS INTRODUCED INTO the House of Lords on 6 December 1966, immediately before a question on the transport of flammable substances. Their lordships would soon learn that the train from Darlington to King's Cross frequently carried an inflammable prelate. Ramsey had every intention of using the House of Lords to influence a wider body of opinion than that of the church people within his diocese. Although he expected to present a cross-bench view of Church opinion on matters of domestic and foreign policy, he was bound to be affected by current legislation passing through the House. There were debates when the colour of his politics and economics was clear, but during his time the majority of legislation was of a strictly moral nature so it mattered less whether the Labour Government under Harold Wilson was in power, until 1970, or a Conservative administration, led by Edward Heath thereafter. In making Christian opinion articulate both in Parliament and elsewhere Ramsey enabled the Church to influence politics without claiming political rewards.

The House also gave Ramsey access to a second club for dining and meeting people, a facility he used to its utmost; it was similar to the Athenaeum of which he was a member.

Between his maiden speech on 19 July 1967 and his final one on 22 March 1972 he spoke, intervened, or proposed amendments on forty-four occasions. This does not reflect his presence in the Chamber for he slipped in and out whenever he could on visits to London. In debates Ramsey had a persistent and stubborn streak which did not let other peers subdue or overrule him. He was always well equipped with evidence to challenge ill-thought-out legislation or the ramblings of peers who had not done their homework! He detested pomposity and patronising as, for example, on an occasion when Viscount Dilhorne, said Ramsey 'moved his amendment in a charming ecclesiastical fashion'.

The test for Ramsey came quickly. On one issue, the most

controversial of its time, he was a target for slings and arrows, in addition to fulsome or conditional support. The whole human race is deeply divided over the question of the moral legitimacy or illegitimacy of abortion. The explanation of this wide divergence of view between different groups of the human race is, in the first place, that the sanctity of human life is more highly valued in some communities than in others, and in the second place that there is disagreement as to when human life may be said to begin or, in older language, when does the soul enter the body? A human being is an embodied rational spirit. The rational spirit develops in and along with its body. In infancy it is an infantile rational spirit. But when does all this begin? There are three possible answers, that it begins at birth, that it begins at some stage during pregnancy, that it begins at conception. The Christian tradition settled for the third answer. Chiefly it is because of the conviction that by the act of procreation, the human parents, consciously or unconsciously, deliberately or accidentally, co-operate with God in bringing into being a human person, and neither they nor anybody else have a right to halt the process, once begun, and the process clearly begins at conception. This position would seem to lead inevitably to a total prohibition of abortion. The life of one human being may not be destroyed for the sake or the convenience or even the preservation of another.

It is often overlooked that it was only by a Statute of 1803 – Lord Allenborough's Act – that the procuring of an abortion became a statutory crime. In the twentieth century there was the Infant Life (Preservation) Act 1929, which marked the gathering, not yet galloping, momentum for a change in the law. In 1961 a Medical Termination of Pregnancy Bill was introduced by Kenneth Robinson (Labour MP for St Pancras North, and Minister for Health 1964–1968) into the House of Commons but it was talked out.

The Church Assembly Board for Social Responsibility formed a committee to study the subject. Ian Ramsey was appointed chairman. To familiar minds and faces – R.M. Hare, Basil Mitchell, Garth Moore, Josephine Barnes, and Gordon Dunstan (Secretary) were added Mr G.F. Abercrombie, formerly President of the College of General Practitioners; Miss Audrey Catford, Head Medical Social Worker, Charing Cross Hospital; Dr Portia Holman, Senior Physician in Psychological Medicine, Elizabeth Garrett Anderson Hospital; and Canon H.M. Waddams of Canterbury Cathedral. The Bishop of Exeter, Robert Mortimer, was a Consultant Member.

The report, *Abortion. An Ethical Discussion* was published in 1965, the year in which a bill to amend the law on abortion was introduced in the House of Commons by Mrs Renée Short (Labour MP for Wolverhampton North East) and given a first reading. It did not survive the parliamentary session. Later that year a new bill was introduced by Lord Silkin and given a second reading. His bill would legalise abortion not only for (a) the sake of the mother's health and safety, but also (b) if there were a substantial risk that the child, if born, would suffer from such physical or mental abnormalities as to be seriously handicapped, or (c) in the belief that the health of the patient or the social conditions in which she is living (including the social conditions of her existing children) made her unsuitable to assume the legal and moral responsibility for caring for a child or another child as the case may be, or (d) in the belief that the patient became pregnant as a result of intercourse which was an offence under specific section of the Sexual Offences Act 1956, or (e) that the patient was a person of unsound mind. Ramsey's committee could not support (b), (c) and (d) unless 'by reason of these matters, the mother's health and well-being is seriously threatened'.

The broad conclusions of Ramsey's committee, after surveying the matter afresh in the light of traditional discussions and of present proposals, was that in certain circumstances abortion could be justified:

This would be when, at the request of the mother and after consultation, it could be reasonably established that there was a threat to the mother's life or well-being, and hence inescapably to her health, if she were obliged to carry the child to term and give it birth. And our view is that, in reaching this conclusion, her life and well-being must be seen as integrally connected with the life and well-being of her family. Whether such a threat existed – and to decide as to a threat plainly includes the weighing of future probabilities – would be for the medical practitioner concerned to decide in the light of a full discussion with such a consultative group as we have envisaged, a group which would bring together different professional and personal interests.

In our view such a consultative procedure would cover those cases where justification for abortion would rest upon there being an assessable risk of a defective or deformed child, as well as cases of incest or rape; though the ground of the decision would be the prognosis concerning the mother as affected by the pregnancy in question; not the possibility of deformity itself, not simply the fact (if established) of the act of incest or rape. Further, it is our hope that the consultations which we envisage would not only establish a moral tradition in each particular hospital or hospital group, but might also help to create uniformity of practice throughout the country. They would help also to avoid that disingenuity in law or medicine which any inadequate reform is almost certainly bound, in practice, to invite. Finally – and this is of great importance – in cases where abortion is not indicated, they would give the patient access to the skilled medical and social services which can afford her the encouragement, help and support which she may need to continue the pregnancy and give birth to the child.

In 1966 an Abortion Bill was introduced into the House of Commons by Mr David Steel (Liberal MP for Roxburgh, Selkirk and Peebles) where a middle course was aimed for between the contending lobbies and thus to produce a consensus bill. An important clause was inserted that 'no person shall be under any duty, whether by contract or by any statutory or other legal requirement, to participate in any treatment authorised by this Act to which he has conscientious objection.'

Ramsey made his maiden speech on 19 July 1967 during the second reading of the Medical Termination of Pregnancy Bill and he moved a number of amendments on 26 July and again in October, one of them to ensure that cases of handicapped children should be explicitly referred to in the bill. The 'Ramsey report on abortion' had already been mentioned in the debate and having its chairman, now a bishop, in the House of Lords enabled Ramsey to draw attention to the findings in the report. One was that doctors may take account of the woman's actual or reasonable foreseeable environment when deciding whether an abortion is called for. This provision, the so-called 'social clause' was the subject of considerable controversy during the debate. Ramsey pointed out that it was not, as some peers thought, a separate ground for abortion, but an indication to those professionally involved as to what factors may reasonably be taken into account.

Ramsey was used to speaking and was not restrained or deflected by opponents. Occasionally he lacked precision, clarity and sharpness when proposing amendments, which had the effect of appearing to dilute his case resulting in a few defeats.

The Abortion Act became law in 1967 but there was considerable disquiet at the way it was interpreted in a liberal direction. In its first year there were 54,819 abortions. By 1972 the number increased to 156,741 which represented fifteen per cent of all live births. A flow of non-resident women was already entering England and Wales to undergo abortions. In *Church and Society in England 1770–1970*, E.R. Norman has an observation:

> although the general attitudes in the Abortion Report, 1965, were those the legislation of 1967 in effect adopted, the influence of the Church was not decisive. It was convenient. It enabled the secular humanist liberalism of those who sought reform for reasons which had nothing to do with the interpretation of Christianity to get their way without too much embarrassing religious opposition – except from Roman Catholics. The Church of England's formal teaching remained unchanged however; the force of conservative opinion was in general sufficiently strong to prevent a collective declaration for humanist morality, whatever the theologians might hope one day to see.

When Religious Education in Schools was debated on 15 November 1967, Ramsey had recently been appointed chairman of a commission on the subject. He treated the debate as if he were collecting evidence. For the first, and far from the last, time peers heard expressions of 'vision', 'insight' and 'exploration'. Viscount Eccles, a former Minister of Education, was particularly struck by Ramsey's assertion that indoctrination on the one hand, and instruction about religion on the other, were not the only two alternatives:

> Let me put a third possibility like this. Whatever anybody teaches has to be taught in a context. Words have their meaning only in use: and I do not just mean a verbal context: I mean the whole context of the school environment, the teacher, his or her experience, and so on. Education in this way always emerges from and out of a context, to be a living experience, whatever it is.

Religious education, as I see it, best emerges in a context of questions about man, about the universe, about problems of their own lives which children, even at the earliest age, have to be encouraged to ask.

It is because religion, if properly taught, gives man this habitual sense of his greatness, that there will always be a final defence for religious education. In other words religion stands for a depth, a new dimension, in human existence and also for a spirit of inquiry, or a spirit of genuine controversy which that sense of depth generates and encourages. Religious education does not argue for a supernatural which is vacuous and meaningless; or, if it might, it should not and never reasonably does . . . The important point is this. When we discuss the pros and cons of religious education, let us not think or talk in terms of outworn ideas or methods or conclusions, but in a way which sets religious education in the context of contemporary developments and ideas, involved both in education and in religion.

Ramsey was recognised as a champion of and for the communities of the north-east. He demonstrated his familiarity with people he knew and met, by weaving into his remarks specific places and areas where, for example, the impact of pit closures on households was grim, or the poverty he encountered in rural villages. That is why he spoke with some authority in such debates as the second reading of the Coal Industry Bill (12 December 1967) and on Fuel Policy (14 February 1968). He welcomed the Government's promises for redundant miners and other alleviating measures, but pressed for new diversified industries for young men 'and not industries that depend largely on female labour, as some of the new industries do. They should be integrated industries and not branch factories out on a limb which, in a small colliery village, everyone thinks will be the first to close when the clouds approach.' Ramsey rebuked those who thought miners were obstinate Luddites. From his visits to miners' lodges he was convinced that:

they were not all concerned to have the coal industry artificially protected for ever. They had no nostalgia for mining. But they were concerned, as I am now, that new industries of the right kind should be steered to the north-east, so that they could have the satisfaction of genuine work and be able to meet the responsibilities of their homes and their families in the communities which mining had created.

He had special sympathy for older men and had personal memories:

> At the age of fifty-eight, men's lives will so often seem, when that
> pension comes, to be at an end. This is no luxury of an early
> retirement. As a boy I saw enough of men like these, and walked with
> some of them, from the mining and engineering industries, whose
> spirits were utterly broken, whose lives were shattered, and who
> trudged 'down and out', from one works gate to another, yearning to
> be offered even a brush with which to sweep up; and they were never
> given it . . . The man at fifty-eight, out of a job, even with financial
> provisions such as this Bill gives, needs more than that general
> consolation, and also something more than money can buy, in order
> that he and his family may have a life, rather than a bare existence. If
> we have broken his spirit, money will be only a charity which is a
> travesty of the name and an insult to man's personality.

He wanted the Churches to do all they could to help restore a sense
of purpose and hope for men, 'but my point is that the responsibility
of the State cannot finish with this Bill.'

The White Paper on fuel policy affected Ramsey's 'people'. He
provided three examples of how the ordinary working man in his
club or outside the employment exchange saw the position. The
excessive delay in reaching any decision about the type of power
station at Seaton Carew did not inspire confidence, created rumours
and harboured discontent. Ramsey wondered if there were sufficient
marriage of fuel and transport policies:

> Long distance electrification, which has also proved to be one of the
> most successful developments which British Railways have pioneered,
> has now been dropped from Weaver Junction to Carlisle. That may
> be a right decision when all the features are reckoned with, but my
> relevant question is this. Was it ever considered, in coming to that
> decision, that it would mean a preference for oil, and consequently the
> loss of a further possible use for coal, electricity-wise?

Ramsey noticed that in the White Paper the expansion of oil was the
main cause for the declining demand for coal. However the country was
wholly dependent on foreign sources for oil, which, as the White Paper
indicated, 'this raises difficulties both in relation to the balance of
payments as well as difficulties arising from political unsettlement in the
Middle East'. Ramsey wanted some Government re-thinking to be done.

Ramsey was forthright in a debate on Youth and the Nation (21 February 1968). He was sceptical of easy solutions, of imposed central policies and, whilst denouncing paternalism, he took a swipe at the problems being met by a 'do-gooding' which 'occurs because it suits the doer rather than the needs of those who are only too often regarded as the object – and the word 'object' is significant – of the exercise.' His chief concern was with the groups of young people:

who in a mood of deep dissatisfaction with society, with no little intelligence and, sometimes, high sensitivity, rebel. They seek a satisfaction which society fails to provide: and among these, of course, are those who become drug-dependent. I was talking recently with some pharmacologists, and some of those responsible for university health services. In this discussion it seemed to me quite clear that many of those young people, whether in university or elsewhere, who 'take a trip' with drugs, seriously misguided though they be, often do this as means of self-discovery, endeavouring to make possible a personal exploration in a world where contemplation and privacy are all at a discount. Or it is done in search for identity in a world of stereotypes. Or again they see in drugs a means which they believe, in a world of shibboleths, may give them new insight into themselves, their relations with other members of society and the world in general. They may be – I think they are – utterly misguided but the significance of their actions should not be lost on us, for the tragedy is that there should exist in society these youthful yearnings which at the moment fail to be harnessed to, and fail to provide the stimulus for, any major constructive task.

Ramsey pressed the needs of young people on his junior clergy. What could they do for those who may become the tragic flotsam and jetsam of society, often who leave school unemployed, or those who have deep unsatisfied yearnings? There were parishes who were tackling these areas of deep concern and tension, and Ramsey did all in his power to encourage plans and initiatives and bring, if only a few, to fruition.

Ramsey asked a Question (18 March 1969) whether the Government was aware that broadcasts from the Durham Constabulary Radio Network interfered seriously with the reception of BBC Radio Durham throughout the whole area of the county, and what steps were being taken to resolve the problem. Baroness Llewelyn-

Davies informed him that new frequencies would be brought into use within one month.

During the Committee stage of the Divorce Reform Bill (10, 11 and 15 July 1969) Ramsey was troubled about the social responsibility of the legislation, particularly on women:

> Where can we get any guarantee whatever, in the case of poor people, that the wife divorced against her will, will have money, without necessarily going through the ordinary channels of social security and so on? This is the end of what I have to say and the incredible suggestion. Would it be absolutely incredible to think that the State, having agreed to irretrievable breakdown as the criterion for divorce, should in suitable cases match that with State provision for a wife who is discarded in that way, without her having to go with the general case of people who have to apply for National Assistance? I should be grateful if those considering these financial possibilities could look into that suggestion, incredible and extraordinary though it might be, so that the wife of a poor husband could, as of right, get some finance from the State which has decided – it may well be in its wisdom – to have this new outlook on divorce and the way of obtaining it.

When the significance and implications of Demonstrations were debated (11 December 1969) Ramsey widened the debate from students and long-haired violence to worrying trends such as nurses protesting against inadequate salaries by sleeping out on Ilkley Moor, or villagers in County Durham whose request for a bus service was met with stereotyped rejection in a machine-like manner, and from his personal experiences:

> As chairman of a hospital management committee I got the impression that many, if not most, Ministry circulars, especially those relating to finance, were devised to keep my colleagues and myself from exercising any novel policies whatever. Just how much initiative we had was a very difficult question to answer. Of course there was always the Regional Board to blame. And when it reached them, they could always blame the Ministry; and the Ministry blamed the Treasury. Then one saw a kind of stony malaise, a kind of dissatisfaction, settling over all. In the local setting, we went on with our usual routine, hoping some day for an explosion; although it was perfectly clear that if it occurred we should have to make it ourselves.
>
> The only way I myself got a decision, when my application had

reached some kind of joint planning committee the length of whose title was clear symbol of inefficiency and delay, was by a threat not only to appeal to the Minister but to sit in his Department until a decision was reached. You may say 'silly', 'unreasonable!' Perhaps it was, but it worked where nothing else had worked. That is the unfortunate truth.

Ramsey supported demonstrations for 'at their heart, (they are) witness to the everlasting spirit of man; and a society which, by its large-scale planning, or its large-scale business, oppression, risks, insensitivity, ignorance, or neglect is bound to threaten that spirit and to be seen to be threatening. This is a sober reflection, and when demonstrations remind us of it, let us be encouraged to grapple better, which means more effectively with the needs and human problems that underlie these demonstrations.'

When confronted with a problem or crisis, Ramsey worried away at it until it was solved. His daughter-in-law, Gail, puts her finger directly on this trait:

> I likened Ian Ramsey to a small and very enthusiastic terrier. This sounds rather flippant, but anyone who has lived with one of the small breeds of terriers (a Cairn or a Westie perhaps) will recognise the comparison. When digging (from whence comes the description 'terrier') they are determined and utterly dedicated to the hole under their paws. They cannot easily be distracted and will continue to dig until they are satisfied. Ian had the same indestructible determination to see that his work was done to the best of his ability and gave himself wholly to the task. Sadly, there were too many holes to dig and too many squirrels to chase. He lacked the terrier's saving grace – they know when they have done enough for that day.

It is almost an aphorism that we spend about a quarter of our lives growing up and three-quarters growing old. In 1970 it was not yet common to consider the ever-growing ageing population and the effect they would have on the Government in particular and society in general. A White Paper on 'The Age of Retirement' was debated on 28 January 1970. Ramsey wanted to see co-operation between the Government, the Churches, and those responsible for the national economy and industrial life. He advocated an entirely new approach, not only to the age of retirement, but towards fostering radical changes in attitudes to work and life, equally to changes in wage and salary structures:

> It has been traditional for remunerative employment, by and large, to provide a purposive pattern within human existence; a status and a distinctive role for the worker, and a network of lively relationships with colleagues or workmates. And so a sudden cessation of employment means that purpose is lacking, and there is a loss of status, a loss of relationships which have been the very fibre by which the man has lived.
>
> There is the picture of the man who suddenly discovers overnight that his skill, his energy, his capacity to make rapid decisions are no longer needed by anybody: he is retired and is virtually dead. A cheque and a gold watch, or perhaps, more ominously, an easy chair and a clock, and all the pleasantries of the office party can so easily seem to be but the sugar on a pill, a pill whose taste becomes all the more unpleasant as the years go by.

Ramsey was beginning to think of setting up a group to study this new feature of society. The critical period for adjustment was the period just before retirement. He began to make enquiries and found a number of firms, for example Rolls Royce and Pressed Steel, who had admirable pre-retirement courses. What of post-retirement? Adult and further education work was not in its infancy – the Workers' Educational Association was a pioneer – but would the Government and local authorities back proposals with money? Ideas for the Churches' active participation were growing in his mind and he began to discuss the issue with clergy.

By 1971 the House of Lords was looking like a second home, so often was he there and speaking in debates. Some of them overlapped his other commitments, such as Mass Media Communication (3 February 1971) which Lord Ritchie-Calder, Ramsey and others were considering on the Social Morality Council.

Ramsey put down a Motion on Long-Term Prison Sentences, which was debated on 17 February 1971. His concern was less the term itself but the conditions under which such sentences were served. The abolition of hanging had increased the number of long-term prisoners. He opened the debate at 3.00 p.m. and made his concluding speech at 8.16 p.m. He bombarded his peers with facts and figures and reports, evidence of his own readings and research. It was not a debate leading to conclusions and recommendations but one providing opportunities for Law Lords and those with experience of prison reform, and moralists, to air their views. A very worthwhile occasion.

There were other debates during 1971 where he was in the vanguard, representing workers in the north-east (Wilberforce and the Economic Situation, 3 March) and the controversial Industrial Relations Bill (6 April 1971) of which he was severely critical, courting the ire of Lord Thorneycroft. Ramsey pleaded for the Government to broaden its views and to pay careful heed to all those on whom industrial relations depended, and not to think of the opposition of the trade unions as cussedness. He put forward a proposal that a mandatory code of practice should be the sole way forward. Although he wished to repair the breaches and to heal the wounds of industrial conflict, there was no doubting where and on which side he stood. Giving the House a lecture on the colourful history of conflict between employers and workers in County Durham did not always go down well for it savoured of party politics, yet that was not the case. If Durham was his diocese the whole of the north-east was his constituency and he seemed to speak for 'his' people as if he were one of them:

> May I illustrate, to show that it is not an empty suggestion that I am making. I should hope, for instance, that such a code of practice might include a legal right of shop stewards to have day release, industrial relations training . . . It would contain provision for many more joint management-union training schemes. It would contain a vast improvement in the industrial relations training for graduate managers, who normally have only technical qualifications. It would provide a legal right for every worker to have access to joint consultative machinery. It would include a legal right for every worker not only to be given information about his company – and this should not be hedged around with all the qualifications in the present Bill – but, especially, about the company's financial position and future problems. If balance sheets are too hard to understand now, I should hope they would be easier in twenty years' time. Furthermore, the worker should hear all this directly from his manager and his full natural work group with opportunities for discussion. Such a code of practice might include the emergence of alternative strike methods

and, perhaps, the creation of local groups of experienced conciliators or arbitrators, who could be on the scene quickly in any dispute before serious issues emerged. Those are but suggestions as to what a code of practice might contain, and for me the fact that this Bill contains a reference to a code of practice is its saving clause.

Apartheid, race relations and Rhodesia were recurring topics on which Ramsey had something to say. He spoke in the Address in Reply to Her Majesty's Speech (3 November 1971) criticising the sentence which had been passed on the Dean of Johannesburg, Gonville ffrench-Beytagh: 'The sentence makes it perfectly clear that next to the doctrine of apartheid what earns our equal and outright condemnation must be the laws and legal framework by which that inhuman doctrine is maintained and encouraged.' In the same speech he referred to the intricate and tangled situation in Northern Ireland:

> Unquestionably, as we shall all agree, it has a religious ancestry, and of some of the religious causal factors we can be heartily ashamed. I say that with relatives in Ulster, with friends in the Orange Order and with pupils and friends in Catholic seminaries. I hope that the Churches in Ireland, which themselves cross the Border and in principle know no Border, may be able to do something effective and practical to take an initiative in this situation.

In 1969 Ramsey had undertaken a lecturing and preaching tour in Ireland. Before he went he intimated that he wanted to meet all 'Christian' sides in what were euphemistically referred to as 'the troubles'. He had long conversations with the Roman Catholic and Church of Ireland Bishops of Derry, and priests and laity of both Churches, and with senior Presbyterians and Methodists.

Ramsey had met Trevor Huddleston, Ambrose Reeves, Joost de Blank and other heroic leading opponents of apartheid, whose names stuck in the gullets of Afrikaaners in South Africa. He was fortunate in having close at hand in Durham, Kenneth Skelton, 'God's gadfly' in Rhodesia. He was accordingly very well briefed when it came to debates on 'Rhodesia: Settlement Proposals in the Lords' (11 and 12 December 1971). He was fearless, never quaked before his 'seniors', never took advantage of his 'juniors' in knowledge or experience. He was no favourite of the then Lord Chancellor, Viscount Hailsham, and a number of other Conservative peers. It was foolish to accuse

Ramsey of being short of information on any subject under debate, for he was quickly on his feet to rebut any accusation. Neither could Ramsey be pushed into a position advocated by a number of extremist political voices. He approached the subject from a different perspective:

> Proposals and plans never, of themselves, bring any settlement, any more than a treaty between two nations prevents a war. Only people, not proposals, effect a settlement. When it comes to people – and as Lord Goodman frankly admitted, he has not persuaded the Rhodesian government to a more liberal way of thinking – I am not surprised to find in these proposals no evidence whatever of a radical change of heart expressed in the determination to implement the proposals under the vision of an integrated Rhodesia. I find not even a faint shadow of that vision here, and yet without that, these proposals might be only ten printed sheets of folded paper. Indeed, looking for the guarantee which the Five Principles envisage, sadly, I find only evasiveness and ambiguity, sinister phrases and suspicious qualifica-tions. It might be said, 'Let us leave it to the Rhodesian people themselves'. That sounds so reasonable and so sensible, and so simple. Not so! For when we put proposals to anybody – and here may I dare to hope to mediate between the noble lord, Lord Wade (formerly Liberal MP for Huddersfield West, and President of the Liberal Party), and the noble and learned Lord on the Woolsack – it is normally inferred that we are commending them. When we are not, special provision is made, and we have qualifying phrases like 'without prejudice'. The result is that when we are asked, without any qualification, to agree to putting these terms to the people of Rhodesia for their judgement, the implication is that we commend these proposals *ex animo*, and that we see them as embodying the guarantees of which the Five Principles spoke.

It is not difficult to see how and why Ramsey was capable of 'getting across' those peers, of whom there were many, who were also lawyers.

Ramsey was on his feet again during a debate on a report on 'Violence in Southern Africa' (19 January 1972) when he also referred to the detention of Mr Garfield Todd in Rhodesia. Ramsey was on the receiving end of a shoal of abusive letters and referred to this in the House:

If someone says to me, 'What about reconciliation and prayer?' I answer that reconciliation is never a matter of silence, of smooth words. All reconciliation is costly – very costly, indeed; as costly as the Cross itself. The first step to reconciliation is to make the facts plain for all to see. Nor must prayer be seen as an alternative to action, for prayer without appropriate action is almost blasphemy: and what we must painfully seek is some action which will be congruous, congruous with our understanding of God and the Gospel and its story.

Ramsey initiated another debate, by proposing a motion on 'Education in a Multi-Racial Britain', on 15 December 1971. Once again he was continuously in the House when he opened the debate at 3.55 p.m. until he made his closing speech at 9.00 p.m. The 'Ramsey report', *The Fourth R*, was the background for what he had to say. This was an occasion, one he favoured, of taking an initiative and allowing every possible view to surface which it did with speeches from peers including Viscount Combermere, Lords Champion, O'Hagan, Belstead, Ritchie-Calder, Willis, Boyle, Brockway, Gridley, Gladwyn, Walston and Baronesses Gaitskell, Phillips, White. For Ramsey this was debating at its best, an end in itself, concluding with his motion, by leave, being withdrawn.

Ramsey's last appearance in the House was for a debate on 'The Arts: Work of Regional Associations', when he pleaded for the arts in the north-east. He wanted local associations to become increasingly autonomous 'so that they can play an ever-effective role in this search for a new culture and this pilgrimage towards a better humanity.'

'Humanity' was the alpha and omega for Ramsey. He knew how to use a scalpel with precision when dissecting ideas, propositions and movements in thought, religious and secular alike. His intuitions were not always right, his actions not always wise, his conclusions not always successful. But he resolved to face public issues of society with discernment and the power that comes from the Gospel. He had a fluent tongue which propelled endless ideas in the House as elsewhere.

Ian Ramsey lived by words of Dietrich Bonhoeffer:

To do and dare – not what you would, but what is right. Never to hesitate over what is in your power, but boldly to grasp what is before you. Not in the flight of, but only in the deed there is freedom. Away from timidity and reluctance! Out into the storm of event, sustained only by the commandment of God and your faith, and freedom will receive your spirit with exultation.

CHAPTER 11

Light and Shade

THE INFLUENCES ON RAMSEY'S LIFE, thought and ministry are various and manifest. There were fewer heroes, people who exerted over him a lasting and living influence and of whom it may be said, in words of Walter Pater, 'He is in truth, in the power, in the hands, of another, of another will ... Attracted, corrected, guided, rewarded, satiated, in a long discipline that "ascent of the soul into the intelligible world".' Three people merit explanation and expansion for the light and shade they cast on Ian Ramsey.

First, Joseph Butler (1692–1752) the English moral philosopher and theologian who became successively Rector of Stanhope, Bishop of Bristol (1738), Dean of St Paul's (1740) and Bishop of Durham (1750). Butler recorded that he set before himself the search after truth as the business of his life. It is not difficult to discover the reasons for Ramsey's indebtedness and laudation of Butler by setting out six of Joseph Butler's characteristics, which, with the exception of one of them, were imbibed to the full by Ramsey. Firstly, Butler's vindication of the originality, independence, and authority of conscience. This truth was the bedrock on which his whole system, whether in the Sermons or in the Analogy, reposes. Secondly, his deep sense of personal religion and of direct obligation to a moral and personal God which so greatly distinguishes his writings from most of his contemporaries. While they approached God from the side of the logical intellect, regarding Him primarily in the light of an intellectual necessity, the inevitable complement of any rational theory of the universe, Butler advanced to the belief from the side of conscience, found in God, far more than an intellectual abstraction or a logical necessity, a moral judge and governor, of whose nature and purposes conscience spoke to man with no indistinct or uncertain sound. Thirdly, a characteristic which enhanced his writings to ones of permanence and value. The conspicuous fairness and impartiality with which he states his case; his anxiety not to exaggerate but rather to underestimate and understate the evidence for the position he is maintaining; his scrupulous and undeviating record and attention to fact. Fourthly, Butler's method which was much insisted on by W.E. Gladstone, statesman and Prime Minister:

> No writer has ever insisted more strenuously than Butler that, on the one hand, the amount of the belief which is yielded to any conclusion must be measured by the amount and character of the evidence which can be adduced in support of it but that, on the other hand, in all practical matters (and religion is, of course, concerned directly with practice) we have to content ourselves with a kind and amount of evidence which falls far short of demonstration. It behoves us, consequently, to act in this as we do in all other practical matters, and instead of complaining that the evidence is not greater or more complete than it is, to try and ascertain honestly and fairly on which side the balance of evidence lies, and having done so, guide our conduct in accordance with the results thus arrived at.

Fifthly, like some modern Socrates, Butler reiterates with emphasis and insistence the message – 'Know thyself . . . Recognise, indeed, thine own powers and capacities, but recognise no less their limitations and deficiencies . . . Lay no claim to an omniscience thou dost not and canst not possess.' This doctrine comes very near to being the central doctrine of his system. If by their deeds ye shall know them, Ian Ramsey is at his weakest here. Sixthly, Butler was engaged in philanthropic activity and attempted to make the rich more sensible of their obligations towards the poor and destitute.

Joseph Butler was never afraid to exercise reason, or to submit calmly and seriously to examination of the facts which he considered established, however formidable and disquieting they might appear. He yet never abandoned his fundamental religious beliefs and principles – that God is, that He is just, that He is good, that He is Love, and He cares for people and seeks and longs to redeem and save them.

Ramsey wrote a lengthy article on Butler, published in the *Oxford Magazine*, September 1952.

The next hero was Charles Earle Raven (1885–1964) who Ramsey knew well and of whom he wrote a remarkably perceptive portrait for the British Academy of which Raven had been a Fellow (*Proceedings of the British Academy* (1965)). Raven was variously Dean of Emmanuel College, Cambridge (1909), Rector of Bletchingley and Joint-Secretary of COPEC (Conference on Christian Politics, Economics and Citizenship) (1920), Canon of Liverpool Cathedral (1924), Regius Professor of Divinity, Cambridge (1932), Master of Christ's College, Cambridge (1939 to 1950), and Vice Chancellor of the University (1947–1949). Ramsey's judgement embraces both the light and the shade of Charles Raven, as this extract conveys:

> For Charles Raven the life of a college (Christ's, Cambridge) was ideally an interweaving of three strands – learning, friendships and faith, and his own life could be given a similar characterisation. There were his scholarly interests in theology and science, and his lifelong desire to inform each with the cares of the other as to join what so many would put asunder; the sensitivity and warm-heartedness which made him generous in friendship also lay behind his social concerns and reforming zeal; and evident in his learning and in social concerns alike were the insight, the burning convictions, and the restlessness of the prophet and visionary. Sunsets and moonlight, a moth emerging from its pupa, or the patterns of a bird's feathering – all these provided him with glimpses of the eternal; and God also met him in splendour when he saw in Liverpool a young couple lovemaking on a seat by the roadside on St James's Mount. When in the same city he saw the proprietor of a dingy shop in shirt sleeves dispensing packets of fish and chips wrapped in newspaper to a crowd of shawl-clad women, again there was, he tells us, 'All of a sudden the glory; and God fulfilling His eternal task, giving to His children their daily bread'. In this way, nature and human nature constantly revealed God.
>
> He had to the end something of the endearing impulsiveness of the small child; but he had also the intellect of a giant, and the product was a powerful and quite outstanding personality. Yet while no one could hear him and be unmoved, his was a vision so unusual as to earn for him for most of his life a sense of loneliness where appreciation meant much, and where criticism could be particularly wounding. With his rare sensitivity, rich humanity, and zest for life; with the intellectual honesty, moral courage, and reforming zeal of the prophet; and with the large concerns of the evangelist, he always saw life as a struggle whose sufferings are deep and whose loneliness can be profound. He once remarked that it is the old, and not the young, who are haunted by the greatest doubts. Not surprisingly his favourite biblical passage was Romans viii with its vision of the whole creation

groaning and travailing together in pain and yet in this very pain and suffering finding the redeeming love of God, which works all things together for good, and from which not even death can separate us.

In the preface to *The Creator Spirit* (1927) he remarks significantly that he is 'prepared to fail again in a great venture than try to win success for a small one'. For the Christian, failure and success are each judged, however, in relation to a faithfulness which fulfils both, and undoubtedly throughout his life Charles Raven was faithful to the demands of life in all its fullness. If he was too involved in life to see it steadily, he certainly saw it whole. He was, like Paul, 'not disobedient unto the heavenly vision', and also, like Paul, he knew 'that we must through much tribulation enter into the Kingdom of God'.

Ramsey's links with Raven were at Cambridge and the Modern Churchman's Union, of which Raven was a Vice-President, Ramsey a member of its Council, though they had in common a dislike of that brand of liberalism which seemed to be destructive of faith rather than concerned constructively with establishing its reasonableness. Raven was an early follower and interpreter of Teilhard de Chardin, scientist and seer. No one was less 'churchy' than Raven. There were blind spots and moral weaknesses, but those who knew him and loved him, felt in him the power of God. There was a public controversy on the Christian attitude to war before its outbreak in 1939, when Raven virtually accused Archbishop William Temple of York of apostasy. He received a private letter from Temple, 'The trouble is, Charles, that you're thin and I am fat'. Ramsey comments, 'Controversy had been cut through by friendship and Temple's laugh often echoed in Christ's even in the war years.' There were glorious reconciliations in Raven's life.

This brings us to a third, and the most important 'hero'. The Church of England is somewhat lukewarm towards its heroes of faith who are written largely on the pages of history – the hallowed character of the saint, the high passion of the martyr, the militant charity of the missionary, the consecrated labour of the scholar, and the disturbing presence of the prophet. The veneration and recognition of saints is something which must be controlled but cannot be directed by authority. There is the danger, not avoided by the Roman Catholic Church, of adding too many names and weakening the example of holiness. Holiness is the gift of God and ecclesiastical authorities cannot dictate where He shall bestow it. He raises up His saints where and when it pleases Him, the faithful recognise His work and the part of authority is to make sure that the recognition is well founded. The saints are God's continual gifts to show us that the vocation to which He calls us is not impossible of fulfilment.

Recognition of saints in the Anglican Church since the Reformation was included in the 1928 Kalendar and though an improvement upon that of 1662 no single saint of later date than 1390 found a place. Northern saints – Cuthbert, Columba, Oswald, Ninian and Hilda were included. This did not prevent a number of institutions – university and theological colleges and religious orders – observing with proper collect, epistle, and gospel, people of God belonging to them or their history. Brooke Foss Westcott is commemorated on 27 July at King's College, Cambridge where he was Fellow; and Charles Gore on 18 January at Cuddesdon Theological College. Other names include Edward King (8 March); Arthur Stanton (28 March); John Keble (29 March); John and Charles Wesley (24 May); Evelyn Underhill (15 June); Charles Simeon (13 November); Josephine Butler (30 December) and, for our present purpose William Temple on 26 October. Ramsey gave the Second William Temple Lecture – 'William Temple: Some aspects of his thought and life' – at William Temple College, Rugby, 22 June 1968, (printed in *The Bishoprick* November 1969). In 1967 Ramsey became Chairman of the Governors then housed in the old rectory at Rugby, of which the formidable pipe-smoking Miss Mollie Batten was Principal, and who he appointed as one of his Examining Chaplains in 1968. It was unusual, perhaps unique at the time for lay persons to be so appointed. In addition to Mollie Batten, Ramsey appointed Dr R.F. Hobson, Consultant Psychiatrist, and Dame Enid Russell-Smith, Principal of St Aidan's College, Durham.

When William Temple (1881–1944), Archbishop of Canterbury, died on 26 October 1944 'we bow'd our head and held our breath.' The late Norman Sykes, Dixie Professor of Ecclesiastical History, University of Cambridge, and another good friend of Ramsey's at Cambridge, caught the prevailing mood:

> The sense of loss was universal and profound. Not only Anglicans but Christians of all Churches; not only Englishmen but citizens of many

peoples; not only those wise and mighty in the world, but an unnumbered host of the humble and meek, felt the loss to themselves, and all pronounced it irreparable. It was not only that the Archbishop of Canterbury had died, but a prophet, teacher, leader, and a friend, upon whose like we could not hope to look again, had been taken away in the plenitude of his strength, as it seemed, and at the moment when, least of all times, he could be spared. For Temple had been able to speak to the condition of our age.

(Theology November 1948)

He too upon a wintry clime
Had fallen on this iron time
Of doubts, disputes, distractions, fears.
He found us when the age had bound
Our souls in its benumbing round;
He spoke . . . (and) there was shed . . .
On spirits dried up and closely furl'd
The freshness of the early world.

(Matthew Arnold: *Memorial Verses*)

William Temple was, perhaps, more variously distinguished than any of his post-Reformation predecessors. He combined the characters of a philosopher, a preacher, a politician, a popular orator, and a literary man and was eminent in every one of them. His industry was astonishing; the range of his sympathies not less so; and he possessed an attractive personality and popular manners. His fine voice and disciplined excellence, many-sided experience, wide range of friendships, gift of humour, flawless simplicity of manner and life, enabled him to hold with general approbation the great position he had attained. Temple was not in the academic sense a scholar. Modern science was outside his range. He said large things in a large way. This made him usually tolerant of convictions which were not his own, when held by those whose intellectual power, scholastic qualifications and Christian character he was compelled to respect. Those with little or no allegiance to Christianity and the Church dubbed him 'the People's Archbishop'.

Despite his strength, personality and renown Temple accumulated enemies in political circles because of his socialist and economic utterances in word and print. At his funeral crowds of watching working people were there to share grief and sympathy. What would they have thought if they had known what Winston Churchill had to say, as recorded in the diary of Sir Alexander Cadogan (Cabinet Secretary during the war years), 'News came of death of Archbishop of Canterbury. PM delighted'?

Where do we find Ian Ramsey in his thought-provoking and admiring, though not without critical evaluation of William Temple? Not in background, for Temple was born in the 'purple' at the Bishop's Palace, Exeter, where his father was bishop, later translated to London and the archbishopric of Canterbury? Not in educational progress, as Temple was educated at a preparatory school and then Rugby? Not in a sermon when he was Headmaster of Repton, when he said to the boys 'Have we ever realised that to follow Christ is to share the outcast's life?' But he had never known what it was to be an outcast, not even experienced ordinary life in a terrace house like Ramsey, which was the lot of the majority of northern people in industrial towns and cities. Ramsey's youth gave him not simply lifelong sympathy, but also empathy with the underdog, the under-privileged, the victim, the man, woman or child who was ''ard done by'!

For his William Temple lecture at Rugby, Ramsey relied princi-pally on two books of Temple, *Christianity in Thought and Practice* (1936) covering philosophy and religion, personality in theology and ethics, and ethics for individuals and groups; and *Christianity and Social Order* (1942), covering the Church's right and duty to 'interfere' in social questions, how it should do so, its past social role, primary and derivative Christian social principles, the 'natural order' and a priority of values. An appendix deals with a specific programme of social reconstruction in capital ownership, industrial democracy, investment, credit, land and in international trade. This was an outstanding success, regularly re-printed and re-published with forewords by prominent politicians, a landmark still capable of being read with edification.

In his William Temple lecture Ramsey commented on Temple's concept of truth and his approach to Christian social morality:

(Christian truth) A great deal is sometimes made of an alleged change in William Temple's thought towards the end of his life, and not least, as it is said, of the Second World War and Barthian theology, and while there is no evidence that he ever reckoned with the philosophical positivism and empiricism that emerged in the mid-thirties, he may have drunk in some of the spirit of the age which was critical of large-scale metaphysical schemes . . .

At the same time I am bound to think that in his broad concept of Christian truth Temple need not have changed, nor do I think he did change, and I certainly felt he did not. It seems to me that he gives us an insight of permanent validity for the Christian faith – that Christianity is exploratory in character – exploratory of a vision which the Gospels and all genuine elements of a Christian tradition disclose, a vision which is wide enough to include nature and grace. God and the world, logos and flesh. Whether it is in the matter of Anglican-Methodist relations, or 'intercommunion today', or any other contemporary controversial topic the great divide as I see it is between those who would take a view of theology as close-knit and inelastic, and those who see theology as to-and-fro of exploration mapping as best we can that which has caught hold of us in Christ and His Church. There is in my mind no doubt as to which side of the fence we would find Temple standing; nor have I any doubt that from such a beginning Temple would be concerned to explore the whole universe and in this sense to be engaged in a metaphysical endeavour while not creating a metaphysical system.

(Social morality) Social problems have proliferated in their complexity, and the character of industrial problems has changed beyond belief. Yet Temple's comprehensive view of religion is still needed in our own day. At the same time I think that we come increasingly to see that never again will any one person be able of himself to devise a conceptual structure to interpret, as Hegel did, the detail of art, science, literature, ethics and sociology. Perhaps the last traditional metaphysician in this sense, if not Hegel, was Whitehead whom Temple greatly admired. With the future there can be no metaphysical prodigies, and it seems to me that a world view will only be reached as and when those specialising in different disciplines and fields of knowledge come together to explore problems which lie on the frontier of all their subjects. But did not Temple himself see knowledge as a dialogue, and argue that union will only be found in the creative inspiration of God? After all, the dialectic which had always fascinated Temple is, at the end of the day, no more than conversation and discussion. Temple would point us to a social morality which emerges not only by any rule of thumb methods but as a result of creative decisions being reached in multiple groups and under the inspiration of a common vision.

Is this Ramsey in Temple's image or Temple in Ramsey's image? Close scrutiny suggests they are further apart than Ramsey is prepared to concede. Moreover, Temple's two series of *Readings in St John's Gospel* (1939 and 1940 – 412 pages in all) separate 'Saint William' from 'Brother Ian'. 'With St John I am at home,' declared Temple. These readings intended for devotional meditations are evidence that the Fourth Gospel was part of the warp and weft of his mind. Some even thought them the best devotional work by an Anglican since William Law's *Serious Call* (1729).

Much more interesting, perhaps important, is to hold up Temple and Ramsey to the effects of a penetrating searchlight. Two largely unpublished lectures on William Temple were provided to this biographer by the Revd Alexander ('Alec') Roper Vidler, one time Warden of St Deiniol's Library, Hawarden; Editor of *Theology*; Canon of Windsor and from 1956 until 1966 Fellow and Dean of King's College, Cambridge, retiring to his old family home, 'Friars of the Sack', at Rye. Vidler was politically Labour and ecclesiastically Liberal, scholar and historian, a natural rebel, always a writer. He joined a society of celibate priests in 1923 – the Oratory of the Good Shepherd – to which he remained faithful. In Vidler's candid perceptions of Temple, whom he knew personally, there is much that relates equally to Ramsey, and worth exploring, appraising and applying to him. Vidler looked at Temple's character, achievements and teaching ('In the Light') but also recognised and probed his limitations ('In the Shade'). Vidler used to ask himself why – in spite of his great and warm admiration and affection for Temple, who should have been just the man to speak to his condition, did not do so? 'I find this a somewhat baffling inquiry, yet he was a Christian upon whose life and teaching the Cross wasn't at all clearly or deeply imprinted.'

There are uncomfortable similarities as well as evident dissimilarities in their characters. What light do they shed on unfathomable aspects of Ramsey's personality? Vidler's words are quoted at some length:

> William Temple was not only a successful man on whom Providence smiled abundantly, but he was also – from the start, it would seem – a unified man, an integrated man: and this inevitably limits his appeal

to those of us who are not unified or integrated and who are never likely to be in this age. Temple was always one and the same. He was not complex. Part of his charm was his simplicity, his consistency. Yet it's a question whether part of the cross that many of us have to bear in this age is a lack of unification, of being pulled this way and that, an ineluctable absence of settlement. If so, then Temple's simplicity and consistency of character, while it was a manifest source of strength, also limited his appeal and his witness. Temple's predecessor as Archbishop of Canterbury was Cosmo Gordon Lang. Reading J. G. Lockhart's biography of Lang is to discover at least two contradictory men in him, and that he was both aware of the fact and much tormented by it. He was quite a different man when, on the one hand, he was at Lambeth and in the corridors of power, and, on the other hand, when he was secluded from the world in his retreat in the west of Scotland immersed in self-examination. He was a much more complicated, and a more mysterious, character than Temple, and in a certain sense the Cross was more clearly imprinted on his character. Lang was a great Prelate in a way Temple never appeared to be, but at the same time he was more acutely aware of the vanity and transitoriness of all earthly grandeur: at least, so I surmise. It has been said of Cardinal Manning that he was 'a man tortured by the personal ambitions he was ever struggling to tread underfoot', and something of the sort could have been said of Lang. But Temple seems to have been altogether free from any torture or tension like that.

With regard to Temple's thought, his theological teaching and his preaching, there's a smoothness about it, a roundedness, a sweet persistent reasonableness, that is in very sharp contrast with, for example, Kierkegaard or Karl Barth and many a lesser divine. Temple doesn't disturb or shake your mind, baffle and bewilder you, at once repel and draw you, as the greatest theologians do. While Temple had a finely balanced or balancing mind, yet in the scales of his mind world-affirmation weighed down world-renunciation, and this per-haps was a consequence of his theology having been incarnational rather than soteriological. I don't mean of course that he was so naïve as to be a perfectionist or a utopian or a 'secular' Christian. Indeed, I would say that Temple had an awareness – a Platonic awareness – of the reality of 'the other world', of the eternal and the invisible, that is rare among the generality of Christians in this century. All the same he did more than any other leader of the modern church to encourage a preoccupation with the affairs of this world.

This leads me to, perhaps, the key to both Temple's appeal and to his limitations. He was, if anyone ever was, *anima naturalier christiana*. He was a man of faith naturally – inevitably – not as a result of stress and strain or of agonising. He couldn't help believing. He once said – not of course thinking about himself but about other people – 'If we love God, what we like will be the right thing. This is the reason for the perfect spontaneity and simplicity of really saintly men. They do not need to guard their actions or their words; they can speak out whatever is in them, they can follow all their impulses, because their whole being is permeated by the Spirit of Christ.' In that sense Temple was a really saintly man – a man who travelled to God in the light. Hear what the seventeenth century Scottish divine Archbishop Leighton, whose writings Coleridge described as the most inspired outside the canonical Scriptures, said about this: 'Some travel on in a covert, cloudy day, and get home by it, have so much light as to know their way, and yet do not at all clearly see the bright and full sunshine of assurance; others have it breaking forth at times, and anon under a cloud; and some have it more constantly.' Temple was one of those who had it constantly. But just for that reason he does not speak to the condition of those who have to travel in the shade – 'in a covert, cloudy day'. I take it that Temple didn't experience what mystical theologians call 'the dark night of the soul' nor the dark night of the intellect.

Nonetheless, no one ever matched Temple's Oxford University Mission in 1931 whilst he was Archbishop of York. Sceptical and indifferent audiences were transfixed and transformed. The Mission 'stopped the rot' in the Christian life of post-war Oxford. Temple projected his faith and life as a force essential to the salvation of mankind. When Ramsey led a Mission to the University of Oxford in 1969, his talks in the Sheldonian Theatre were above the heads of many students. Afterwards he reflected, 'The novelty of this Mission probably lay in its endeavour to proclaim the Gospel while honestly facing the fact that there is no single strand of Christian doctrine, and that Christians differ, sometimes quite severely, in their understanding, for example, of the Bible, of the Church, and of the Ministry. It was an endeavour to combine a firm assurance with a relaxed attitude to theology.' David Edwards is correct when he points out that, 'once again his personal qualities shone out, not only in the main meetings, but supremely in the private committee where he was told that he was being too clever and too critical. He took this rebuke so well that some who had been complaining were silenced by the thought that a truly humble man of God was in Oxford.' Ian Ramsey was indeed humble, also a thoroughly good man, who had thrown the whole weight of all he had to give on the side of Christianity. But did he, for some reason, in spite of all his hard work and unquestionable merit convey the attraction of Christ? No person saw more clearly the permanent need of religion in the human spirit, and no one was more sincerely convinced of the truth of the Christian religion. But did he bring to religion chiefly his intellect, and so had intellectualised its ethic, leaving its deepest meaning to those who possessed, what he appeared to lack in his intellectual discipleship, the quality of mysticism? Is that why he dazzled, but did not always illuminate the darkness or throw a white beam ahead of heavy-laden and far-journeying humanity on the road which led to a better order of things than the present system?

A Christian, whose seeing and reading of souls is always done in the shadow of the Cross is less likely to be taken in than one who is disposed to look on the bright side of things. Would he, would Temple, have been speechless and tongue tied when meditating upon that famous painting of the *Crucifixion* by Grünewald, in which John the Baptist is depicted directing an exceptionally long index finger to the Cross? Ramsey was probably a better judge of people than William Temple.

Adopting and adapting Vidler's thinking, Temple and Ramsey were once-born rather than twice-born Christians. Was this a limitation? The once-born are the majority of those who occupy pews or seats in the churches. But the once-born do not touch the depths of Christian experience nor is the Cross of Christ imprinted in their witness, as is the case with the twice-born. It is the twice-born who have exerted the most powerful influence for Christ and the Gospel – St Paul, St Augustine, Luther, Wesley, Kierkegaard, John Donne. Yet Temple and Ramsey are united in being Christians, for whose lives and examples people thank God. They were more free from egotism than most people, whereas that lingering disease usually continues to beset the twice-born.

CHAPTER 12

A Life – Checked or Completed?

T HE YEAR 1972 WAS THE END of one journey and the beginning of a new adventure for Ian Ramsey. For most of his life Ramsey kept a very full daily diary usually written up each night. His writing was always small and the diary can only be read with a strong magnifying glass. Each day there is reference to the weather followed by an account of what he did, decisions made, who he met, usually references to his family, often including gratitude to God for the day, and what had been achieved, and sometimes ending with a 'God bless' and a sign of the cross – +. A very few and partial extracts follow:

> January 1. 'A most enjoyable day' as Mum (mother) said going up the stairs & so it has been. We 'sleep in' while there is an opportunity & then go for lunch in the flat where we have a splendid pheasant (one of those Lord Lambton sent) – Christmas pudding – fruit before – a really lovely lunch with Mum & a good start to the New Year. Mummy (wife) & I then go for a walk round the bowling green and as on many occasions my mind goes back to that view of Auckland Castle as seen in the book bought at Oxford on that wet Saturday when the news came through … (Letter from Prime Minister nominating him for the See of Durham). I dictate letters & then see TV plays as well as going to the post & tonight I've done the Oxford article at long last. Thank God for a good start to the New Year …

From January to March the pace of activity was undiminished in the diocese and outside it, meetings often and everywhere, the perpetual allure of London for House of Lords and major organisations of which he was President or Chairman, Oxford for lectures and informal gatherings, sermons to prepare, books to finish and articles to be written and a perpetual flow of books arriving on his desk for review. Synods – General and Diocesan, committees and meetings, and new opportunities and initiatives. Above all there were people, those who needed his advice, and friends everywhere – and letters, letters, letters.

Ramsey wrote his 'Easter' message in March for publication in the April *Bishop's Letter.*

Easter — a time of hope and promise. To Mary Magdalene the scene in the garden was originally flat and dark, obscured by mist and tears. Then came the salutation 'Mary', and the flat and bleak situation took on depth and warmth, darkness became light and the mists had cleared. Mary now saw not someone she took to be the gardener; her eyes were opened, and she saw the risen Christ. So, too, on the roads to Emmaus — one of Bishop Moule's favourite stories commemorated in the memorial window at Auckland Castle — the perplexed, disheartened travellers share their difficulties with the Stranger and then at the supper table in the cottage 'their eyes were opened and they knew Him . . .' May Easter be for us all an occasion when, in the same way, our eyes are opened, the light dawns, the mist disappears, the darkness is illuminated, and perplexities and sorrows are transformed. May the inspiration of the risen Christ enable us to see eternity in time, life through death, love's redeeming work being fulfilled for each one of us, as for the society in which we live and for the world of which we are a part — so that looking ahead in faith and confidence we see days of darkness as a time of hope.

April 1 (Easter Eve)
    Writing this on April 5th . . . For although I'd a good night I woke with a touch of the pain I had on Tuesday and between 7 & 8 a.m. it got progressively worse. Mummy rings for Dr Ferguson who then sends for Dr Robertson and by something like 8.30 or so I'm strapped in a chair, carried downstairs — Mummy, Vivian, Mum kiss me as I leave the Castle & the ambulance brings me to the General Hospital . . . I'm brought to a side ward of Ward 14. The Monitor is started, many injections. I'm given drinks from a bowl with a spout on or through a straw but I lie peaceful & my main memory is of my hand being held — communication indeed through few words. So we commend the future to God — whatever in His purposes these events signify — faith, trust . . .

At no time in his diary did Ramsey acknowledge that he had had a severe heart attack.

April 2 (Easter Day)
    Little by little improvement comes. Harry (McClatchey) looks in and as with Mummy & Vivian the holding of the hands symbolises &

speaks of much. The monitor is showing a good pattern & I start on a very restricted diet. Dr Mizra takes the blood tests daily, there is a nurse from Malaysia & others who are very much local people . . . It is wisely agreed that I have no visitors except for the family & the Bishop of Jarrow – I'm so glad to think that Alec (Jarrow) will be in charge of things. Daffodils from the bowling green & a lovely card . . . my mind goes back to another Easter in hospital 38 years ago.

April 3 (Easter Monday)

Arnold Hadwin does a most touching appreciation of my work – 'a wider concept of pastoral care' he calls it. It is words like this, which in this part of the world I know to be genuine, that bind me closer & closer to the faith & hopes & lives of the people: both within the Church & beyond it. *The Evening Despatch* comes indeed as I've just been given the bedpan, and when the little student nurse asks me (as I think) whether I need paper – & of course I say yes! – it turns out to be the *Ev. Desp.* At 3 p.m. Mummy & Mum come – & Mum brings me my Easter gift of a deluxe Biro. Gail & Paul (daughter-in-law and son) look in as well . . . how much the messages of hand and eyes and lips mean on such occasions. So little need be said – but here are moments of vision, disclosure of what abides . . .

April 4 (Tuesday)

Though I am wired up and sellotaped again this morning, I've been brought over to a bigger side-ward on the other side of the corridor where *inter alia* I can hear on occasion the trains going up to Weardale and Witton Park, no doubt, for the Etherley tip. I also pick up a portable TV & I was able to see something of the British Empire programme & the news . . .

April 5 (Wednesday)

In the new side ward I see the clouds scurrying across the blue sky – and I continue to read for the most part Somerset Maugham's short stories of the East. Many, many letters and cards come and I am greatly moved and sustained by all the enquiries, visits, with messages and the prayers. Tom Swinney (Vicar of Witton-le-Wear and Chaplain to Bishop Auckland General Hospital) comes to give me Communion & I have a strong feeling of being in fellowship with so many others who are united with us in prayer. Look at TV again – but it is only the first part of a Dorothy Sayers' story. I then go down after seeing the news – the fighting in Vietnam, and the very significant plea to Roman Catholics and others that the initiative of the Westminster Government should be given a fair chance.

April 7 (Friday)

I buy a copy of *The Telegraph* and I see Jack Norwood's death (Master of Sherburn Hospital & Canon of Durham) – so sketch out a little appreciation for the Bp's Letter. See some TV, the Virginian & the news, but begin *Mist over Pendle*.

April 8 (Saturday)

Today I left the bed for the first time for a week as I used the 'commode' – finding it much easier than the bed pan. Barbara (Vivian's fiancée) & Vivian come this morning and bring many letters again, including those from Darlington & Sunderland Corporations. My calories have been increased to 1,000 per day – the same food but more of it . . .

April 9 (Sunday)

Progress, thank God, continues. I begin to read Charles Snow's *The Corridors of Power*. Knowing Charles & the House of Lords it certainly becomes very vivid . . . I commend myself to God – all of us – for all time . . .

April 12 (Wednesday)

Thank God for another good day. The nurse tells me that she nearly didn't come into work this morning because she won £237 at Bingo in Spennymoor last night! 'The Hospital – a place of Truth' – I've often thought of the title of that Report as I've laid here.

April 13 (Thursday)

Up in the chair for ½ hr. tonight – so my first step to progress. All the papers have carried details today of parts of the speech which was read for me at Nicosia – the BMA Conference. On the whole good reports.

Ramsey returned to Auckland Castle on Friday, 21 April. He had to spend time in bed but was allowed to get up for several hours each day. On 29 April he said Mattins with his family for the first time since Good Friday. In May he was still confined to the Castle, not yet receiving permission to tackle the stairs, but was taking short walks around some of the rooms on the first floor, and getting used to moving about again.

May 8 (Monday)

Some bright spells today but a dull night with rain. Dr Ferguson is pleased with my progress and I can now have 6 hrs/day up, an increase of an hour but no stairs yet. I still feel vigorous as get back to bed tonight. Talk to Harry . . . Lord Eccles sent me a copy of the speech he made which contained a reference to my speech in the Lords. Given *The Observer* which said in relation to the Abp's (of Canterbury) possible retirement that the problem was my illness – inevitably speculation that I might not be asked to go south though I'm making excellent progress, that if the Abp soldiers on it will be because of my illness, the time needed to groom a successor. But for my illness, Pendennis remarked, it was all but certain I'd have taken over early next year . . . So the expected speculation develops – Bob Runcie mentioned as the 'dark horse' . . . and here I am . . . but would it ever have been right to neglect work desperately wanting to be done because I might then become Abp of Canterbury? Surely not, and I did nothing beyond what a Bp of Durham should do, & what needed doing. But I saw I couldn't continue like that . . . I couldn't work at half steam to make Canterbury possible. Whatever the future now holds, God grant me strength to fulfil it in a worthy way.

The episcopal wheels of the diocese were well oiled by the Bishop of Jarrow and Bishop Kenneth Skelton (who was awarded the CBE in the New Year's Honours List), and everyone rallied to assist in every way possible. By June Bishop Hamilton informed the diocese that, 'The Bishop is now not only allowed to go downstairs but has even been given permission to go out and even to go for short drives in his car. This is a clear indication that he is getting steadily stronger and that before too long he may be able to undertake a little light work.' But Ramsey had no comprehension of the meaning of 'a little light work'. By July he was at his desk again. In the August *Bishop's Letter* Ramsey admitted he could not continue indefinitely the kind of programme:

> I have tried to carry out over the last five years. To put the matter in the baldest way: an enquiry I had initiated a month before I fell ill revealed that my number of working hours, not including meal times, when calculated from report sheets, averaged 90 per week. Again in the matter of correspondence, a week's letters at Auckland came out on average at 210 in and 230 out. It was clear that some rigorous forward planning was desperately needed. My illness gave me a chance if not to stand back to lie back, and to ponder how I could arrange matters better. But let me say at once, what I trust hardly needs saying, that I would never be a party to practising semi-retirement! My hope

in short is that by a certain amount of re-organisation and planning
the diocese, the church at large, and myself will all be beneficiaries.

Even as these words were written Ramsey was diving into his work
and expanding his commitments. In sad fact he was not swimming
but drowning. In August his old and trusted friend, Gordon Dunstan,
visited him, 'I had tea with him and Margaret, relaxed and at home
in Auckland Castle. He said he had learned his lesson: he would not
go back to the old killing round. But he did. Too soon he was on
the London train. St Paul once said he was not disobedient to the
heavenly vision. Ian might have said that he was not disobedient of
a moral claim.'

These months of recovery had been precious ones for Margaret
Ramsey. It was the only time since his Consecration that they had
spent such time together. His entry in *Who's Who* listed family and
home; reading maps and (once) Bradshaw. For Ian and Margaret it
was recreation and re-creation at Auckland Castle. But the itch of
activity was all too soon scratched again.

Ramsey was a star and starred speaker at the Church Leaders'
Conference organised by the British Council of Churches with a
substantial Roman Catholic participation. Five hundred leading
members of the British and Irish churches met from 11 to 15
September 1972 in the Selly Oak Colleges, Birmingham, not to
legislate, pass resolutions and agree messages, but to join together in
considering in depth with a minimum of formality the crises which
Christianity faced. Not since the Reformation had such a representative gathering of leaders assembled. Anglican Archbishops, Roman
Catholic Cardinals, Moderators or General Secretaries of the Presby-
terian, Methodist, Congregational, Baptist and other Reformed
Churches were there. From the first moment it was a conference
where divisions and conflict were not bowed into corners. Speakers
and lecturers ensured that splits in theology and divisions in doctrine
were out in the open. David L. Edwards, then Canon of Westminster
and Rector of St Margaret's, Westminster, first thought of the idea,
and wrote an account of the Conference, *The British Churches Turn
to the Future*, which he dedicated to the memory of 'Ian Ramsey
philosopher and bishop whose life disclosed to many what the truth
is in Jesus.' Ian Ramsey's eighty-minute lecture on 'The Crisis of

Faith' given on Tuesday 12 September, was the glory and summation of his thought and appears as an Appendix to this work.

Three further diary entries.

October 3 (Tuesday)

Another full day – God give me health & strength. (Interviews with five people). Tea and then off to Ebchester for the Confirmation. Ponder the Rotary Club talk, the schools talk & the sermon for tomorrow . . .! The Labour Party Conference at Blackpool is in full swing. Denmark by a large majority votes to enter the European Community – which is a relief all round, not least in Denmark! God bless +

October 4 (Wednesday)

A perfect 'September' day with warmth and sunshine like that of a summer's day. Thank God for all I've been able to do. Off at 9.15 to the Hermitage School at Chester-le-Street . . . I take the Assembly with prayer, hymn, talk and prayer – talking of the different kinds of decision. Coffee & photographs for the papers and then I talk to one of the classes showing them the 'regalia' (of a bishop) & answering some good questions. So off to Peterlee for the Rotary Club where I speak on U.S.A. which is much appreciated . . . Back to rest when I do the sermon for tonight when I've collated David Davison to Sherburn Hospital with a great attendance. I see Bishop George West & pay well-deserved tribute to him. Home to hear of a difficult telephone call to deal with.

October 5 (Thursday)

Another perfect 'September' day after the mists clear, then it is warm and sunny with a clear blue sky. I mention to Mummy that I'm glad Gail and Paul are coming on Saturday. Sort papers in the car to Darlington: catch the 9.44 – v. comfortable and I'm in KX after lunch at 1.10 (2 minutes late). Over to ESU (English Speaking Union) where I rest and then do letters. Across to SCM (Student Christian Movement) with *Preface* for IRM (Institute of Religion and Medicine) volume – get other letters posted & then to BBC where I see John Lang on tomorrow's business. With Howard Root & John Lang to Shepherd's Bush for the Viewing Session where we ask some very significant questions about the character of apologetics on TV & radio. Back in car for about 11 p.m., here at ESU – but too late to ring Mummy. London three year's running today. I send letter to Gail and Paul.

Ramsey spent the day of 6 October chairing the Central Religious Advisory Committee at Broadcasting House. John Lang was there and with Ian Ramsey shortly before his final heart attack:

> After the meeting he asked to be allowed to stay on for a bit, because he had some preparations to make before his next engagement. A few minutes later Mr F.L. Tomlinson went into the room to clear up after the meeting. He greeted the bishop, who began to reply but suddenly fell forward across the table. Mr Tomlinson got medical help with the utmost speed, first a nurse and then the ambulance. I got back from my office as the bishop was being carried, unconscious out of Broadcasting House. I went with him to the Middlesex Hospital fearing he might already be dead. In fact he was not and the waiting doctors at first got a slight reaction from his heart. It was a false hope, however, and quarter of an hour later I was told he had died.

The 1800 King's Cross to Newcastle had an empty seat to Darlington that evening.

As a boy at home Ian Ramsey had had his own little desk. One day when his mother was dusting it she found he had stuck a little sixteenth century prayer inside. He was aged ten at the time. His mother and father said this prayer every night and Ian and Margaret used it all their lives:

> O Lord support us all the day long of this troublous life until the shades lengthen and the evening comes, and the busy world is hushed, the fever of life is over, and our work is done. Then, Lord, in Thy mercy, grant us a safe lodging and holy rest and peace at the last.

CHAPTER 13

The Improbable Bishop

IAN RAMSEY'S STATURE WAS immediately recognised in a broadcast tribute by the Archbishop of Canterbury, Michael Ramsey, on Sunday 8 October 1972. The diocese of Durham was devastated. People found it difficult to bear their loss because that loss was 'personal'. Two priests speak for many: the Revd A.W. Hodgson, Vicar of St Oswald's, Hartlepool, had served the whole of his ministry in traditional working-class parishes:

> We were preparing for a stewardship mission when the rural dean rang to tell us of Bishop Ian's death. I gathered everyone together for prayers and then sent them home. I went for a long walk through Hartlepool's dockland and sobbed my heart out, and then re-wrote the Sunday sermon using Elijah and Elisha. At his successor's (John Habgood) consecration there was a very emotional feeling. I broke down during the hymn 'Be thou my vision'.

He was not alone, for the congregation was thinking of their lost leader. The Revd Jeremy Martineau, curate of St Paul's Jarrow and Ramsey's Industrial Adviser, reflects:

> He was humorous, friendly, genuine, spiritual, intellectual, and fully human. Even dictating these words about him brings back important memories and touches deep emotions. I felt very angry indeed with God for his untimely death. He made sense of our faith in today's world and was not bound by traditional forms and language. In that way he inspired me to be somewhat of a radical myself, which I suppose I am by nature but he gave me the permission to be who I am.

Even today there are clergy studies with a photograph of Ian Ramsey – 'my bishop' – on the desk. An endless cascade of tributes came from people Ramsey had 'touched' and 'influenced', sometimes in ways of which he was completely unaware. His presence was sufficient. The General Secretary of the National Union of Mineworkers for the Durham Area wrote, 'His popularity with working people was undoubtedly founded upon his ability to understand them and their problems, and miners in particular will remember his courageous advocacy of their cause over the years.' A wave of sorrow passed over whole communities. Mrs Ramsey was the recipient of hundreds of memories and tributes of 'Ian, our Bishop'.

Ian Ramsey's funeral was followed by cremation and his ashes rest in the mediaeval splendour of the Chapel dedicated to St Peter in Auckland Castle, near to the burial places of bishops John Cosin (1594–1672) the restorer of The Bishoprick; Joseph Barber Lightfoot (1828–1889) who never forgot 'the Bishop in the Scholar, nor the Scholar in the Bishop'; and Brooke Foss Westcott (1825–1901) 'Everybody's Bishop', not least to the miners of Durham.

There were six Memorial Services, the first one at Durham Cathedral on 13 October with an Address by the Archbishop of York, Donald Coggan. One of the words he used was 'affirmation':

> It is, I believe, a misuse of the pulpit to make it, on such an occasion as this, merely a place where a panegyric is uttered, however sincere that panegyric may be. 'In the midst of life we are in death' – how vividly this has been brought home to us! But for the Christian that statement is not one of unrelieved gloom. Far from it. For when we are most perplexed at the death of a great man 'before his time', as we put it; when we long that a William Temple or an Ian Ramsey might have been given another decade or two in which to pursue his work and continue his contribution to the Church and to society, we recall our belief that, in God's Kingdom, there is no waste. To that belief we hold, even when our eyes are dimmed; and by that belief we steady ourselves, we who are left to carry on the work.

After the Blessing, the Procession moved though the Nave, and the Choir sang 'I will lift up mine eyes . . .'

At Bishopwearmouth Parish Church, Bishop Kenneth Skelton opened his Address with these words:

> It was the final session of the Church Leaders' Conference at Birmingham, barely a month ago. The Secretary of the Methodist Conference was summing up his impressions. He spoke of being thrilled by the address of the Bishop of Durham. 'I followed him most of the way', he said; 'and then at the end of the road, when he appeared to be ascending into the mount of vision, the mists came

swirling down. He was last seen with his back towards us, undoubtedly making off in the general direction of God.'

We smiled: but to some of us the words brought a chill of fear.
What if indeed he was, not just turning towards God, for he was
always in that position . . . but setting his foot on that final ascent
which involves every man in turning his back on his friends – and
from which there is no return?

At Christ's College, Cambridge on 22 October the Bishop of Ely,
Edward Roberts, quoted Edmund Burke with prescience, 'Great men
are the guideposts and landmarks in the State' – and the Church!

Ian Ramsey's roots were not forgotten. There was a Memorial
Service at Bolton Parish Church on 29 October with a sermon by
the Ven. Len Tyler, Principal of William Temple College, who spent
seventeen years of his ministry in Lancashire.

The national Memorial Service was held at St Margaret's Church,
Westminster, on 17 November 1972. Those participating came from
organisations Ramsey had chaired and served, and the prayers were
adapted from prayers used by him. As at the Durham Memorial
Service, so at Westminster, people did not hold back their tears and
emotions when the final hymn was sung – 'For all the Saints . . .' The
Archbishop of Canterbury's Address was momentous and moving,
and merits extensive quotation:

> It is never easy to speak about a dear friend or a great man, and it is
> doubly hard to speak about one who was both. I have known other
> men who had something of Ian's winning warmth of heart and others
> who had Ian's liveliness of mind; but I have never known one in
> whom the warm heart and the lively mind were so completely of one
> piece. That was the secret of his influence as a theologian. He cared
> intensely that theology should listen to other disciplines if it is to have
> something intelligible to say in the contemporary scene. He cared no
> less that those who speak about Christian faith should do so with
> sensitivity to the many who find faith hard or incredible. These gifts
> made Ian Ramsey nearly unique amongst the theologians of our time
> in winning the attention and respect of people trained in other minds
> of mental discipline. And for Ian this outreach on the frontiers of faith
> could never be an intellectual process alone. It meant outgoing
> friendship with people of many professions, a ceaseless engagement of
> heart and mind alike, a ceaseless giving of himself.

So when Ian left the academic life of Oxford for the very different tasks of a Bishop of Durham there was, for all the vast change of scene, a striking continuity of work and character. In Durham it was quickly apparent that he cared greatly about the community and its problems and was thinking vigorously about them. Those who worked in the mines and the shipyards, trades unionists and managers alike, those who took part in local government or education or medicine or the social services, saw in the bishop one who understood and cared, with a concern for people as well as for ideas and causes. So there was a renewal in a fresh form of the historic link between the See of Durham and the community, for Ian had a sense of the past as well as the present, and he was never happier than when he welcomed crowds of visitors to the bishop's historic home and showed them the memorials of his great predecessors.

Inevitably Ian Ramsey's leadership was reaching far beyond his own diocese. The work of the Doctrine Commission, the production of the report on education entitled *The Fourth R*, the work of other groups of his own creation, a succession of speeches in the House of Lords made with the weight of considerable knowledge – amid all this his impact as a Christian leader was growing, and it was a leadership of a kind which no one else could give. But a frightening problem began to occur.

Is it possible for one man to lead the pastoral work of a diocese with its outreach to the community and at the same time to be taking part in national affairs and at the same time also to conserve the work of study, reading, thought, and teaching? Not many bishops have tried to combine these three roles at once, and those who have tried know that survival is only possible if there is a rigorous discipline in excluding things which do not matter and limiting painfully the things which do. Alas, it was impossible for Ian to admit the advice and experience of those who know something of the problem, because it had become a deep and inseparable part of his character never to say 'no'. And in the office which he held, never to say 'no' means before long to lose the power of discrimination and to be living in a whirl of mental and physical movement. The whirl became the whirlwind which swept Ian, like Elijah of old, to Paradise.

Yet perhaps if it were otherwise Ian would not be Ian. Perhaps the saying of 'no' to any request of a fellow human being and the planning of priorities for himself were impossible for one to whom any incidental encounter, any person met, could be a thrilling disclosure, a bursting forth of one of God's secrets. Such was the man, with mind and heart ceaselessly engaged with people and ceaselessly engaged with truth and ready for truth to break out anywhere in a blaze of glory. That was the Ian God gave to us, and we are thanking God today for one of the best of His gifts that we have known, a gift not like any other. Our loving prayers surround Ian's brave family at this time, and for Ian we pray that he will now have the vision which our Saviour promised to the pure in heart.

When considering which bishops made the biggest impact on the Durham *community*, Michael Ramsey named Brooke Foss Westcott and Ian Ramsey as the two who 'it would not be surprising if history comes to remember'. Taking the twentieth century as a whole it is possible that, so far as the 'community' is concerned David Jenkins might be added. The name of Herbert Hensley Henson stands alone, illustrious and controversial in Church and State.

On 22 November there was a Memorial Service at Oriel College, Oxford. Professor Basil Mitchell gave the Address on 'The Improbable Bishop' which provides the title not only for this final chapter, but for this biography:

Ian Ramsey was active in so many fields that no single individual could possibly have encountered him in all of them. His friends knew that for most of the time he operated outside their range and that he did a great deal more than could reasonably be expected of any man. Yet they could not doubt that whoever met him in whatever connection found him the same man, responding with spontaneous warmth and friendliness to those about him and concerned in a practical way for their interests.

He became for many so familiar and so dependable a figure that it was easy to forget what an improbable man he was. In thought and manner and expression he was highly individual – nothing he wrote could conceivably have been written by anyone else and his characteristic phrases almost demand to be read in his own accent and intonation – but he never attempted to impose his personality upon those with whom he worked . . .

In discussions with doctors, scientists, lawyers and other experts Ian Ramsey was at his best, patient, quick in comprehension, humorous, fair and firm; impossible to shock and very difficult to disconcert. His improbableness was a great help here. No one ever looked or sounded less like a bishop or even a professor, so that from the start people were able to set aside their preconceptions and see and hear the man;

33. 366 Manchester Road, Clifton, Ian's boyhood home. Paul Ramsey's photograph

34. St John's, Farnworth Church where Ian was confirmed. Paul Ramsey's photograph

35. *High Quarry, Harcourt Hill, North Hinksey, Oxford which Ian had built for the family and his parents. Print from friend in 1959*

36. *Christ's College, Cambridge today. Fellows' Garden and Fellows' Building where Ian had his rooms as Chaplain. Paul Ramsey's photograph*

37. The Lord Lieutenant of Durham – Sir James Duff, Her Majesty the Queen and Ian on their way from the Castle to the Cathedral on Maundy Thursday 1967. Photograph given by Mrs R.R. Sidgwick of Brandon

*38. Durham Cathedral from near Prebend's Bridge by the River Wear.
Paul Ramsey's photograph*

39. Ian in Coronation Cope, which he relished wearing, at Auckland Castle

40. *Ian leading a Diocesan Pilgrimage to York, at York Station in 1968*

41. *Auckland Castle today. Paul Ramsey's photo, with kind permission from Bishop of Durham*

42. Clock Tower gateway to Auckland Castle grounds today. Paul Ramsey's photograph, with kind permission from Bishop of Durham

43. Auckland Castle Chapel through the main gates today. Paul Ramsey's photograph, with kind permission from Bishop of Durham

44. Ian's portrait in the Throne Room at Auckland Castle.
Paul Ramsey's photograph, with kind permission from Bishop of Durham

45. Bishop Joseph Butler's portrait in the Throne Room at Auckland Castle.
Paul Ramsey's photograph, with kind permission from Bishop of Durham

46. Ian and Margaret at Auckland Castle in September 1972. Paul Ramsey's photograph

47. Ian and Margaret's Memorial at St Peter's Chapel, Auckland Castle.
Paul Ramsey's photograph, with kind permission from Bishop of Durham

finding that he would listen to what they had to say, however abstruse and technical, and that he eschewed premature conclusions and artificial reconciliations, the experts quickly lost any suspicions that remained. He was seen to be totally lacking in the timorous anxiety which leads some churchmen to evade the rigours of careful empirical inquiry.

'Improbableness' was a natural asset. May this be stretched to include indiscrimination? Charles Vereker admired Ramsey whilst questioning his inability to refuse any invitation which came his way: 'Such an attitude involved the loss of the power of discrimination . . . it seems possible, however, that in Ian's case to be indiscriminate was a Christian virtue. He gave his life for it.' (Ian Ramsey: Prodigality and Passion *Crucible* January, 1974)

Following Ramsey's death it was surprising how quickly the ecclesiastical vultures gathered over their prey. The sour *Crockford Preface* 1973–74 was not unrepresentative:

> By the death of Dr Ian Ramsey, Bishop of Durham the Church has lost a loveable personality, a man of great gifts, and one who in lifestyle brought something new to the episcopate. Within six years his influence and reputation grew to astonishing proportions. His early death was the result of his inability to refuse requests for help. Much as we admired and liked him, however, we have doubts whether in a few years' time his intellectual contribution to Anglican theology will seem quite as great as it is now rated. He was the spokesman of a period of theological disintegration to which a positive veneer is given by the use of the term 'pluralism'. Dr Ramsey rightly set himself, as a philosopher, to grapple with the situation created by the Logical Positivists, trying to enter their thought forms and speak their language. Such a relation with current philosophy has been a feature of Christian endeavour from at least the time of Justin Martyr. It is attended by the danger that the result will be something that is more justifiable in terms of current philosophy than profoundly Christian. That was a weakness of the Idealists in their day, and there are those who saw it in Ian Ramsey's work also. The next generation but one will be in a better position to judge.

In Church and State alike we have difficulty honouring people, particularly if they carry the pre-fixed burden of 'Right Reverend Lord Bishop'. Fame is bestowed and clichés are lavished upon celebrities, who strut, smile or grin briefly, or arrogantly, at us for a fleeting moment before they disappear. We have forgotten how to pay tribute, to express a sense of gratitude and respect which we feel toward a very few people in our institutions and communities. It may be that this inadequacy is traceable to an intense egalitarianism which has rendered us cautious of any proclamation which seems to make one person more honourable than the next. Together with all his limitations and weaknesses this biography **salutes**, **celebrates** and **proclaims** Ian Thomas Ramsey as one the great glories of the Church of England. The petition 'Let light perpetual shine upon him' is met in Ian Ramsey as a pilgrim and pioneeer. Light is what is primarily associated with him. Richard Hooker said, 'Ministers of good things are like torches, a light to others, a waste and destruction to themselves'.

God gave to the Church someone whose inexplicable hyperactivity led to a short episcopate and an early death. Should his all too recognisable faults be seen as by-products of his availability, serviceableness, charity and generosity? The Church of England, left with such startling suddenness without him, felt bewildered and bereft. A life cut short? That is a human way of looking at loss. The fruitfulness of a life, the evaluation of a ministry and episcopate, cannot be measured by its length. There is another and worthier standard of judgement for human lives than the number of years. 'A righteous man, though he die before his time, shall be at rest.' Was this perhaps a clue to an understanding of God's purpose in his passing? Were we being taught that never and in nothing should a Church, required to be faithful to its Master, come to rely too much on even the noblest of persons?

May it be that in the wisdom of Almighty God, Ian Ramsey's work was actually completed? Did he, like Job, discover in the end that we cannot demand explanations of God? Surely we have seen in the Cross, that suffering which appears fruitless and frustrating can be transformed in the hands of God into redemption and glory.

> From earth's wide bounds, from ocean's farthest coast,
> Through gates of pearl streams in the countless host,
> Singing to Father, Son and Holy Ghost.
> Alleluya! Alleluya!

Text of lecture on 'The Crisis of Faith'

given by the Bishop of Durham
Ian Ramsey
At the Church Leaders' Conference, Selly Oak Colleges,
Birmingham, on Tuesday, 12 September 1972

To link 'crisis' and 'judgment' is a well-known and well-worn device as etymologically sound as it has proved often to be empirically shallow, and when associated with a *deus ex machina* theologically unedifying. So for myself in this context of *crisis* and *judgment*, crisis and decisiveness, I rather picture a crisis of faith as a decisive time, a time of decision between two eras. What then are the ingredients which enter into the present to make it the critical, decisive time that it is? What routes have brought us to this watershed, this Continental divide between two eras? What must be our response under God and inspired by His Gospel in Christ – to the complex and deeprooted issues which confront us?

Let us begin by looking at some of the issues, and first, at the growing implausibility of a prescriptive theology. For long years theology, and for the moment I use the word with deliberate vagueness to cover *inter alia* the language of the scriptures and of doctrine, was supposed to participate in the givenness of God Himself. Its words were supposedly authenticated and guaranteed by the revelation they expressed. In that sense theology was a part of the revelation of God – so that in a literal direct sense there were revealed truths. Revelation not only referred to an activity of God in Christ; it referred to particular God-given propositions as well. God did not only act, He spoke; He not only spoke, He dictated. On this view, it is not surprising that theology should seek to control and prescribe the conclusions in every other subject while being itself unaffected by discoveries about the world. Determinative of other knowledge, it was a purveyor of truths which all other studies must accept.

Here was theology as the queen of the sciences demanding a strict obedience of her subjects. Empirical studies were held to be either unimportant or, if they conflicted with the tenets of theology, not only wrong but blasphemous.

It is perhaps hard for us to realise that this was a generally accepted view as recently as a century ago. Hence the significance of Charles Darwin's *Origin of Species* in 1859. Whether scientifically reliable or not, it was sufficient that here in principle was the possibility of conclusions about creation, providence and the destiny of man arising from empirical observations. A former Bishop of Peterborough, Dr Spencer Leeson spoke movingly of the influence of Charles Darwin on his father's faith: 'One day a friend put *The Origin of Species* into his hands. This wrecked his faith; chiefly because it was not reconcilable with the biblical account of creation, and as the biblical revelation hung together and was all of one piece, if part of it fell out, the rest would fall out too. If Adam never existed, he did not sin; if he did not sin, man was not fallen; there was therefore no need for Christ to come. If the Bible was wrong in science, how could we be sure it was right in theology?' Dr Leeson continues: 'We fail in justice and in sympathy if we make light of the real agony of mind through which he and many of his contemporaries passed.'[1] But the seriousness of the challenge was not that it denied certain empirical conclusions that hitherto had been regarded as unassailable. It was that the view of the biblical text, and by implications of theology, which that conclusion presupposed, was now being rejected.

Part of the reason for our contemporary crisis of faith is that despite all the challenges over the last century, and of course with notable exceptions like Thomas Arnold and F.D. Maurice – and that is the point, they were exceptions – the prescriptive character of theology not only remained unquestioned, but was the more resolutely affirmed. Faced with the challenge of empirical knowledge, men became negative not to say neurotic, insensitive not to say incensed, in the defence of the status quo. I have often wished that a century ago we had had the mass media of today which, whatever be their defects, would at least have ensured that in every home there was a hearing of all sides. True, the nineteenth century would have been to many even more shattering than it was; but there could not have been the same self-confidence and hollow victories. As we face the crisis of our own time, the reaction of our predecessors to the crisis of a past age is a terrible warning. Not only did they fail to face up squarely to searching issues; their sidestepping merely postponed until today the crisis which should have been faced yesterday.

As late as 1891 Robert Gregory, Dean of St Paul's, could join with seven other deans in issuing a statement on the 'Truth of the Holy Scriptures' in which they said 'the Holy Scriptures "are inspired by the Holy Ghost: that they are what they profess to be: that they mean what they say: and that they declare incontrovertibly the actual historical truth in all their records both of past events and of the delivery of predictions to be thereafter fulfilled."'[2] Somewhat earlier, in 1868 when the Honours School of Theology was established in Oxford, Dr E.B. Pusey could feel that the setting up of this separate honour school safeguarded the uniqueness of theology within the university system. 'Theology', he declared, 'is a subject quite apart . . . in it the question is not one of mere knowledge of facts, or of opinions, or of philosophies, or of philosophical theories, but of a revelation of God for the salvation of man.'[3] It was still supposed, in other words, that theology was guaranteed by its object. Here again we see how a failure of analysis concealed from men the crucial problem and compromised the very commitment and conviction they valued as their lives. Theology is certainly concerned, as the Gospel is concerned, with 'a revelation of God for the salvation of man', and the scriptures are certainly 'inspired'. But this does not mean that theology has itself a God-given character, that its words carry in themselves the authority of God Himself. Yet one element in the critical situation today is that there are still many Christians who take up the standpoint of Dean Gregory or Dr Pusey. Those Christians who take an alternative view seem to their fellow Christians to be faithless unbelievers; and this infighting encourages many contemporaries not only to disbelieve what we say, but to be convinced that we ourselves don't believe what we say. Our epistemological muddles play as much havoc with relations between Christians as they do with our relations with unbelievers. It may be worth remarking here that I will not be arguing for a liberalism of an outdated brand. The older liberals were men of broad views and great integrity, and on the whole they saw the problems, and asked the right questions, at a time when a question mark was thought to be almost a symbol of blasphemy. But their answers tended to be shallow and superficial largely because with no sense of the variegations of language (a point to which I shall return presently) they took science as definitive, so that not surprisingly a sense of mystery not to mention the distinctiveness of the Christian faith seemed to evaporate and disappear.

So the first feature of our present situation which needs a thorough thinking through is a problem in the theory of knowledge: the relation between revelation and its expression, between revelation and talk about revelation, between what is God-given and how this is articulated. What is at issue in what is often represented as a tension between belief and unbelief, conviction and scepticism, is rather two different views of theology and its relation to revelation, and if we are to face the present crisis responsibly we have to grapple with these two views of theology, the attitudes they foster, and the character they give to the Church, its ministry, its evangelism and its moral reasoning. For far too long we have failed to get to grips with what is this basic underlying issue. What undoubtedly has made the attitudes of Dean Gregory and Dr Pusey increasingly implausible has been the development of historical studies over the last century and a half. These studies have made it plain that theology cannot have a monolithic and self-guaranteed character; that there is no precision-built theology to be prescriptive. It only gained this appearance in the past by Christians taking cognisance of only a partial selection of the relevant facts with different Christians taking different selections and making sure they never met each other. Critical historical studies however make it impossible for instance to hold that there is but one view of the Christian ministry which itself contains the whole truth; that alternative views are just verbiage. Again, the idea that doctrinal controversy yields clear unambiguous views of (say) Christological or Trinitarian truth can hardly be sustained. It is high time that theology as she is preached and theology as she is practised in liturgies listened to theology as she is taught. A Nelson's eye attitude has run through preaching and liturgy for far too long.

The second ingredient of the present situation which calls for a faithful and frank response is the growing importance assigned to the empirical and the secular.

One particular result is that it becomes increasingly unsatisfactory and difficult to read off at all easily God's purposes in nature and history – a point which is obvious enough to the critical reader of the Old Testament and which lies behind John Wisdom's famous remark: 'The existence of God is not an experimental issue in the way it was'. The point may be put in words from *The Fourth R*: 'On the one hand there was the theological view that God controlled the events of nature – rain or sunshine. Natural calamities were viewed as punishment, national prosperity as reward. God was directly involved alike in man's prosperity as in his failures. Further, it was God who gave men the victory in battles against nations. Yet for some four hundred years men have been developing very different interpretations of nature, human nature, and history. The new ways of talking about the world, about human nature, about history, not only seem never to need the concept of God, but often seem to be in head-on collision with all the ways of talking traditional to the theologian.'[4] All this has an obvious bearing not only on traditional Christian teaching but on the articulation of our prayers – a point I touch on later. But nowhere have the collisions and tensions emerged with more unmistakeable force and clarity than in the area of human nature and human behaviour, not least because of the comparatively recent developments in psychology and the behavioural sciences generally. At one time, sin and wrongdoing seemed to be clear and unambiguous. But not only developments in psychology, more lately developments in the biological and medical sciences, and in endocrinology in particular, have led to an acknowledgement of new factors which must be reckoned with when we appraise human behaviour. Glandular excretions and biochemical imbalance are of undeniable importance in any full understanding of human behaviour; it may not always be John himself but his testosterone which is to be blamed for John's sexual irregularities. Sin in the sense in which it is to be assimilated – though I realise not too readily – to moral wrongdoing will always be, in part, a frontier problem between biochemistry and psychiatry.

The practical and social implications of these moral developments are legion, and they more often than not conflict with the built-in attitudes which are the legacy of a past approach. For instance, it was once supposed that left alone in the isolation of a prison cell, a person would come to his senses, be brought to penitence, and all would be well. What so often happens is that when judgments such as this are now rejected on empirical grounds, the rejection is taken to be a rejection of Christian theology, and so it would be, and will be, if this is all Christian theology has to say.

What these reflections thus underline is the need to ask ourselves, against the deeper understanding of human behaviour which it is now possible for us to have, how far can the old personal, social and theological generalisations be reiterated? Better: how do we move towards a better understanding of human behaviour both in terms of theology and biological and behavioural studies? Here, undoubtedly, is one of the most threatening as well, I hasten to add, as one of the more promising aspects of the contemporary crisis of faith. How can we avoid being naïve and superficial about God and humanity alike? – For that is the terrible risk we run. Nothing does greater harm to our witness than to let fall from our lips whether in prayer or teaching the commonsense of a past age masquerading as theological assertions, which not only never latch on to the empirical situation, but use such large-scale language which shows itself both ignorant and insensitive about the circumstances that are being judged. I have pointed out elsewhere that the criticism of being judgemental, often being levied against Christian social workers and clergy, and indeed Christian people generally, reduces in its main thrust to a criticism of an *a priori*, authoritarian theology imposed in an ignorant and insensitive fashion on to the superficial features of a human problem.

So, the second feature of our contemporary situation contributes two problems to its critical character. First, there is the problem of making judgments about nature, history and human nature, a problem which demands for its solution a new matching of theological and empirical language. How do we reach judgments which do justice both to the Gospel and to the vastly increased empirical knowledge we now possess about man and the world?

But that problem presupposes another – and an even more far-reaching one connected with the shifting of theological interest to the secular, for thanks to neurotic churchmen of a past age, this has now reached a climax precisely at a time when secular studies are enjoying an unprecedented and in large measure a spectacular success story and feel they can afford to stare the theological gift horse in the mouth. So, theology having now met up with empirical studies, far from this being a joyous reunion for two prodigal sons whose father, Descartes, against his own better judgment had encouraged to go on their separate paths, the questions which now haunt Christians are radical and far-reaching: is not our secular knowledge of the world, the knowledge supplied by the natural and behavioural sciences, self-sufficient? Is there any empirical evidence of God being active in the world at all? On what grounds can we convincingly articulate about the activity of God in nature and history? In other words, the growing interest of Christian theology in the Incarnation, and therefore no matter how reluctantly and indirectly in the humanity of Jesus, a Jesus who is *Lux Mundi*, the growing concern of theology with the empirical and the secular, a splendid tradition to which men such as James Ward, F.R. Tennant and Charles Raven – to mention no others – have been outstanding contributors, has reached a climax at the very time when empiricism in science and philosophy seems to be leaving no room for the transcendent, no logical place for mystery, no place for that to which theology tries to do justice. Is this new approach to theology, then, coming to birth at a time when theology is doomed to be stillborn in the hands of an empirical midwife? These are far-reaching questions to which we must address ourselves with urgency if we are to come out of the crisis on the right side.

We have now been brought conveniently to a third feature of the contemporary situation – the contribution of philosophy to the present crisis. Having had to shorten this document by more than one third of its length, it is here that I have exerted the greatest self-denial. That as recently as forty years ago there could be a philosophical study of Hegel, which was a best seller at Oxford and which spoke of the coincidence of religion and philosophy, is an old but not an exaggerated story. That was the day which thought in terms of a Christian philosophy whose framework was absolute idealism; the climate in which, of recent theologians, William Temple especially was nurtured. But it is also an old but not exaggerated comment which recalls that this same absolute idealism could be viewed either as a disguised enemy or a treacherous friend. For while it essayed a world-view of magnificent coherence and comprehensiveness with undoubtedly Christian components, it could do nothing for the distinctiveness of Christianity, nor did it give any central place to a gospel of redeeming love in Christ. It has been argued that Temple himself finally surrendered his Hegelian hopes in the light of Barthian theology and the events of World War II. My own view would be that while he came to see that the idea of a Christian philosophy would be something very different from the kind of blueprint which traditional metaphysics, and in particular absolute idealism would offer, he never surrendered completely the hope that there might be some overall Christian perspective but one showing a greater empirical seriousness than absolute idealism ever displayed, displaying a broader sense of reasonableness than ever Hegelian dialectic contemplated, and not least doing greater justice to the unsearchable riches of Christ, and the sinfulness of man. But Hegel and William Temple apart, it would never have been supposed forty years ago that there was an imminent crisis to the rapprochement of philosophy and theology. Further, it is only fair to our predecessors to say that the prevailing philosophical fashion, and contemporary cultural attitudes, encouraged them to be patronising towards the scientific and the empirical. But by now the empirical strength of science and philosophy has broken down the sandbags by which defenders pathetically thought that they were fighting the battle of faith when in fact they were merely resisting its claims and preserving their own insularities. Our gratitude that the situation has now been opened up, that we now have a crisis which cannot be sidestepped, should go in no small measure to logical positivism. We may regard Wittgenstein, I suggest, as he who represents the development of logical empiricism over some thirty years, as, in the providence of God, the Cyrus of our time.

But the challenge of the earliest logical positivism was all the more devastating since it was not concerned with the truth or falsity of theology but with the prior question of its meaning. Indeed, it now became a compliment to a subject to deny that its assertions were true, for that denial at least implied that the assertion was meaningful. Theology did not receive many such compliments. Yet it is somewhat over twenty-five years ago that I implored the Oxford Society for Historical Theology, not to mistake the empiricist's bark for his bite, but to take empiricism seriously, as having a positive contribution to make to theological studies, and the development of empiricism over the period has, I believe, made that plea more, rather than less, important.

Now the crucial question which recent empiricism raises for theology is this: granting that there is no longer a positivist's veto against a meaningful theology – what is the logic of religious discourse? What is its empirical anchorage? What is the character of religious discourse and to what sort of situations does it belong? At the same time the hints which recent empiricism gives us are two:

1. There is no single brand of reliable reasoning: language is very variegated. At one time it was supposed that there was only one pattern of reliable argument. For Aristotle, this was given by the syllogism especially when all syllogistic reasoning was supposed to be reducible to a single form. For Descartes, the only brand of reliable reasoning was mathematics, and philosophy itself had to conform to that pattern. For the positivists, whether of the nineteenth century or our own day, the ideal was the language of experimental sciences. But no one any longer supposes that reliable reasoning is restricted to a single pattern of argument, nor that there must be only one explanation of a particular state of affairs. On the contrary, it is recognised that there are many different patterns of reliable reasoning, e.g. in mathematics, history, poetry, theology and that there can be a logical multiplicity of explanations – points sometimes encapsulated in the slogan 'Every assertion has its own logic.' We go to theology then expecting to find many interwoven strands, each strand being an endeavour to talk in one particular direction of the moment of vision from which the language takes its rise.

2. Secondly let us be on our guard against supposing nouns, e.g. episcopacy, priesthood, ordination, consecration, grace, for example to stand for isolable topics and commodities which are, and must for ever and always be, their 'meaning'. Rather, in order to see what is being talked about, we must consider words in the context of sentences, themselves in the context of disclosure, which itself is given its full concrete situational setting. Personal situations may well provide helpful parallels to those situations in which religious language is grounded, and here the interests of the empiricist and those of the existentialist can come close to each other. So much for contemporary philosophy in relation to the crisis of faith. That I shall not succeed in giving an exhaustive analysis of the present crisis follows not only from my own inabilities but from the complexity and diversity of the features that go and have gone to its creation. But I would be even more inadequate than I can hope to be if I neglected two other features. The one concerns the question of authority; the other contemporary social attitudes, and my overall argument is that

not only do both supply us with ingredients for any analysis of the present situation but – as with our reflections on philosophy – begin to point us forward and at least to encourage us as we grapple with current difficulties.

Fourthly, then, the matter of authority. Our problem today – whether in theology or morality, whether in making personal, or social, or political judgments – is how do we embody in our judgments, our organisation, our planning and our structures, the authority which fulfils and releases and speaks of freedom rather than the authoritarianism which oppresses and restricts and speaks of tyranny; recognising that part of the devilish attraction of authoritarianism is to be clear and forceful in its views and to yield striking success by criteria as immediate as they are superficial, a success in other words that is only matched by the long-term disasters which it brings in its train. We may also recognise that nothing is likely to make men authoritarian more than the idea that they are uttering a God-given language; in these circumstances, men not only forget they are men, not God – they also forget that their God is not a God whose dealings with men makes them mere larynxes and vocal chords for the production of divine noises. God's grace in Christ Jesus is a relationship which makes that supposition as blasphemous travesty of the facts. But here again we see how inter-connected and criss-crossed our present problems are: for it is all too easy to misread the Bible in such a way as to conclude that God uses men as mere mouth-pieces. Unless we are either very unsophisticated or very sophisticated, passages in the Bible which use the word 'God' as the subject of a sentence are hazardous in the extreme: for they read as if God had been observed to say and do precisely what is there described. They conceal the fact that the words are the writer's interpretation of a situation, not his reporting of observable features as news of the world and God. If all this seems by this time trite and obvious, I can only say that unfortunately much of our reasoning about God, man and the world proceeds on the assumption that far from being obvious, it is plainly false. This is another measure of the Herculean task which confronts us.

Fifthly, let me by a few random strokes of the brush – some four in all – paint some features of the contemporary social scene with which any assessment of the contemporary crisis for faith must reckon.

First, as far as religious education goes – and of course we always, and rightly, hedge our generalisations with acknowledgements to the conscientious, well-trained, well-informed and devoted teachers of which there have always been some – the superficial and unnecessarily dogmatic teaching of the Christian faith has led to the Christian faith meaning very little indeed to the population in general, even though for about a generation we have had the 1944 Act. As for believers, I am bound to ask whether the situation has been helped by a traditional Catechism which, however excellent as a syllabus, is absolutely disastrous when indicative of a method, since it presupposes a way of learning which, of all others, is least likely to help a pupil to make what is learned part of themselves. Where in fact do we look for an approach to the Bible and doctrine which has learned from the problems, mistakes and difficulties of the last century and a half? Does a broad common intention and outlook unite ministers and clergy on the one hand and teachers on the other? Are we over-stocked with theologically educated or even just theologically well-informed laymen? I am not here apportioning blame – though we may all have our views about that – I am simply recognising a feature to which we must not be blind if we are ever to emerge from our present crisis on the right side.

Secondly, children and their parents look on, and move in, a society where the Christian faith and the Churches apparently mean so very little, at least in the sense that monopolies, trades unions and management, national and international sport, mean very much. Is it then surprising that there is every encouragement to scepticism? Further, the very fact that different world views are openly canvassed and discussed obviously contributes to a general sense that no one view matters very much, and a religious view seems to matter least of all especially if it bears little, if at all, on the world around us. I recall some words of Sean O'Faolain as he looked back on the faith into which he had been born. It was a faith, he says, which revelled 'in the liquefaction of common life, the vaporisation of the mortal into the mystical, the veiling of the natural in the fumes of the supernatural, always at the expense of failing to develop the character of man as social animals.' He continues: 'So then, far from providing me with codes, values or rules for living in this pragmatical pig of a world, as Yeats calls it, all that, as far as I could see, the faith into which I was born offered me was a useful set of formalities, rather like a passport stamped with a lot of visas, guaranteed to get me as quickly as possible through this unpleasant world to my happy destination in the next. Since I was fated to become a writer concerned with the character and behaviour of men and women, I could not but feel that this kind of mystical concept for common actuality was something that would have to be put severely in its place if I ever hoped to write one truthful word about the human condition.'[5] No doubt there is here an element of misunderstanding, misrepresentation and exaggeration. But we have something to learn from the overall point.

More particularly, as we saw, for some 300 years there has been a growing gap between the Christian faith and scientific studies and, more lately, technological development, between the Churches and life, between the Gospel aspirations and the work patterns of man in an increasingly industrial society. The soup kitchens and the recreational facilities for instance in Jarrow some forty years ago were needed and valued; but there should well have been a more vigorous theological critique which related the social and industrial scene to the quality of human life and the nature and destiny of man. This would of course have necessitated a communication between the Churches and an industrial and technological society over bridges that had not only not been built over some 300 years, but where a refusal to build had been a point of principle, not to say honour, on both sides. For the one wanted to be free of the ecclesiastical tyranny and control which had atrophied its development, and the other was content to believe itself as a subject and an institution so much apart that its concern was entirely elsewhere.

There are, thirdly, other features of society we must briefly recall. Not only is the radical character and rapidity of social and industrial change producing great insecurity and unsettlement, it is matched in these islands by the loss of our world bearings as well. The old tag that we have lost an empire and not yet found a role is not only politically shrewd. It reminds us how, for many, the Empire and later the Commonwealth gave the sense of their having a place in the world; they were solidly built into the universe and had a mission to fulfil in it. Little by little the links have been broken, and there is now a sense of being not only politically but cosmologically adrift.

Insecurity in the docks, insecurity for executives as well as trades unionists, serious as that is for everyone, becomes also the point at which these deeper needs are laid bare.

Again, fourthly, the necessarily large-scale patterns of government or industry – necessary at least if we are to benefit from computers, trade patterns, growth in productivity and so on – inevitably bring with them an erosion of the place of the individual. Hence, the many features of our present society which express, at least in part, a desire for self-affirmation, which may be a subject for self-identity and self-realisation no matter how misguided; features, too, that show a desire to escape from the imprisonment of planning, and even the imprisonment of rules. Drugs, the Skinheads, Hell's Angels, the vandals – everybody across to those who wish to be 'somebody' by distinctive dress, or hair, or ways of living, all of them exemplify this deep-seated need. Let us note the recent words of someone who recalled coming out some years ago from 'Rock around the Clock' at the Elephant and Castle. He was asked why the occasion inspired and got hold of him. His answer: 'You felt big; nothing could stop you; you were the Government and the King. You found in your work and in your life you could go so far and no further – so you had to do something to get rid of it' i.e. the frustration. Again, with some of our contemporaries: 'We just go (they say) to Blackpool or Margate or the Pop Festival. Others, when they go places, may wonder what to go in, what sort of accommodation to get, they may want to plan details. Not us. We just go.' A one-sided reaction perhaps. But couldn't we in the Church do with a bit more of this spontaneity of action and could we not make it plainer than we do that the faith is in fact fulfilling and not oppressive? We have been brought full circle. For the problem with which we are presented is how to make our presentation of the Gospel less authoritarian, less oppressive. How do we ensure that our discourse, our liturgies, our structures make more evident the Gospel, reflect better the light of the knowledge of the glory of God which we have ourselves seen in the face of Jesus Christ?

So much then for the ingredients of the crisis in which we find ourselves. What do we see as the ingredients of a faithful response?

The first and all-important need is to come to a better understanding of revelation and the character of theology suited to it. More broadly how do we ensure that we talk sense, and how do we make good sense rather than bad sense of what lies at the heart of our religious faith and convictions?

If a brief autobiographical reference will be allowed, it was when I had to ask myself such questions in a youthfulness surrounded by logical positivists and challenged at every point to elucidate the meaningfulness of religious discourse, that I came to see that such discourse cannot do without alluding to the facts and features of the world around us, yet cannot be satisfied with such empirical cashing alone. It must appeal to empirical criteria and more: but not more such criteria, or else there is no transcendence; nor to similar criteria but in another world, for that is to buy sense and reference at the cost of intelligibility. Faced by this predicament, I came to talk of disclosure as that by which the transcendent makes itself known in and through things spatial and temporal, whether subjectively as that in ourselves which is more than our observable behaviour, or objectively as that we speak of in terms of the Word of God. In other words, as we look around us, some so-called 'facts' are there to be discriminated and looked at – these are the stock-in-trade of informative, descriptive language – in the case of persons, eyes, ears, hair and skin, as Bishop Berkeley reminded us in *Alciphron*; but some other facts declare themselves, make themselves known to us, they capture our attention – disclose themselves, and that is how we recognise persons, personal activity, spirit, to remind ourselves again of Berkeley.

In short theology and all religious claims, Christian or any other, in the end appeal to disclosures, moments of vision, flashes of insight, though these phrases conceal the point that a disclosure may not be at all spectacular, but rather possess the impressiveness and growing significance of a silence. Hence two metaphors – 'the ice breaks' (a spectacular discontinuity) and 'the light dawns' (a gradual awakening). Perhaps I should add that I speak of revelation when such disclosure occurs in a Christian context. It is in such situations of vision and disclosure where a flat, impersonal, narrowly empirical situation takes on depth and another dimension, that theology arises. Theology trades in models and metaphors each of which occurs within, and arises from a particular disclosure situation, and each of which licenses discourse by which we can be articulate about what the disclosure discloses. So theology becomes a complex interweaving of different strands of discourse each proceeding from different models, and each at different points and in different ways being qualified so as to indicate their disclosure basis. For all the strands are attempting to be articulate in one way or another about a vision.

The resulting discourse is then subject to formal and material checks and criteria. Thus, for example, that discourse is better than another which is the more coherent, consistent, comprehensive and simple; and we shall constantly ask, of each area of discourse, what is the character of its empirical fit: how well does this enable us to interpret the world?

But one way or another, theology has to be regarded as multiple and not linear; not primarily descriptive of fact, but primarily pointing to situations by trading in terms of plain language, which it uses in such a special way as to provide a particular inroad into a disclosure. All this means that theology is much less stereotyped than once was supposed. Far too much of our theology is read as though it were monolithic not multiple, and prosaic, formal, descriptive, matter-of-fact language and as readers of Bishop Barry and *The Times* will recall, doctrines of the Last Things provide the obvious example, though we have also to become accustomed to a logical intricacy and diversity about any apparently uniform area of discourse such as Eucharistic theology. In short, we can all welcome the so-called 'Death of God' controversy in so far as it is concerned with the death of a certain kind of God-language.

The relation between a disclosure and the discourse by which we are articulate about it between the moment of vision and the theological articulation can be illustrated by what was said about the discovery of Tutankhamun's tomb. A contributor to *The Listener* on 13 April 1972 writes: 'The greatest day was when the tomb was opened and the ante-chamber was found to be substantially intact. After that, anything he (Howard Carter) found had, almost by definition, to be a lesser climax. The objects can never be quite as dramatic as the drama of their discovery.' Here is the contrast between the discovery and the disclosure on the one hand, (and I do not apologise for linking the two words), and its elucidation on the other, talk of what it is that, at the moment of discovery, struck us. The same kind of point is embodied in what Robert Frost wrote of poetry: 'Poetry begins in delight and ends in wisdom.' Faith begins in delight and ends in doctrine and the more lush and prolific the theology we profess the more cautious we should be in uttering it for we shall be furthest from its origin in delight. How many of our doctrines delight those who hear them, and they will not do so unless they delight us.

Such an approach to theology, which sees theology as a multiple attempt to be articulate about a vision, not only makes no pretence that theology is a subject apart. Rather does it ground theology in disclosure situations which arise around matters of fact and empirical patterns. So while theology necessarily goes beyond the secular, all theological articulation starts from secular and never despises it. Jacob's ladder, embodying communication between heaven and earth, had its feet on the ground though we may suppose at the top disappeared in the infinite distance. True, our faith starts with God but theology only begins when words pass our lips. It is plain that here is a view of revelation and of the relation of theology to other subjects, radically different from that which we found unsatisfactory at the outset.

What is authoritative here is that of which we are aware – that which is given – in the disclosure. But our talk of this is never in the same way given. We are committed theologically to a constant exploration of paths old and new, and a constant mapping and cross-referencing.

In this connection, I may hazard the suggestion that we must look for an inclusive not an exclusive analysis of the distinctiveness and the uniqueness of the Christian faith. Like all religions, it will appeal to a disclosure of the eternal in the temporal: its uniqueness and distinctiveness arises around the claim that in Jesus of Nazareth the Christ, God's activity has to be characterised not only in universal terms (as when we speak of God as Creator and Sustainer of the Universe), not only in personal terms (as when religious men speak of the miraculous, or of God's 'choosing' a people) but in uniquely personal terms, where the uniqueness is interpreted inclusively, as, for example, in the Pauline doctrine of the Remnant, or in terms of ‘ανακεφαλαιωσς (summing up) as in Irenaeus or λογος in the Greek tradition. The crisis of faith will not be met by segregating the Christian faith, nor by denying that there is a candle of the Lord set up in every man. The Christian best pictures the world's religions as bearing light of different colours while holding that all light is fulfilled in the white light of Christ.

But – a well-known missionary hymn not withstanding – we must no more suppose that non-Christians are in perfect darkness, than we must suppose ourselves to be in perfect light whose candlepower is given on the bulb. Yet that point has radical implications for Christian evangelism and missionary work not to say the sale of church buildings.

Now if we are to emerge from this crisis on the right side, there are two major items on our agenda:

(i) We must find ways and means of creating, for our contemporaries as for ourselves, moments of vision and disclosure. For without these there is no cash value to be given to anything we say or do. Without such occasions of insight there can be no foothold for religious discourse in general, or for the Christian faith in particular. Our contemporaries will then rightly conclude that Christian institutions are at best no more than phenomena with an impressive past and little future, catering for those who happen to like the kind of social behaviour to be found in our Synods and Assemblies, our Churches and Chapels, our Schoolrooms and Parish Halls. Our primary and urgent need, on which all else depends, is to make possible occasions of insight, moments of vision and disclosure, occasions when our society could re-discover a sense of the sublime. Mary Warnock has recently written: 'The concept of the sublime, which is not particularly widely discussed at the present time, is all the same of the greatest importance. When many people were religious they had the sublime, to some extent, tamed, and available to them on Sundays. But now most of them have not, and without it their lives may suddenly seem too banal and too completely intelligible to be worth living.

Their imaginations are starved by the well-explored material limits of their lives, because one can't separate the notion of the sublime from that of the limitless or infinite.'[6]

I see a great significance at this point in the present popularity of Festivals and my remarks here will provide a bridge to the second major item on the agenda. Festivals provide the means by which, today, the haunting vision can be recreated around key ideas, symbols, which are sufficiently open-textured to transmit a true power, the power of inspiration from which discourse can be derived. Further, as artists and technicians, composers and players give form and context to the ideas and symbols, people mingle together and discuss them, and thus begin to lay the foundation for the frameworks, the cathedrals of ideas and corporate action, in which power can be and must be expressed for a reasonable religion to influence social change and development. The Festival, as a social ingathering of symbols, is thus the catalyst – the necessary bridge – between the vision and its explication, between inspiration and institutions, between the moment of vision and the report we give of it, the revelation and our talk about it. In other words, what the Church needs today is a permanent attitude of Festival. Concerned for the moment of vision as well as its articulation in ideas and action, the Church must be even more concerned for what lies between them both for the social ingathering of symbols, old and new, that the Gospels and the arts and the sciences can provide. It is the symbols which lie at the heart of Festival, that hold together the vision and its interpretation, and so keep us from sheer 'enthusiasm' on the one hand, and an authoritarian theological stereotype on the other. The theme of Festival brings us close to that of prayer. We are moving rapidly to a time when our forms of prayer will have to make more evident than they do the logical structures which they embody so that they cannot so easily be misread or misunderstood and can be all the more expressive of the vision which should lie at their heart. Basically, a prayer should be discourse apt to the evoking of a disclosure, consistent and coherent with our ideas of God, man and the world, and linked effectively with some practical action. Yet how can this be when so many of our ideas of man and the world, and so many practical possibilities have emerged from science and industry over the years when they have not even been on speaking terms with the Christian faith? We need a critical and sensitive examination of the phrases in our prayers and a radical experimentation in forms of prayer, and in symbols for worship, and these may helpfully start from secular images which as at a time of Festival belong to moments of vision. I recall how in Canada a barbecue stove, a secular symbol of fellowship and joy in the universe, became that in which incense was burnt and over which were offered to God the prayers of the congregation. On some other occasion bread and wine could easily have taken the place of steak and baked potatoes.

(ii) The second item on our agenda runs in double harness with the first. The first was the need for moments of vision, disclosure, occasions of festival; the second is for a theology and institutions which match and make evident their basis in such a vision. But this means an emphasis on theological reticence rather than theological loquacity, in an endeavour to do greater justice to the mystery and infinitude which should characterise the moment of vision, and which extravagant theological utterance only too easily dispels. In short, there must be radical changes of theological attitude and expectation, a new understanding of the point and significance of theological controversy, a new idea of what is desirable theological agreement, and radical changes in our idea of different Churches and their relationships. We must sponsor a multiple theology and we must eschew uniformity as an analysis of union.

Lest my remarks be misunderstood, let me immediately make an important supplementary point. This does not necessarily imply that we must be relativists in theology, or loose federalists in Church organisation. It does not necessarily imply a take-it-or-leave-it attitude about theology or the Church. For the cost of a multiple theology, and the cost of variety in unity is not only a constant vigilance, but a constant exercise in co-operation, in mutual edification that both edifies and builds up. In short, with a multiple theology we must always be concerned with cross-references between the various strands, with locating strands in their moment of insight, with constructing what I called above the most coherent, comprehensive, consistent and simple map we can, and of testing it for empirical fit; and with a federal unity there must be constant grappling together with common projects and problems – not least the theological project I have just mentioned. Meanwhile we shall remember that it is certainties which have divided as they always divide; what unites is – not certainties – but the common vision which leads us all to recognise our common ignorance as we look from our shore over the infinite sea towards a moving horizon which opens towards the future. It is then not a day for the mere reiteration of theological conclusions but for encouraging new attitudes and methods. In this way we contrast decidedly with the Patristic and the mediaeval periods where, as Professor Nineham has reminded us, Christian thinkers were, on the whole, systematisers and codifiers, not dreamers or poets.

In this connection let me advert briefly to our contemporary moral unease and turmoil. Part of our trouble today with moral issues is not that all past principles are outworn, but that while situations remain macroscopically in the large the same, e.g. curing a patient or having sexual intercourse, microscopically in the small we now know that these situations have many more ingredients than once we supposed, ingredients of which the natural and behavioural sciences have much to tell us. In these circumstances some principles still remain above question. But with others it is more important to see what insights they embody than to think of merely applying them, though once we have made a moral decision no matter how novel a new moral principle or rule becomes available. The crisis in Christian morality is not met either by merely mouthing old principles or by suggesting that principles have no place in Christian moral decisions. Above all else we have to make clear what is the logical function, the basis in an inspiring vision, a sense of obligation of any moral rule we use in our discussions and rules are only invoked constructively when a thoroughgoing empirical analysis of a situation has shown them to be needed and called for their assistance.

Here again, it is more a time for learning new methods, new ways of reasoning than for merely reiterating old conclusions even though these be wise and reliable, if not misused. What this means in practice is that it is the day of the multiple group for moral and political decisions, the interdisciplinary which David Jenkins has wisely suggested we better call transdisciplinary groups. Such groups will be, I suggest, a regular feature of our Church life – will be indeed the means at one and the same time of proving our convictions, grappling with problems, learning better our faith and ministering the grace of God to man and society. Such groups will recognise the need both for a classical theology which gives us the necessary professional background, and also for what has been called a contextual theology where in a transdisciplinary group, believers develop the facility for latching on to the multiple discussion of a problem. Such a discussion not only aims at a creative decision, but in reaching such a decision discovers also new developments in theology, new possibilities of theological articulation. It is in this contextual theology that there will be found the growing points of our faith and the intimations of a new culture, a culture Christian, scientific, technological and humane. Incidentally, while being careful to distinguish the logic of scientific discovery and theorising, and the logic of religious discourse, we can note that the supposed enmity disappears when the old rigorous attitudes and authoritarian claims for both disappear. Both can then be seen as responses to wonder, as the articulation of a vision, as understanding the ways of God whether as Creator or Redeemer. Theology may learn from the new outlook in science how to display in its utterance, what for long has accompanied the exposition of scientific cosmologies – a sense of wonder, a response to the infinite, the spirit of relentless enquiry that aptly accompanies the exploration of a vision, and science may learn from the new outlook in theology that supplement which enables it to talk of the one world, to display moral and social responsibility, and to point forward to a humane technology. I cannot exaggerate the necessity for transdisciplinary groups, nor their significance, nor their theological and educational value any more than their novelty and difficulty. To me they represent a structure that anticipates the future. They even have evangelistic possibilities though this will not be their primary purpose. Let us notice however that the crisis brings with it the need as well as the possibility of a new type of evangelism. Evangelism, as I have remarked, may well occur in the multiple group where evangelist and evangelised grow together. Be that as it may, it is not enough – nor of course has it ever been – to preach the Gospel, still less if it was supposed that preaching the Gospel meant no more than uttering some conclusions, however true those conclusions were; though this is not of course to put any limits on what God can do even with what, in the obvious and non-biblical sense, we may call the foolishness of the preaching. But the difficulty today of preaching and teaching with an integrity that respects biblical, and historical, and doctrinal scholarship, not to mention secular studies, fortunately leaves us to see that a new strategy altogether is needed if we would make evident to our contemporaries the Gospel of Christ and see that it informs and sustains man and society. Such a strategy must extend to new patterns of ministry, new types of training for ministry, and new ecclesiastical structures as well as new social, political and industrial groups.

To put the whole matter in another way, what is needed is a new concept and pattern of leadership. Leadership must no longer profess to give ready-made answers to all questions of importance. What is important is to ensure that in every problem the points at issue are made plain, a radical treatment is given, the roots displayed, that we are articulate about the Gospel in such a way as to give an authoritative but not an authoritarian grounding to the principles which are used, and all this in the hope that a creative decision will emerge whose light is that which glorifies the Father and alone gives a clear lead. We do not give a lead, though those who ask us for one often suppose we do, by reiterating conclusions which those around us wish to hear or wish to have without the trouble of reaching them. We give a lead only by displaying in our utterances or otherwise, that which inspires us. 'The power of God is the worship He inspires,' said Whitehead. Christian power, we may infer, is the inspiration of God's love in Christ: Christian leadership must display this which leads us – the light of Christ – and this can be more evident from the quality of our struggles and our co-operative endeavours than it is from any claim to have already arrived where we are sitting at ease in Zion dispensing packaged answers. As pilgrims and pioneers we are still *in via* and we must run around as in a Munich stadium, caught up – whether we care for it or not – in the political turmoils of the world. But, as in the stadium of Hebrews 12, 'Our eyes must be fixed on Jesus', on whom faith depends from start to finish and that faith can be evident from the way we run, and the way we struggle together, if only we do.

I hope I may briefly dispose here of two metaphors that are used to despair of the current situation when (as it is said) the trumpet sounds an uncertain note, and the hungry sheep look up in vain to be fed. The implication is sometimes that the only food suited to the sheep, and the only food they desire is a prescribed diet of food devoid of roughage: which a moment's reflection will tell us is entirely unhealthy. Rather should shepherds and sheep be engaged on a common endeavour, weather-beaten by the winds of change, of converting unpromising land to green pastures. As for the trumpet, let us recall that St Paul in this metaphor was protesting against unintelligibility not diversity; whereas our main trouble today is that trumpets are sounded on all sides all too clearly and all too readily. The moral however is not that we exclude some rather strident and ear-splitting notes but trace all the notes back to their blowers to see whether with patience and wisdom a new and altogether unexpected harmony may be created. A crisis of faith there is; but if we respond aright we can play our part constructively in the emergence of a new culture and a new era, and meanwhile we can show that the Gospel points to an authority, a security, and purposiveness which is fulfilling and not tyrannical – that for which our society is searching. So, crisis though it is, I see no cause for depression and despair, still less for nervousness and fright, neurotic and reactionary responses such as were evident in the nineteenth century. Today I see the possibility of advancing with all the vision of the pioneer, the pilgrim, the man of faith, who endeavours to talk of as best he can, and in his practice to display as best he can, that which inspires him, that which called forth and constantly renews his commitment, and points him towards fulfilment. It is a critical time, but for that very reason it is a time in which we should be glad to be alive. 'This is the day which the Lord hath made; let us rejoice and be glad in it.'

14 September 1972
CLC/47

Notes

1   Quoted *The Fourth R*: pp. 32–33 from S. Leeson, *Christian Education* (Longmans 1947), pp. 97–8.
2   *The Fourth R*. pp. 31–32. The quotation included in the Reference is from an article of mine in *Theology*, December, 1964.
3   Loc cit. pp. 29–30.
4   *The Fourth R*. p. 42.
5   *The Listener*, 11 May 1972. p. 606.
6   *The Listener*, 11 May 1972, p. 614.

Restricted Bibliography

The large and extensive archive of Papers of Ian Ramsey is in the Durham Dean and Chapter Library. There is a small collection of material in the Peart-Binns Episcopal Biography Archive in the J.B. Priestley Library (Special Collections), University of Bradford.

The focus of this work is Ian Ramsey as Bishop of Durham from 1966 to 1972. A complete bibliography would contain several hundred entries with the largest proportion covering his thought on philosophy, theology, religion and science, most of which was explored, developed and sustained before his Durham episcopate. Accordingly, apart from listing his own books, those he edited and contributions to some symposia, this bibliography is limited, with exceptions, to the Durham years.

Books – sole author

Miracles: An Exercise in Logical Mapwork (Inaugural Lecture, Oxford). Oxford, 1952.
Religious Language. London, 1957.
Freedom and Immortality. London, 1960.
On Being Sure in Religion. London, 1963.
Models and Mystery. Oxford, 1964.
Religion and Science: Conflict and Synthesis. London, 1964.
Christian Discourse: Some Logical Explanations. Oxford, 1965.
Words about God. London, 1971.
Our Understanding of Prayer. London, 1971.
Models of Divine Activity. London, 1973.
Christian Empiricism. (ed. Jerry H. Gill). London, 1974.

Books edited/jointly edited

The Reasonableness of Christianity by John Locke. Stanford, 1958.
Prospect for Metaphysics. London, 1961. ITR – Introduction: On the Possibility and Purpose of a Metaphysical Journey.

The Miracles and the Resurrection. London, 1964. ITR – Introduction: Miracles: An Exercise in Logical Mapwork.

Biology and Personality: A Symposium. Oxford, 1965. ITR – Introduction: Biology and Personality: Philosophical Reflections.

Christian Ethics and Contemporary Philosophy. London, 1966. ITR – Discussion of R. Braithwaite: Moral Judgments and God's Commands: Towards a Rehabilitation of Natural Law.

Personality and Science (with Ruth Porter). London, 1971. ITR – Human Personality.

Contributions to Symposia and other publications

The Authority and the Church Today (in) *Authority and the Church* ed. R.R. Williams. Conference between theologians of the Church of England and the Evangelical Church in Germany. London, 1965.

A Personal God (in) *Prospect for Theology* ed. F.G. Healey. London, 1966.

Talking about God: Models Ancient and Modern (in) *Myth and Symbol* ed. F.W. Dillistone. London, 1966.

Theology Today and Spirituality Today (in) *Spirituality Today* ed. Eric James. London, 1967.

Polanyi and J.L. Austin (in) *Intellect and Hope* ed. T.A. Langford and W.H. Poteat. Princeton, 1968.

Contributions to *The Bishoprick* (Quarterly Journal of Diocese of Durham)

1967 May		*Sermon* preached at Inthronement on 15 December 1966.
	August	*Presidential Address to Diocesan Conference* 27 June 1967.
		Sermon preached by Canon J.S. Boys Smith, Master of St John's College, Cambridge in York Minister on All Saints' Day, 1966 at the Consecration of Ian Ramsey as Bishop (of Durham).
	November	*Some Reflections on Current Liturgical Experiment: Holy Communion – Series II.*

1968	February	*Theology Today and Spirituality Today.* Revised and abbreviated version of paper given to the Parish and People Conference at Durham 1967.
	May	*The Church and the Secular City.* *The Placement and Movement of Assistant Curates.* Council for the Recruitment and Training for the Ministry.
	August	*Anglican Thinking and Explorations into Unity.* An address given in Newcastle at a meeting during the week of Prayer for Christian Unity, 1968. Notes and Queries. Canon W.S.T. Wright's criticism of Ramsey's Article in February issue; and Ramsey's response.
	November	*Anglican/Methodist Proposals.* *Bishop's Directions regarding Confirmation.*
1969	February	*Palm Sunday: The Sunday next before Easter.* From sermon broadcast by BBC on Palm Sunday 1968.
	May	*Violence in Contemporary Society.* Substance of a speech in the House of Lords on 12 February 1969.
	August	Introduction to articles by Canon W.S.T. Wright (Series 2 Communion) and Canon Professor H.E.W. Turner (The Eucharistic Presence. An Evangelical Exploration).
	November	*William Temple – Some aspects of his thought and life.* The Second William Temple given at William Temple College, Rugby, 22 June 1968. *On Not Being Judgmental.* The Third Margaret Allen Memorial Lecture delivered in Edinburgh to the Scottish Pastoral Association in November 1969.
1970	May	*Processions and Witness.* Part of the Address given to the Convocation of York, 13 January 1970 (slightly amended for publication).
	November	*Science and Religion: Past and Future.* Sermon preached to the British Association in Durham Cathedral, 6 September 1970.

1971	May	*The Industrial Relations Bill.* Substance of a speech in the House of Lords, 6 April 1971. *The Crockford Preface.*
	August	The Miners' Gala, 1971. Speech at the Miners' Gala on 17 July 1971.
1972	August	*Moral Problems facing the Medical Profession at the present time.* Inaugural Lecture for the B.M.A. Conference in Cyprus in April 1972. (Lecture delivered in Ramsey's absence.)
	November	*Sermon* preached by the Archbishop of York at the Memorial Service to Ian Ramsey at Durham Cathedral on 13 October 1972.
1973	February	*Address* by the Archbishop of Canterbury at the Memorial Service for Ian Ramsey in St Margaret's, Westminster on 17 November 1972.

The Bishop's Letter

Monthly – Diocese of Durham: October 1966 to November 1972.

Archbishop's Commission on Christian Doctrine

Reports during his years as (first) Chairman 1967-1972.
   1968 Subscription and Assent to the 39 Articles.
   1971 Prayer and the Departed.
   1972 Thinking about the Eucharist.

Church Assembly Board for Social Responsibility

Reports of Committees of which Ian Ramsey was member (M) or chaired (C).
   1959 Ought Suicide to be a Crime? (M).
   1962 Sterilization: An ethical enquiry (M).
   1965 Abortion: An ethical discussion (C).
   1965 Decisions about Life and Death, A Problem in Modern Medicine (M).

House of Lords

Ian Ramsey was introduced into the House of Lords on 6 December 1966. The following list of his speeches and interventions in the

Lords, was kindly researched by Paul Ramsey in the pages of *Hansard*, who generously provided me with copies.

Maiden speech – 19 July 1967.

1967	July 19, 26	Medical Termination of Pregnancy Bill (Committee stage)
	October 23	Abortion (No 2) Bill (Report stage)
	November 15	Religious Education in Schools
	December 12	Coal Industry Bill (2nd Reading)
1968	February 14	Fuel Policy
	February 21	Youth and the Nation
1969	February 12	Violence in contemporary society
	March 25	Voluntary Euthanasia Bill (2nd Reading)
	July 10, 11, 15	Divorce Reform Bill (Committee)
	November 26	Springboks' Tours and Race Relations Acts
	December 10	Demonstrations: Significance and Implications
	December 17	Murder (Abolition of Death Penalty) Act 1965.
1970	January 27	Experiments on Animals: The Littlewood Report
	January 28	The Age of Retirement
1971	January 20	Church of England, Disestablishment Proposal
	February 3	Mass Media Communication
	February 17	Long-Term Prison Sentences (Motion)
	March 3	Wilberforce Report and the Economic Situation
	April 6	Industrial Relations Bill (2nd Reading)
	May 11	Industrial Relations Bill (2nd Reading)
	November 3	(On) Address in Reply to Her Majesty's Speech
	December 1, 2	Rhodesia: Settlement Proposals
	December 15	Education in a Multi-Racial Britain
1972	January 19	Violence in Southern Africa
	February 23	Tributes to the late Marquis of Salisbury
	March 22	The Arts: Work of Regional Associations

Miscellaneous (by Ian Ramsey unless otherwise stated)

'The Quest for a Christian Philosophy' *Modern Churchman* February 1941.

'Love and Equality' *Modern Churchman* November 1947.

'The Paradox of Omnipotence' *Mind April* 1956.

'Persons and Funerals: What do Person Words Mean?' *Hibbert Journal* July 1956.

'Ethics and Reason' *Church Quarterly Review* April–June 1957.

'The Logical Character of Resurrection Belief' *Theology* May 1957.

'The Two Moralities' *Journal of William Temple Association* December 1957.

'The Family in Contemporary Society.' The Report of a Group convened at the behest of the Archbishop of Canterbury. London 1958 (Ian Ramsey a member).

'The Feast of Meeting'. A sermon preached before the University of Oxford on 2 February 1958 *Church Quarterly Review* January–March 1959.

'Charles Darwin: The Origin of the Species' *Leicester Cathedral Quarterly* January and April 1960.

'Religion and Science: A Philosopher's Approach' *Church Quarterly Review* January–March 1961.

'A New Prospect in Theological Studies' *Theology* December 1964.

'Towards the Relevance in Theological Language' *Modern Churchman* October 1964.

'Charles Earle Raven, 1885–1964' *Proceedings of the British Academy* 1965.

'Towards a Rehabilitation of Natural Law' *Christian Ethics and Contemporary Philosophy* (1966).

'Faith Alert' The Lambeth Conference 1968. London, 1968 ed. Ian Ramsey and Michael Perry.

'Fullness of Life – Ian Ramsey, Bishop of Durham'. *All One Body* Interviews with Bishops of the Anglican Communion. Ed. Timothy Wilson London 1969.

'Joseph Butler 1692–1752, Some Features of his Life and Thought.' Dr William's Trust London, 1969.

The Fourth R: The Durham Report on Religious Education. London 1970 Ian Ramsey (Chairman of Commission).

'Christian Ethics in the 1960s and 1970s' *Church Quarterly Review* January 1970.

'The Influence of Technology on the Social Structure.' Lecture to the Royal Society of Arts. *Journal of RSA* August 1971.

'The Crisis of Faith.' The greater part of the address Ramsey gave to the Conference of Church Leaders at Selly Oak, Birmingham on 12 September 1972. *Theoria to Theory* Volume 7 No. 1 January 1973.

The British Churches Turn to the Future by David L. Edwards. London, 1973.

Censorship Crucible January 1974.

Publications about Ian Ramsey.

Ian Ramsey. Bishop of Durham – a memoir by David L. Edwards Oxford, 1973.

Ian Ramsey: To Speak Responsibly of God, Jerry H. Gill, Allen & Unwin, 1974.

'Ian Ramsey' in series of *Makers of the Modern Theological Mind*, William B. Williamson, ed. Bob E. Patterson. World Books, Waco, Texas, 1982.

(Booklet) *Ian Ramsey in preliminary perspective* by David L. Edwards. Durham, 1984.

'Ian Ramsey' in *Apostles Extraordinary. Celebration of Saints and Sinners* by Geddes MacGregor. San Francisco, 1986.

'The Authority of a Moral Claim: Ian Ramsey and the Practice of Medicine' by G.R. Dunstan *Journal of Medical Ethics* 1987 No. 13.

The Improbable Bishop: Ian Thomas Ramsey – Bishop of Durham 1966–1972 by John S. Peart-Binns *Modern Believing* April 2005.

Index